D1686725

Ostendorf
International Sales
Terms

International Sales Terms

by

Patrick Ostendorf

Professor of Commercial Law
University of Applied Sciences, Bielefeld

Second Edition
2014

C. H. Beck · Hart · Nomos

www.beck.de

ISBN 978-3-406-64875-5 (Beck)
ISBN 978-1-84946-609-7 (Hart Publishing)
ISBN 978-3-8487-0471-2 (Nomos)

© 2014 Verlag C. H. Beck oHG
Wilhelmstr. 9, 80801 München

Printed in Germany by
fgb · freiburger graphische betriebe GmbH & Co. KG
Bebelstraße 11, 79108 Freiburg

Typeset by Reemers Publishing Services GmbH, Krefeld

All rights reserved. No part of this publication may be reproduced, stored in a retrieval system, or transmitted, in any form or by any means, without the prior permission of Verlag C. H. Beck, or as expressly permitted by law under the terms agreed with the appropriate reprographic rights organisation. Enquiries concerning reproduction which may not be covered by the above should be addressed to C. H. Beck at the address above.

Preface

International sales law is both a complex and consistently evolving area of law: The United Nations Convention on Contracts for the International Sales of Goods (CISG) is gaining pace as a well accepted piece of uniform sales law, and other international instruments (sponsored both by private and public institutions) on the European as well as on a global level are contributing to the ongoing harmonization of international sales law and related areas of law. Nevertheless, domestic laws – that are regularly unknown territory from the perspective of at least one of the parties to an international sales contract – still play a substantial role both with regard to gaps left behind by the international instruments and in relation to the interpretation and enforceability of individual contract clauses. Against this background, international sales contracts entail from a legal point of view both risks and opportunities: Risks because international commercial contracts give rise to specific legal problems and pitfalls that do not exist on the domestic level. Opportunities, given that the existence of an international link of a commercial contract provides the parties – compared to a purely domestic transaction – with substantially greater contractual freedom. However, in order to avoid risks and to benefit from opportunities, a general understanding of international sales law and an awareness of existing differences between domestic legal systems and their impact on standard sales terms are of the essence. This book tries to identify both opportunities and risks from the perspective of a commercial seller: The annotated international sales terms suggested in this book are tailored for a specific governing law that appears to be flexible as well as easily accessible for lawyers and business people from a variety of different legal backgrounds. At the same time, it is the aim of this book to illustrate the interaction between standard contractual clauses contained in international sales contracts and the governing law in a broader sense.

For the second edition of this book, a variety of more recent developments had to be taken into account. The International Chamber of Commerce (ICC) has published a new edition of its widely used trade terms, the Incoterms 2010, as well as new Rules of Arbitration (2012). The European Commission has proposed a draft for a new Common European Sales Law (CESL) that may (once enacted) constitute a potential alternative for the CISG, and has adopted a recast of Council Regulation (EC) No 44/2001 on jurisdiction and the recognition and enforcement of judgments in civil and commercial matters (the "Brussels I" Regulation). Relevant amendments of Swiss domestic law, in particular with regard to applicable limitation periods for warranty claims (Art. 210 Swiss Code of Obligations) and the statutory policing of general terms and conditions (§ 8 Swiss Federal Act on Unfair Competition) have been enacted. Also, the ongoing Euro crisis poses the question whether the draftsman of international sales contracts should insert appropriate terms into standard form contracts that may limit potential risks triggered by a complete or partial breakup of the Euro zone. Finally, since the publication of the first edition of this book, a multitude of publications on the subject of international sales terms have hit the shelves that had to be taken into consideration just as new case law applying the CISG.

Preface

This book could not have been written without the experience that I gained during my work as a lawyer with a specific focus on international sales and distribution law at Orth Kluth Rechtsanwälte in Berlin and Düsseldorf and the ongoing fruitful exchange and discussion with both colleagues and clients. I should also like to thank my editor at C.H. Beck, Dr Frank Lang, for his ongoing valuable support.

This book is based on the materials that were available to me up to 31 July 2013.

Patrick Ostendorf   Bielefeld, 20 September 2013

Table of Contents

Preface V
List of Abbreviations IX
Introduction XIII

A. General Part 1

　I. Role and impact of the law governing a sales contract 1
　II. The suggested choice of law for the present International Sales Terms 4
　III. The CISG 6
　　1. Part I of the CISG: Scope of application and other general provisions 7
　　2. Part II of the CISG: The formation of the sales contract 9
　　3. Part III of the CISG: Obligations, rights and remedies of the parties 11
　IV. Swiss law as the supplementary governing law of choice 27
　　1. Overview on the relevant issues 27
　　2. Relevant Swiss contract and tort laws 28
　　3. Validity of the contract 29
　　4. Limitation of actions 32
　　5. Set-off 34
　　6. Assignment 34
　　7. Contractual penalties and liquidated damages 35
　　8. Concurring claims under tort (product liability) 38
　V. Outlook: The Proposal for a Common European Sales Law (CESL) – a potential alternative for the CISG? 39
　VI. Relevant laws beyond the governing law of the contract 41
　　1. Mandatory rules: General issues 41
　　2. Proprietary aspects: The transfer of property in the goods sold 46
　　3. Competition and antitrust laws 47
　　4. Export control regulations 50
　　5. Exchange control regulations 54
　　6. Product liability towards third parties 55

B. The Main Contract Document 57

　I. The benefit of a countersigned main contract document 58
　　1. Requirements for the incorporation of general terms into international contracts 58
　　2. The "battle of forms" problem 59
　II. Price 61
　III. Payment Terms 62
　　1. The legal position under the CISG 62
　　2. The preferred payment method: The letter of credit 63
　IV. Delivery and Trade Terms 67
　　1. The role of standardized trade terms in international sales transactions 67
　　2. The Incoterms © 2010 68

C. The International Sales Terms 75

　I. General Provisions 75
　　1. The suggested clause 75
　　2. Annotations 75
　II. Payment Terms 77
　　1. The suggested clause 77
　　2. Annotations 78

Table of Contents

III.	Delivery Terms	80
	1. The suggested clause	80
	2. Annotations	82
IV.	Retention of Title	86
	1. The suggested clause	86
	2. Annotations	86
V.	Product Defects	88
	1. The suggested clause	88
	2. Annotations	90
VI.	Exclusion/Limitation of Damages Claims	98
	1. The suggested clause	98
	2. General background	99
	3. Annotations	102
VII.	Limitation of Actions	109
	1. The suggested clause	109
	2. General background	110
	3. Annotations	113
VIII.	Export Control Regulations	116
	1. The suggested clause	116
	2. Annotations	117
IX.	Avoidance by the Seller	118
	1. The suggested clause	118
	2. Annotations	118
X.	Confidentiality Obligations	119
	1. The suggested clause	119
	2. Annotations	119
XI.	Force Majeure	121
	1. The suggested clause	121
	2. General background	121
	3. Annotations	123
XII.	Entire Agreement, Written Form, Severability and Anti-Assignment Clause	124
	1. The suggested clause	124
	2. Annotations	124
XIII.	The governing law of the contract	130
	1. The suggested clause	130
	2. Annotations	130
XIV.	Arbitration and Litigation	134
	1. The suggested clause	134
	2. General background	135
	3. Annotations	139

Appendix 147

    I. The Sales Documentation Put Together 147
CISG   II. The United Nations Convention on Contracts for the International Sale of Goods 156
    III. Excerpts from the Swiss Code of Obligations (Obligationenrecht) and other relevant Swiss statutes 174

Index 179

List of Abbreviations

ABGB	Allgemeines Bürgerliches Gesetzbuch (General Civil Code, Austria)
A.C.	Appeal Cases
AcP	Archiv für civilistische Praxis
AGB	Allgemeine Geschäftsbedingungen (General Terms and Conditions)
AJP	Aktuelle Juristische Praxis
All ER	All England Law Reports
Am J Comp L	The American Journal of Comparative Law
Am Rev Int' Arb	American Review of International Arbitration
Antitrust L J	Antitrust Law Journal
Arb Int	Arbitration International
ASA Bull	ASA (Swiss Arbitration Association) Bulletin
AWG	Außenwirtschaftsgesetz (Foreign Trade Act, Germany)
AWV	Außenwirtschaftsverordnung (Foreign Trade Regulation, Germany)
BB	Der Betriebsberater
BeckRS	Beck Rechtsprechung
BG	Bundesgericht (Federal Supreme Court, Switzerland)
BGE	Entscheidungen des Schweizerischen Bundesgerichts (Official collection of the decisions of the Swiss Federal Supreme Court)
BGH	Bundesgerichtshof (Federal Supreme Court, Germany)
BGHZ	Entscheidungen des Bundesgerichtshofs in Zivilsachen (Official collection of the decisions of the German Federal Supreme Court)
B.L.R.	Building Law Reports
BR/DC	Baurecht/Droit de la Construction
Bus L Int'l	Business Law International
BW	Burgerlijk Wetboek (Civil Code, the Netherlands)
CA	Court of Appeal (England & Wales)
Campbell L Rev	Campbell Law Review
CC	Civil Code (Switzerland)
CCL	Commerce Control List
CCCL Journal	Journal of the Canadian College of Construction Lawyers
CESL	Common European Sales Law
CFR	Cost and Freight (Incoterms 2010)
CIETAC	China International Economic and Trade Arbitration Commission
CIF	Cost, Insurance and Freight (Incoterms 2010)
CIP	Carriage and Insurance paid to (Incoterms 2010)
CILL	Construction Industry Law Letter
CISG	United Nations Convention on Contracts for the International Sales of Goods 1980
CISG-AC	Advisory Council of the CISG
CLJ	Cambridge Law Journal
CLP	Current Legal Problems
CML Rev	Common Market Law Review
CO	Code of Obligations (Switzerland)
Colum. J. Transnat'l L	Columbia Journal of Transnational Law
Cornell Int'l L J	Cornell International Law Journal
Comm	Commercial Court (England &Wales)
CPT	Carriage Paid To (Incoterms 2010)
CUP	Cambridge University Press
DAP	Delivered At Place (Incoterms 2010)
DAT	Delivered At Terminal (Incoterms 2010)
DB	Der Betrieb
DDP	Delivered Duty Paid (Incoterms 2010)
Dick L Rev	Dickinson Law Review
EAR	Export Administration Regulations (USA)

List of Abbreviations

EBLR	European Business Law Review
EC	European Community
ECR	European Court Reports
EEA	European Economic Area
EEC	European Economic Community
EGBGB	Einführungsgesetz zum Bürgerlichen Gesetzbuch (Introductory Act to the Civil Code, Germany)
EJCL	Electronic Journal of Comparative Law
EJCCL	European Journal of Commercial Contract Law
EJLR	European Journal of Law Reform
ERCL	European Review of Contract Law
ERPL	European Review of Private Law
EU	European Union
EuZW	Europäische Zeitschrift für Wirtschaftsrecht
EWCA	Court of Appeal of England and Wales
EWCA Civ	Court of Appeal of England and Wales, Civil Division
EWHC	High Court of Justice of England and Wales
EWS	Europäisches Wirtschafts- und Steuerrecht
Ex	Court of Exquequer (England & Wales)
EXW	Ex Works (Incoterms 2010)
FAS	Free Alongside Ship (Incoterms 2010)
F.2d	Federal Reporter, Second Series
FCA	Free Carrier (Incoterms 2010)
FIDIC	Fédération Internationale des Ingénieurs Conseils (International Federation of Consulting Engineers)
FOB	Free on Board (Incoterms 2010)
Franchise L J	Franchise Law Journal
FSR	Fleet Street Reports
Ga J Int'l & Comp L	Georgia Journal of International and Comparative Law
GWB	Gesetz gegen Wettbewerbsbeschränkungen (Law against Restraints of Competition, Germany)
IBLJ	International Business Law Journal
IBLR	International Business Law Review
IBR	Immobilien- und Baurecht
ICC	International Chamber of Commerce
I.C.C.L.R.	International Company and Commercial Law Review
ICLQ	International & Comparative Law Quarterly
ICL Rev	International Construction Law Review
IIC	International Review of Intellectual Property and Competition Law
IHR	Zeitschrift für Internationales Handelsrecht
IMF	International Monetary Fund
Ind J Global Legal Stud	Indiana Journal of Global Legal Studies
Int'l Law	The International Lawyer
Int'l L Rev	International Law Review
Int'l Trade & Bus L Ann	International Trade and Business Law Annual
Int'l Trade & Bus L Rev	International Trade & Business Law Review
Int. T.L.R.	International Trade Law & Regulation
IP	Intellectual Property
IPRax	Praxis des Internationalen Privat- und Verfahrensrechts
HAVE	Haftung und Versicherung
HCA	High Court of Australia, Court Reports (Australia)
HG	Handelsgericht (Commercial Court, Switzerland)
HGB	Handelsgesetzbuch (Commercial Code, Germany)
HL	House of Lords (United Kingdom)
Hong Kong L J	Hong Kong Law Journal
Hous Bus & Tax L J	Houston Business & Tax Law Journal
J Bus L	Journal of Business Law
J Int Arbitrat	Journal of International Arbitration
J L & Commerce	Journal of Law and Commerce
JPIL	Journal of Private International Law
KB	Law Reports, King's Bench Division (England)
LCIA	London Court of Arbitration

List of Abbreviations

LD	Liquidated Damages
LG	Landgericht (Regional Court, Germany)
Lloyd's Rep	Lloyd's Law Reports
MMR	Multimedia und Recht
NCPC	Noveau code de procédure civil (New Civil Procedure Code, France)
NJW	Neue Juristische Wochenschrift
No	Number
OGH	Oberster Gerichtshof (Supreme Court, Austria)
OJ	Official Journal of the European Union
OJLS	Oxford Journal of Legal Studies
OLG	Oberlandesgericht (Higher Regional Court, Germany/Austria)
Orgalime	European Engineering Industries Association
OSCE	Organization for Security and Cooperation in Europe
OUP	Oxford University Press
Pace Int'l L Rev	Pace International Law Review
para(s)	paragraph(s)
PECL	Principles of European Contract Law
PILA	Federal Code on Private International Law (Bundesgesetz über das Internationale Privatrecht, Switzerland)
QB	Law Reports, Queen's Bench Division (England)
RabelsZ	Rabels Zeitschrift für ausländisches und internationales Privatrecht
RIW	Recht der Internationalen Wirtschaft
SchiedsVZ	Die neue Zeitschrift für Schiedsverfahren
SGA 1979	Sale of Goods Act 1979 (United Kingdom)
SJZ	Schweizerische Juristen-Zeitung
SMU L Rev	Southern Methodist University Law Review
UCC	Uniform Commercial Code (USA)
UCP 600	Uniform Customs and Practice for Documentary Credits (ICC)
UCTA	Unfair Contract Terms Act 1977 (United Kingdom)
UN	United Nations
UN ECE	United Nations Economic Commission for Europe
UNCITRAL	United Nations Commission on International Trade Law
UNIDROIT	Institut International pour l'Unification du Droit Prive (International Institute for the Unification of Private Law)
UPICC	Unidroit Principles of International Commercial Contracts 2010
US	United States Supreme Court Reporter
USC	United States Code
UWG	Bundesgesetz gegen den unlauteren Wettbewerb (Federal Code against Unfair Competition, Switzerland)
TCC	Technology and Construction Court (England & Wales)
TFEU	Treaty on the Functioning of the European Union
TransportR	Zeitschrift für Transportrecht
Unif L Rev	Uniform Law Review
VAT	Value Added Tax
Vict U Well L Rev	Victoria University of Wellington Law Review
VJ	The Vindobona Journal of International Commercial Law and Arbitration
Vol	Volume
WLR	Weekly Law Reports (England)
YPIL	Yearbook of Private International Law
ZBJV	Zeitschrift des Bernerischen Juristenvereins
ZEuP	Zeitschrift für Europäisches Privatrecht
ZGS	Zeitschrift für das gesamte Schuldrecht
ZIP	Zeitschrift für Wirtschaftsrecht

Introduction

The use of **standardized sales terms** and conditions is indispensable in the operation of the daily business of companies in order to minimize transaction costs and to enable sales departments to conclude sales contracts without having the need to take costly and comprehensive legal advice in any individual case. At the same time, legal problems arising from sales contracts are often multiplied in international transactions. Besides obvious obstacles such as differing languages, legal cultures and legal systems, the parties face specific complexities in case of an international transaction that will not or at least not to the same extent arise from purely domestic contracts. Contrary to a domestic transaction, the parties to an international sales contract need not only deal with the question which laws will govern their contractual relationship and which court or arbitral tribunal should resolve any potential disputes. They must also take a multitude of both domestic as well as foreign laws into account that cover international trade, such as, – but not limited to –, export and import as well as currency exchange control regulations, antitrust laws (sometimes with extraterritorial effect), international taxation rules, insolvency and product liability laws and so forth.

The use of specific **international sales terms** therefore offers two valuable benefits: On the one hand, international trade demands specific contractual provisions that are often not appropriately dealt with by standard sales terms tailored for domestic transactions. Secondly, the parties enjoy with regard to an international commercial contract (contrary to consumer and employment contracts) substantially more leeway to deviate from applicable statutory provisions of their home jurisdiction and to structure a sales transaction according to their specific needs. The latter holds true in particular from the perspective of a German exporter of goods and services given that German statutory law and its interpretation by German jurisprudence to this day applies a particular strict approach as regards the policing of general terms and conditions that deviate from statutory provisions.[1] For instance, it remains doubtful whether a seller can rely on an effective limitation of liability clause contained in standard terms governed by German law[2] although such a clause must be considered as fairly industrial standard in international sales contracts in order to reasonably limit the seller's overall risk exposure.

The parties to an international commercial contract are, at least from the perspective of European private international law but also pursuant to the conflict of laws provisions of many other jurisdictions, in principle free to choose the substantive law which they deem most appropriate to govern their sales contract –

---

[1] For an in-depth discussion of this problem in relation to commercial contracts see inter alia K Berger, "Abschied von der Privatautonomie im unternehmerischen Geschäftsverkehr" [2006] ZIP 2149 ff.; S Brachert and A Dietzel, "Deutsche AGB-Rechtsprechung und Flucht ins Schweizer Recht" [2005] ZGS 442 ff.; more recently W Müller, "Die AGB-Kontrolle im unternehmerischen Geschäftsverkehr – Standortnachteil für das deutsche Recht" [2013] BB 1355 ff.

[2] For an excellent critical appraisal of German jurisprudence with regard to the statutory control of limitation of liability clauses in standard sales terms and conditions see P Tettinger, "Zu den Freizeichnungsmöglichkeiten des Verkäufers einer mangelhaften Sache" (2005) 205 AcP 2 ff.

Introduction

regardless of whether or not the sales transaction has any genuine link to the chosen governing law.³ It goes without saying that the **choice of a foreign law** often entails substantial legal uncertainties and ambiguities⁴ and for this reason requires a comprehensive understanding of the legal system in question, including its interpretation and construction by courts and arbitrators and its effect on contract terms, given that the governing law of the contract will not only determine the scope of discretion enjoyed by the parties to set up their own system of obligations, rights and remedies but will also operate as a gap filler – bearing in mind that even the most comprehensive contract will in all likelihood not fully cover any and all legal issues that may arise from a sales transaction.

Against this background, it is the purpose of this book to provide its user with a set of annotated international sales terms as well as a proposal on how these terms can be effectively incorporated into the individual contract. The suggested terms are predominantly tailored for exporters of goods based in the EU, but they should also be useful for sellers residing in other jurisdictions. Contrary to many other model sales contracts and terms and conditions, the sales terms in this book do also suggest a specific governing law clause. Given the essential impact of the governing law of a contract, it is from the author's point of view essential to draft contractual terms on the basis of a given governing law instead of choosing the governing law as the last step in the drafting and negotiation process. Accordingly, the proposed international sales terms in this book are governed by the United Nations Convention on Contracts for the International Sale of Goods (CISG) and Swiss law as the recommended "supplementary" choice of law with regard to those contractual (and partially non-contractual) issues that are not covered by the CISG.

The **CISG**, an international sales convention (that also forms part of the domestic laws of a multitude of jurisdictions), offers a comparably simple structure. The parties to the sales contract are pursuant to Art 6 CISG also able to amend its application in the way they desire. The advantages of Swiss law as the supplementary governing law on the other hand are twofold: First, Swiss law is often used in international commercial contracts due to its widespread classification as a "neutral" body of law.⁵ Though it is without doubt arguable that this classification confuses the search for a legal system striking a balance between different legal traditions (such as civil and common law traditions) with political neutrality⁶, the frequent choice of Swiss law for international commercial contracts in the past has

---

³ See Art 3 (1) Regulation (EC) No 593/2008 of the European Parliament and of the Council of 17 June 2008 on the law applicable to contractual obligations (Rome I) [2008] OJ L177/6; G van Calster, *European Private International Law* (Hart Publishing, Oxford and Portland 2013) 132. The Rome I Regulation applies pursuant to its Art 28 in relation to all contracts concluded on or after 17 December 2009, see Corrigendum to Regulation (EC) No 593/2008 [2009] OJ L309/87.

⁴ For the advantages and disadvantages of the choice of a foreign legal order see P Mankowski, "Überlegungen zur sach- und interessengerechten Rechtswahl für Verträge des internationalen Wirtschaftsverkehrs" [2003] RIW 3, 4.

⁵ Recent surveys have once again confirmed that Swiss law remains a popular choice of parties to international commercial contracts, see inter alia the ICC 2010 Statistical report, ICC International Court of Arbitration Bulletin, Vol. 22 No 1 (2011). According to this report, Swiss and English law were the most popular choices in ICC arbitration proceedings in 2010.

⁶ See for instance C Fountoulakis, "The Parties Choice of "Neutral Law" in International Sales Contracts" [2005] EJLR 303, 304, who describes the designation of the law of a "politically neutral state" as a popular fallacy from which states such as Switzerland have greatly benefited.

Introduction

fostered its reliability and acceptance particularly in international trade. Secondly, it is familiar to lawyers educated in a civil law system (in particular German lawyers) and offers – due to an absence of any direct policing of general terms and conditions utilized in commercial transactions – significantly more leeway with regard to the use of standard contractual provisions deviating from statutory law.

It goes without saying that a seller cannot always demand the exclusive incorporation of his own terms and conditions into a sales contract. In times of economic recession, the lack of bargaining power and other factors may restrict the insistence on the seller's terms to an even greater extent than usual. In particular foreign public entities calling for tenders for the supply of industrial goods regularly request that their standard purchasing terms must exclusively control the contract and accordingly minimize the seller's ability to influence the applicable contract terms. Even in that case, however, the suggested international sales terms may serve as a **point of reference** in order to review suggested purchasing terms while some of the clauses promoted by this book may at least be used on a stand-alone basis. By the same token, this book offers different alternatives for individual terms at least in relation to the most disputed issues in a sales contract in order to facilitate the negotiation of the contract.

Finally and for the reasons indicated above, it is also the aim of this book to provide both a **general understanding** of the impact of typical contractual clauses used in international sales contracts as well as an illustration of the interaction of other legal systems beyond the suggested governing law (with a special emphasis on Anglo-American law) with those fairly standard "boilerplate" clauses.

Standardized sales terms can never cover the particularities of all possible sales transactions. The terms and conditions in this book are for this reason tailored for the **sale of manufactured goods** that are either intended for resale or production purposes. Sales of raw materials and commodities on the other hand may require specific contractual terms that are not adequately catered for by the annotated international sales terms suggested in this book. Finally, the suggested terms are not appropriate for use in consumer contracts given that mandatory consumer laws both in the EU and elsewhere leave the parties with substantially less contractual freedom with regard to the content of a sales contract and the deviations from statutory law contained therein.

Though this publication was created to provide its reader with accurate information on its subject matter, it cannot replace legal or other expert advice. Given that both relevant case law and statutory provisions are permanently evolving and may substantially alter the legal background of international sales terms, neither the validity nor the suitability of any terms and conditions suggested in this book can be guaranteed.

A. General Part

I. Role and impact of the law governing a sales contract

The law governing sales contracts becomes especially important on two counts even after a contract has been concluded.[7] First, the governing law resolves legal issues arising from a sales transaction that have not been addressed by the parties in their contract. Such gap-filling is usually unavoidable as the parties will almost never address all potential legal issues that may arise from or in connection with a sales transaction. But in addition to its role as a gap-filler in relation to omitted terms, the governing law also influences the construction and interpretation of contractual clauses and – by means of mandatory laws such as but not limited to the policing of general terms and conditions – determines the outer limits of the parties' freedom to deviate from statutory provisions. 1

Notwithstanding the major impact of the governing law on a contract, business people in charge of carrying out a commercial transaction notoriously underestimate its effect on their respective legal position. An agreement on the governing law of the contract (if any) is often made on a last minute basis at the end of (in particular long lasting) contractual negotiations.[8] As a consequence, sales contracts are on a regular basis not tailored to the characteristics of the individual governing law and substantial detriments for the parties may follow. To a certain extent, the same problem affects standard conditions proposed by private international trade organizations that are widely used in the context of international contracts, e.g. the FIDIC conditions[9], the General Conditions for the Supply of Mechanical, Electrical and Electronic Products (Orgalime S 2012) promoted by Orgalime[10] or the ICC Model International Sales Contract (2013).[11] There can be no doubt that these standard form contracts are 2

---

[7] The governing law of the contract is without doubt also of eminent importance during the pre-contractual stage: The governing law not only determines whether a contract has come into existence in the first place but deals on a regular basis also with questions of pre-contractual liability of the parties – even if pre-contractual liability is considered as a non-contractual obligation by applicable conflict of laws provisions, see for instance Art 12 (1) Rome II Regulation (n 318).

[8] P Durand-Barthez, "The "governing law" clause: legal and economic consequences of the choice of law in international contracts" [2012] IBLJ 505.

[9] FIDIC, a private international organization of consulting engineers, has published model contracts that are regularly used for construction contracts but at times also for mere supply agreements. Among other works, FIDIC published the Conditions for Construction for Building and Engineering Works designed by the Employer ("Red Book"), Conditions of Contract for Plant and Design Built for Electrical and Mechanical Plant, and for Building and Engineering Works, designed by the Contractor ("Yellow Book") as well as Conditions of Contract for EPC/Turnkey Projects ("Silver Book").

[10] Orgalime is a private European federation representing the interests of the mechanical, electrical, electronic, metalworking & metal articles industries. The model contract terms Orgalime S 2012 are based on the principles of the General Conditions for the Supply of Plant and Machinery for Export (UN ECE 188) prepared by the United Nations Economic Commission for Europe in 1953.

[11] See ICC Model International Sale Contract (ICC Publication No 738, Paris 2013). For a thorough review of the ICC Model International Sales Contract (1997) see F Bortolotti, *Drafting and Negotiating International Commercial Contracts* (ICC-Publication No 671, Paris 2008) 244 ff.

A. General Part

highly useful, well drafted and can greatly reduce transaction costs. However, standard contracts offered by international private or public organizations generally do not suggest a specific governing law provision.[12] It therefore remains the task of the potential user to choose the governing law and to assess its impact on the contract as well as to effect the necessary amendments (if any) to the suggested model contract clauses. Three rather randomly picked examples may further illustrate this problem:

3 • § 45 Orgalime S 2012 excludes under the heading "Consequential Losses" the liability of both parties with respect to "loss of production, loss of profit [...] **or for any other** consequential or indirect loss whatsoever" [emphasis added]. Pursuant to the commentary published by Orgalime, § 45 aims to exclude the seller's liability for lost profits and loss of production in particular caused by defective contractual goods in their entirety.[13] However, it is questionable whether this goal will be accomplished in the event that English law is the governing law of the contract:[14] § 45 treats loss of production and lost profits as mere sub-sets of "consequential damages". Given that consequential damages are under English law limited to those damages that did not directly flow from a breach of contract, lost profits and loss of production are most likely only excluded pursuant to § 45 if these losses did not occur in the usual "flow of events".[15] As a result, the seller may remain liable for lost profits and loss of production to a much greater extent than originally expected.

4 • § 10 of the ICC Model International Sales Contract[16] provides, in line with similar provisions in a multitude of international commercial contracts, for a cap on the seller's liability in case of **delay in delivery**. The cap on liability for delay suggested by the model contract amounts to 5 % of the contract value whereas a further cap amounting to 10 % will apply in case of a termination of the contract by the purchaser based on the delay in delivery.[17]

---

[12] See for instance § 13.2 UN ECE 188 as well as § 47 Orgalime S 2012 (n 10): Both provisions stipulate the laws of the supplier's country of residence as the governing law of the contract; similarly § 1.2 General Conditions of the ICC Model Sales Contract with regard to legal issues not covered by the CISG. The FIDIC model contracts require the parties to state the governing law in the Appendix of the general conditions. Notable exceptions are the standard contracts provided by the Federation of Oil, Seeds and Fats Association (FOFSA) as well as the Grain and Feed Trade Association (GAFTA). Draft standard contracts of both organizations are specifically tailored for the international sale of commodities and English law as the governing law of the contract. Though England is currently not a member state, these forms also explicitly exclude the application of the CISG.

[13] See (with respect to the preceding version ORGALIME S 2000) *ORGALIME Allgemeine Bedingungen S 2000: Ihre Anwendung und Interpretation* (September 2000) 193 f.

[14] This would in the absence of any explicit contractual agreement stipulating otherwise generally be the case if the supplier of the contractual goods resides in England, see § 47 Orgalime S 2012 (n 10).

[15] See eg *Deepak Fertilisers & Petrochemical Corporation v Davy McKee (London) Ltd & Anor* [1999] Lloyd's Rep 387, concerning the explosion of an industrial plant due to the submission of faulty know how by the contractor: Wasted overheads incurred during the reconstruction of the plant as well as lost profits were considered as "no more remote as losses than the cost of reconstruction" by the English Court of Appeal. This case shows clearly that loss of use and loss of profits are often considered as "direct" rather than "consequential" damages and will in this event accordingly not fall within the ambit of a contractual clause excluding seller's liability for consequential loss. More recently in the same direction *Ferryways NV v Associated British Ports* [2008] EWHC 225 (Comm) paras 81 ff. of the judgment.

[16] See n 11 above.

[17] For a critical appraisal of this clause see J Klotz, "Critical Review of The ICC Model International Sale Contract" <http://www.cisg.law.pace.edu/cisg/biblio/klotz.html>.

I. Role and impact of the law governing a sales contract

If a German seller uses the ICC Model International Sales Contract without showing the purchaser his willingness to amend the limitation of liability clause to his own detriment if requested, and the parties have also not agreed on a deviating governing law clause, § 10 may pursuant to the then applicable German law[18] not be enforceable: Given that § 10 (in a standard form contract) may in this event not be considered as being "**bargained for**" pursuant to § 305 (1) 3 of the German Civil Code, the "strict scrutiny" approach applied by German law in relation to standard form contracts would apply with full force. Due to the fact that § 10 does not carve out liability based on seller's intent or gross negligence (or any other person acting on his behalf), the whole clause may already due to this omission be disregarded in its entirety.[19] Accordingly, the seller would in that event face unlimited liability in case of delay.[20]

- § 11.1 of the FIDIC model contracts stipulates the contractor's obligation to remedy any defect or damage that may be reported by the employer on or before the expiry of a so called "defects notification period". However, though this fact is frequently misunderstood by the parties to a FIDIC-contract, the contractor may remain liable for any defects of the works even after the lapse of the defects notification period until the **limitation period** pursuant to the applicable governing law has expired as well. As the duration of limitation periods under domestic laws differs substantially, the choice of the governing law can have a major impact on the duration of the contractor's liability, though the parties may often not be aware of this problem.[21]

A further problem is caused by the fact that international contract law has been predominantly influenced by **Anglo-American law** – partly due to the fact that the English language became the undisputed "lingua franca" a long time ago also with

---

[18] In accordance with Art 1.2 of the General Conditions of the ICC Model International Sales Contract (n 11), the contract is predominantly governed by the CISG whereas the laws of the country where the Seller has his place of business govern legal matters not governed by the CISG. Hence, in case of a German seller, German domestic law determines inter alia matters of validity, see Art 4 CISG.

[19] German law does inter alia not permit an exclusion or limitation of liability in standard form contracts in case of intent or gross negligence (§ 309 No 7 German Civil Code); this restriction applies also in relation to commercial contracts, see M Schwab, *AGB-Recht* (2nd edn C.F. Müller, Heidelberg 2008) para 795. An exclusion of liability is however possible even in case of gross negligence (but not in the event of intentional misconduct) if the contract was individually negotiated, § 276 (3) German Civil Code.

[20] For a more generous application of §§ 305 et seq German Civil Code by an international arbitral tribunal see however P Hobeck, "Zum Aushandeln einer Vertragsbestimmung in Verträgen zwischen Unternehmen" [2005] SchiedsVZ 108, 111, with reference to the ICC interim arbitral award (29 Jan 2001) No 10279: According to the arbitrators in charge of this case, a cap on liability (5 % of the contract price) contained in a standardized sales contract used by the seller was "considered as being bargained for" even though the seller had insisted on this clause throughout the contractual negotiations. From the arbitrators' point of view, §§ 305 ff German Civil Code did not apply because the parties had discussed the cap on liability repeatedly, the seller did not possess any substantial bargaining power and the clause was never explicitly rejected by the purchaser in the course of the negotiations. It is from the viewpoint of the author however rather doubtful whether a German state court would have taken a similar view in this case; for a notable exception see however OLG Hamburg (12 Dec 2008) IBR 2010, 254.

[21] For the general impact of the governing law on interpretation and enforcement of the FIDIC contracts see R Knutson (ed), *FIDIC: An Analysis of International Construction Contracts* (Kluwer Law International, The Hague 2005).

regard to international commercial contracts. Contract clauses that are (sometimes without much consideration by the parties) regularly used in the context of international commercial transactions often origin in model contracts drafted by Anglo-American lawyers. For instance, legal terms such as "warranties", "conditions", "liquidated damages", "gross negligence", "termination" or "rescission" that can be found in a multitude of international commercial contracts have a specific meaning in **common law** jurisdictions such as the USA and England. The parties to an international sales contract need to be aware of this problem in order to avoid substantial legal uncertainties triggered by the combined use of such terms with a governing law that does not belong to a common law jurisdiction. Courts may in this case be tempted to take recourse to a common law approach when interpreting such a term.[22] The outcome may be an unexpected and often rather unpleasant surprise for at least one of the parties.

II. The suggested choice of law for the present International Sales Terms

7 The choice of the governing law is thus a key element in the process of contract drafting and negotiating. The choice of the CISG[23] combined with **Swiss law** as the "supplementary" law for legal matters outside of the CISG's scope of application is in the author's opinion a reliable and recommendable choice for an international sales contract, among others for the following reasons:

8 • A better likelihood of **acceptance**: The choice of the domestic law of either one of the contractual parties is often hardly acceptable given that the affected party may feel uncomfortable about the fact that the contract is governed by the laws of the "home jurisdiction" of the other party. The CISG as an international instrument offers a genuine compromise. This holds true in particular because the CISG has been influenced both by civil and common law systems and accordingly offers a "common platform" for purchasers and sellers alike worldwide.[24] Contrary to domestic laws, the CISG can for that reason be considered as a truly "neutral" law.

9 • **Reasonable transaction costs**: The choice of a foreign domestic law – in particular in case the parties have chosen a domestic law that is foreign to both of them – may entail substantial transaction costs incurred by the parties in order to obtain the relevant information about the specific content of the applicable law, its interpretation by courts and the interaction with contractual provisions. The choice of the CISG reduces transaction costs. The parties have easy access to large data bases of international case law in the English language and to legal literature dealing with the CISG while information on foreign domestic laws is often much more difficult to obtain.

---

[22] From the perspective of German law see B Triebel, "Auslegung englischer Vertragstexte unter deutschem Vertragsstatut – Fallstricke des Art 32 I Nr. 1 EGBGB" [2004] NJW 2189, 2192.

[23] Given that some 79 member states have as of today (status as of 31 July 2013) acceded to the Convention, the CISG may in the vast majority of international sales transactions apply without further preconditions, see Art 1 lit a CISG.

[24] F de Ley, "The Relevance of the Vienna Convention for International Sales Contracts – Should we stop contracting it out?" [2003] Bus L Int'l 241.

II. The suggested choice of law for the present International Sales Terms

- **Reliability:** In recent years, a widespread tendency to exclude the application of the CISG – in particular by sellers in Germany and the USA[25] – seems to have halted or even reversed.[26] That is most likely due to the fact that business people and their legal counsel are more familiar today with the CISG than they were in the first years after its adoption. The application of the CISG by a multitude of courts located in different jurisdictions around the world has also greatly enhanced reliability: The interpretation and construction of key legal concepts and terms of the CISG – such as the "fundamental breach doctrine" – that were a major obstacle in the beginning years have now, more than thirty years after the CISG came into existence, satisfactorily been clarified.[27] 10

- **Flexibility:** The CISG is a flexible instrument. Pursuant to Art 6 CISG, the parties are in principle free to exclude or amend any of its articles. That has often been overlooked in the past: For instance, German sellers[28] have regularly excluded the CISG in their general sales terms. This has in particular been done, as it would appear, to avoid strict (contractual) liability in case of contract breach. Such an approach ignores however that the principle of strict liability can be replaced by a fault-based principle even in standard contracts[29] if the parties so desire. 11

- If the CISG is the governing law of a sales contract, the parties are well advised to also choose the "supplementary" domestic governing law that will govern those legal (contractual) issues not covered by the CISG. In case the parties omit such a supplementary choice, the "supplementary" law must be determined on the basis of the private international laws of the forum, respectively the special conflict of laws provisions that have to be applied by an arbitral tribunal. This may not only cause legal uncertainty. It can in the individual case also affect the validity of the contract or some of its provisions and thus fundamentally alter the legal position of the parties. Swiss law as the suggested choice for the "supplementary governing law" offers some substantial benefits in that regard: Given that almost all relevant provisions are compiled in one single codification (the Swiss Code of Obligations), Swiss law is – in particular in comparison with common law jurisdictions – from the viewpoint of the author more easily comprehensible with regard to the (limited) legal issues outside the scope of the CISG, such as validity of the contract, set-off, assignment, limitation periods, concurring liability under tort etc. Additionally, the interaction between the CISG and Swiss law and 12

---

[25] Apparently, German sellers have predominantly feared the principle of strict liability imposed by the CISG (compared to the fault principle of the German Civil Code according to § 280 German Civil Code in relation to claims for damages) whereas US sellers were inter alia concerned about additional remedies provided by the CISG that do not exist under domestic US sales law; see with regard to German law inter alia FJ Schillo, "UN-Kaufrecht oder BGB? – Vergleichende Hinweise zur Rechtswahl beim Abschluss von Verträgen" [2003] IHR 257, 259; in relation to US law see inter alia P Windship, "Changing Contract Practices in the Light of the United Nations Sales Convention: A Guide for Practitioners" (1995) 29 Int'l Law 525, 531; M Reimann, "The CISG in the United States: Why It Has Been Neglected and Why Europeans Should Care" (2007) 71 RabelsZ 115, 124 ff.

[26] I Schwenzer, P Hachem and C Kee, *Global Sales Law* (OUP, Oxford 2012) para 5.17 ff.

[27] Contra however M Bridge, "Avoidance for Fundamental Breach of Contract under the UN Convention of Contracts for the International Sales of Goods" [2011] ICLQ 917 ff.

[28] From the perspective of German law see S Regula and B Kannowski, "Nochmals: UN-Kaufrecht oder BGB? Erwägungen zur Rechtswahl aufgrund einer vergleichenden Betrachung" [2003] IHR 45 ff.

[29] See with regard to contracts governed by German law as the "supplementary" governing law U Magnus in J v Staudinger (ed), *Wiener UN-Kaufrecht (CISG)* (Sellier de Gruyter, München 2013) Art 74 CISG para 59.

potential risks and ambiguities resulting therefrom have been largely identified and clarified by case law, respectively resolved by the Swiss legislator.[30] This is, for instance, not the case with English law as the apparently most popular governing law in international trade.[31] Most likely due to the fact that England is not a member state of the CISG, virtually no case law exists that has applied both the CISG and English law (as supplement) to an international sales contract.

13   Swiss law also grants – at least at the present time – **more contractual freedom** than other European legal systems do with regard to standard form contracts, given that neither the Swiss Code of Obligations nor any other statute provide with regard to commercial sales contracts for a specific policing of general terms and conditions. Its appraisal as a "neutral" body of law (even though this classification has rightly been identified as somehow flawed)[32] may also help to foster its acceptance as the "supplementary" governing law of the contract by the respective other party. Most likely due to these reasons, Swiss law constitutes together with English law and the laws of the state of New York apparently the most popular choice in governing law clauses.[33]

III. The CISG

14   It is not the purpose of the following chapter to provide a thorough presentation of the CISG. For a more comprehensive understanding, the reader may consult one of the numerous up to date commentaries and textbooks that have been written on the subject.[34] However, a basic understanding is not only helpful but also necessary in order to understand the legal concepts behind the suggested international sales terms and their impact on the sales transaction.

---

[30] For instance, the interaction between the applicable statutory limitation period for warranty claims pursuant to Art 210 (1) CO and the cut-off period contained in Art 39 (2) CISG poses no more problems given that the Swiss legislator has in 2012 extended the former period from one to two years.

[31] English law is in particular chosen for international commodity contracts – most likely due to the fact that the relevant trade associations – such as, for instance, the Federation of Oil, Seeds and Fats Association (FOFSA) as well as the Grain and Feed Trade Association (GAFTA) – are based in London.

[32] See Fountoulakis (n 6).

[33] See, for instance, the "2010 International Arbitration Survey: Choices in International Arbitration", conducted by the Queen Mary University (London) in collaboration with the law firm White & Case: According to that survey, English law was the most frequent choice by 40 %, New York law by 17 % and Swiss law by 8 % of the responding companies. Swiss and English law were also the two most popular choices in arbitral proceedings conducted by the ICC in 2010, s. ICC 2010 Statistical report, ICC International Court of Arbitration Bulletin, Vol. 22 No 1 (2011). For an overview of further empirical surveys concerning the choice of the governing law in international commercial contracts with similar results see S Vogenauer, "Regulatory Competition through Choice of Contract Law and Choice of Forum in Europe: Theory and Evidence" [2013] ERPL 13, 37 ff.

[34] See in German for instance I Schwenzer (ed), *Schwenzer/Schlechtriem, Kommentar zum Einheitlichen UN-Kaufrecht* (6th edn C.H. Beck, München 2013 – forthcoming); P Schlechtriem and U Schroeter, *Internationales UN-Kaufrecht* (5th edn Mohr Siebeck, Tübingen 2013 – forthcoming); B Piltz, *Internationales Kaufrecht* (2nd edn C.H. Beck, München 2008); in English inter alia P Schlechtriem and P Butler, *UN Law on International Sales* (Springer, Berlin 2009). For more recent commentaries on the CISG in English see SM Kröll, L Mistelis and PP Viscasillas (eds), *CISG – The UN-Convention on the International Sales of Goods* (C.H. Beck in cooperation with Hart Publishing and Nomos, München 2011). For an overview of the more recent case law U Magnus, "Das UN-Kaufrecht – aktuelle Entwicklungen" [2013] ZEuP 111 ff.

III. The CISG

Easy and comprehensive access to the case law of both courts of law as well as arbitral tribunals around the world that have applied the CISG is offered free of charge by the **four major data bases** sponsored and operated (inter alia) by the International Institute for the Unification of Private Law (UNIDROIT)[35], the United Nations Commission on International Trade Law (UNCITRAL)[36], Professor Schwenzer, University of Basel (CISG-online)[37] and the Pace-University, New York,[38] that are all available online. In addition to maintaining the CLOUT-database, UNCITRAL also publishes a digest of case law on each article of the CISG that contains a synopsis of the relevant judgments and arbitral awards worldwide; the most recent version of the digest has been released in 2012.[39] The website of the Pace-University offers a multitude of helpful articles on a variety of legal issues arising under the CISG, written by leading academic scholars and practitioners in the field.[40]

One major benefit of the CISG is its comparably simple composition that allows lawyers and business people alike to become easily acquainted with its content. The CISG is divided into **four main parts**. Part I deals with the scope of application and other general provisions. Part II provides rules for contract formation. Part III governs in particular duties and obligations as well as rights and remedies of the parties arising from the sales contract. Part IV contains some final provisions with very limited practical impact that will accordingly not be discussed any further in the following.

1. Part I of the CISG: Scope of application and other general provisions

The CISG is without doubt the most successful attempt to create a harmonized **global sales law**. At this time, some 79 states[41], namely almost all European countries (with the exception of the United Kingdom,[42] Malta, Portugal and Ireland), the USA, Russia, China, Japan,[43] the most important Central and South American states (including, more recently, Brazil)[44] as well as some African states have ratified the CISG.[45]

---

[35] < http://www.unilex.info/dynasite.cfm?dssid=2376&dsmid=13352>.
[36] <http://www.uncitral.org/uncitral/en/case_law.html>.
[37] <http://www.globalsaleslaw.org/index.cfm?pageID=29>. For ease of reference, court judgments and arbitral awards applying the CISG will be cited in this book with a reference to their CISG-online number whenever possible.
[38] <http://www.cisg.law.pace.edu>.
[39] <http://http://www.uncitral.org/pdf/english/clout/CISG-digest-2012-e.pdf >.
[40] <http://www.cisg.law.pace.edu/cisg/biblio/bib2.html>.
[41] Brazil is for the time being the last state that has acceded to the CISG.
[42] A couple of years ago, there has been widespread belief that the UK will accede to the CISG within the nearer future, see in that regard and with some comments on possible reasons why the accession has not taken place yet A Mullis, "Twenty-Five Years On – The United Kingdom, Damages and the Vienna Sales Convention" (2007) 71 RabelsZ 35, 36 ff. However, it would appear against the background of some apparently fruitless consultations undertaken by the UK's Department of Trade and Industry on that topic that an accession will not take place any time soon, K O'Callaghan and G Hutt, "Harmonisation of European Contract Law" [2011] IHR 137.
[43] Japan adhered to the CISG in 2009; see for the background of Japan's accession H Sono, "Japan's Accession to the CISG: The Asia Factor" (2008) 20 Pace Int'l L Rev 105 ff.
[44] Besides Brazil, most notably Argentina, Chile, Colombia and Mexico.
[45] For the current status see the overview provided by UNCITRAL: <http://www.uncitral.org/uncitral/en/uncitral_texts/sale_goods/1980CISG_status.html>. The overview contains also details on reservations declared by individual states.

A. General Part

18 From the perspective of a state court residing in a member state, the CISG applies to a sales contract if both parties have their residence in different states (the so-called "**internationality requirement**") and either both of these states have adopted the CISG or, in the alternative, the private international law of the forum refers to the law of a state that has adopted it, Art 1 (1) lit a, b CISG.[46] Hence, if the exporter resides in a member state, the CISG will most likely apply even if the residence state of the purchaser is not a member state (provided the parties have not agreed to exclude its application). This is due to the fact that the law applicable at the place of residence of the party performing the characteristic contractual obligation will – at least pursuant to European private international law but also in accordance with the conflict of laws provisions of many other jurisdictions[47] – govern the contract in the absence of any governing law clause stipulating otherwise.

18a Though neither state courts in non-member states nor arbitral tribunals are directly bound by the CISG,[48] the CISG may nevertheless apply indirectly in this case as well if and when the private international laws to be applied by these courts respectively arbitral tribunals point to the material laws of a member state. In this case, both Art 1 (1) lit a and lit b CISG form part of the applicable laws whereas the "rules of private international laws" referred to in Art. 1 (1) lit b CISG should according to the author in such event be deemed to be those of this member state.[49]

19 The **material scope of application** of the CISG is further defined in Art 2 and 3 CISG: The CISG covers neither the sale of goods bought for personal, family or household use (unless the seller neither knew nor ought to have known before or at the time of contract conclusion that the goods were bought for such use, Art. 2 lit. a CISG) nor the sale of stocks, shares, investment securities, negotiable instruments and money as well as ships, vessels, aircraft and electricity.[50] Further excluded are sales effected by way of an auction, execution or other authority of law. Finally, the CISG does neither apply if the purchaser provides a substantial portion of raw materials, semi-finished goods or components that are used for the manufacture of the contractual goods, nor in the event that a **preponderant part of the contractor's obligations consists of the supply of services**, Art 3 (1),(2) CISG. A relevant example of the latter exclusion in practice are "EPC" (engineering, procurement and commis-

---

[46] Art 1 (1) lit b CISG has given rise to some controversies against the background that Art 95 CISG permits the member states to opt out of this provision: In particular, it is still controversial whether a domestic court is bound by the decision of another member state to opt out of Art 1 (1) lit b CISG if the private international laws of the forum state point to the laws of the reservation state, see Schlechtriem and Butler (n 34) para 18. Given that almost all major trading nations of the world have adhered to the CISG (and the CISG will in the vast majority of cases apply already pursuant to Art 1 (1) lit a CISG), this problem has however significantly lost relevance.

[47] EU: Art 4 (1) lit a Rome I Regulation (n 3); Switzerland: Art 117 (2) PILA; Russia: Art 1211 (2) Civil Code; China: Art 41 S. 2 Law on the Application of Law for Foreign-Related Civil Legal Relationships of the People's Republic of China (2011).

[48] A Jansen and M Spilker, "The Application of the CISG in the World of International Commercial Arbitration" (2013) 77 RabelsZ 131, 137.

[49] According to the author's view, it seems unconvincing to treat Art. 1 (1) lit a and lit b CISG in a different manner in this regard. According to Gruber, however, Art. 1 (1) lit. a CISG is inapplicable in arbitral proceedings whereas Art. 1 (1) lit b) CISG must be applied upfront also by arbitral tribunals, see U Gruber, "The Convention on the International Sale of Goods (CISG) in Arbitration" [2009] IBLJ 15, 21 f.

[50] The sale of individual components of these goods – for instance, aircraft engines – does however fall within the ambit of the CISG, see Supreme Court of Hungary (25 Sep 1992) CLOUT No 53.

III. The CISG

sioning) respectively "turnkey" contracts that are concerned with the construction and commissioning of industrial plants: In this case, services provided by the contractor in the form of erecting and commissioning works at the site as well as supervision and maintenance of the plant are often more important than the supply of components and equipment needed for the initial erection.[51]

Although the parties are free to exclude the application of the CISG in accordance with the explicit option stipulated in Art 6 CISG, they must agree on the **exclusion** in an unambiguous (though according to the prevailing view not necessarily explicit[52]) manner: There is widespread agreement throughout the international case law (confirmed both by courts of law[53] as well as arbitral tribunals[54]) that the mere choice of a domestic law that has adopted the CISG is to be interpreted as a reference to the domestic law including the CISG. Furthermore, even if the parties exclude the application of the CISG in their contract, the CISG may still remain important with regard to contract formation matters and its Part II will hence determine whether such an exclusion has been agreed upon at all – in particular if the exclusion of the CISG is stipulated in general terms and conditions.[55] Hence, a good understanding of both the contract formation rules as well as the system of rights and remedies of the parties provided by the CISG is in any event essential for the proper conclusion and execution of an international sales transaction. 20

2. Part II of the CISG: The formation of the sales contract

Part II deals with the formation of a sales contract. Even though the relevant provisions are intended to strike a certain balance between common law and civil law jurisdictions, lawyers from both legal systems will recognize these provisions as being rather familiar. The conclusion of a contract under the CISG requires an offer that sufficiently specifies the details of the intended transaction (in particular the contractual goods, the quantities and the contract price[56]) and expresses the intention of the parties to be legally bound, and a mirroring acceptance by the offeree made in 21

---

[51] See HG Zurich (9 Jul 2002) CISG-online 726. Engineering works performed by the contractor prior to the manufacture of the contract goods will however be considered as part of the manufacture respectively delivery of the goods rather than the provision of separate services, see LG Mainz (26 Nov 1998) CISG-online 563.

[52] See among others OGH (2 Apr 2009) CISG-online 1889; Cour de Cassation (25 Oct 2005) CISG-online 1226.

[53] BGH (25 Nov 1998) CISG-online 353; BG (17 Jul 2007) CISG-online 1515. The prevailing view among US courts still accepts only an explicit contractual exclusion of the CISG, see, for instance, US District Court, Eastern District Michigan (28 Sep 2007) CISG-online 1601.

[54] See Tribunal of International Commercial Arbitration at the Russian Federation Chamber of Commerce and Industry (5 Nov 2004) CISG-online 1360; ICC Arbitration Case No 11333 (1 Jan 2002) CISG-online 1420.

[55] That is due to the fact that the CISG prevails over private international laws, see eg Art 25 (1) Rome I Regulation (n 3). It follows that the CISG will exclusively determine whether general terms and conditions have become a part of the contract even if these terms provide for the exclusion of the CISG – accordingly, also Art 10 (1) and (2) Rome I Regulation are pre-empted by the CISG, see M Schmidt-Kessel, "Kollisionsrechtliche Behandlung der Einbeziehung Allgemeiner Geschäftsbedingungen unter dem CISG. Entscheidung des niederländischen Hoge Raad v. 28. 1. 2005" [2008] ZEuP 605 ff.

[56] Whether an agreement as to the contract price is a condition precedent for a binding sales contract is however still controversial against the background of the contradictory Articles 14 (1) and 55 CISG, see Schlechtriem and Butler (n 34) para 75 f.

A. General Part

reasonable time (if no time is fixed) after receipt of the offer, Art 18 (2) CISG. No requirements as to form exist, Art 11 CISG, and therefore an oral exchange of both offer and acceptance will in principle suffice though member states may pursuant to Art. 96 CISG make a reservation in accordance with Art. 12 CISG "that any provision of article 11, article 29, or Part II of this Convention, that allows a contract of sale or its modification or termination by agreement or any offer, acceptance, or other indication of intention to be made in any form other than in writing, does not apply where any party has his place of business in that State".

22   Both the offer and its acceptance become effective only if they **reach the other party**, Art 15 (1), 18 (2) CISG.[57] A notice of acceptance to the offeror is however dispensable if by virtue of the offer or as a result of practices established between the parties assent may already be indicated by certain conduct (such as the dispatch of the goods or payment of the contract price), Art 18 (3) CISG.

23   Contrary to many civil law systems, but in line with common law principles, an offer can be revoked by the offeror until its acceptance is dispatched, Art 16 (1) CISG. However, a **revocation** is no longer possible if either the offer indicates its irrevocability or the offeree could reasonably rely on the same (in particular on the ground that a fixed time for acceptance was stated), see Art 16 (2) lit a and lit b CISG.[58]

24   A reply to an offer containing additions, limitations or other modifications does not constitute acceptance but a counter-offer, Art 19 (1) CISG. The CISG does however stipulate one significant exception to this rule: Even a deviating reply may constitute an **acceptance** of an offer if the additional or different terms set forth in the reply do not materially alter the terms of the offer. In that case, the offeror can only avoid the binding conclusion of a contract if he objects to the reply without undue delay, Art 19 (2) CISG.[59] Art 19 (3) CISG serves as a rule of interpretation indicating that certain additions or differences are most likely to be considered as material and Art 19 (2) CISG hence does not apply.

---

[57] Additionally, the offeror can at any time withdraw from an offer provided the withdrawal reaches the other party before or at the same time as the offer, Art 15 (2) CISG. By the same token, the offeree can withdraw its acceptance provided the withdrawal reaches the offeror before the acceptance would become effective, Art 22 CISG. The different treatment of a withdrawal of an offer on the one hand and the withdrawal of an acceptance on the other is due to the fact that an acceptance may pursuant to Art 18 (3) CISG become effective without reaching the offeror.

[58] Due to the common law doctrine of consideration, a contract becomes in addition to the general requirement of a "meeting of the minds" binding only if the party in receipt of an offer gives something in return for the contractual promise. Hence, English law even allows a revocation of an offer if the offeror has promised not to revoke it given that no consideration has been given for the promise to hold the offer open, see M Bridge, *The International Sale of Goods* (3rd edn OUP, Oxford 2013) para 12.03. In particular invitations to tender governed by English law often provide, for this very reason, for the payment of a certain amount of money as consideration for the submission of a tender that is intended to be irrevocable for a specified period of time. US law today follows a more modern approach with regard to the doctrine of consideration that leads to similar solutions as the CISG: Pursuant to § 2–205 UCC, a written offer by a merchant that by its terms gives assurance that it will be held open is not revocable, for lack of consideration, during the time stated, or if no time is stated, for a reasonable time up to a maximum period of 3 months.

[59] A delay by more than three working days will most likely be considered as being too late, see P Schlechtriem and UG Schroeter in Schlechtriem and Schwenzer (n 34) Art 19 CISG para 16.

3. Part III of the CISG: Obligations, rights and remedies of the parties

25 For the purpose of this book, the **seller's obligations** and the purchaser's corresponding remedies are the most important piece of Part III of the CISG. Hence, the following introduction into Part III of the CISG will focus both on the seller's obligations to deliver conforming products in good time and on the available remedies in case of their breach. In the end, a short overview over the seller's rights and remedies against the purchaser will be given as well.

a) The concept of a "fundamental breach"

26 The CISG stipulates one major prerequisite for the exercise of some remedies available in the event of a breach of contract: Both an avoidance of the contract as well as a claim for delivery of substitute goods (in case of defective goods) presuppose in principle a **fundamental breach** of the contract by the seller, Art 46 (2) and 49 (1) CISG. A fundamental breach is indirectly also a precondition for a damage claim if the purchaser seeks compensation for a cover purchase pursuant to Art 75 and 76 CISG.[60] Finally, a right of the seller to declare the contract avoided generally also requires a fundamental breach by the purchaser, see Art 64 (1) lit a CISG. Therefore, both the concept and scope of the term "fundamental breach" as further defined in Art 25 CISG will be briefly discussed first.

27 Pursuant to **Art 25 CISG**, a breach of contract committed by either party is fundamental if it results in a detriment that substantially deprives the other party of what it is entitled to expect under the contract – unless the party in breach did not foresee and a reasonable person of the same kind would not have foreseen that result. In line with the other provisions of the CISG, Art 25 CISG does not distinguish between a breach of primary and secondary obligations. Accordingly, the breach of a secondary or collateral obligation can also amount to a fundamental breach.[61] As an example, the breach of a non-compete obligation or of re-import restrictions stipulated in a sales contract have in individual cases been considered as fundamental contract breaches.[62] Furthermore, references to "detriment" instead of "damage" and the parties' expectations imply that the suffering of economic loss is not a necessary precondition for a fundamental breach and reinforce the parties' general freedom to define in the contract at their own discretion what kind of breaches should be regarded as fundamental.[63] However, given that the parties will most likely not "label" all their respective obligations as being either of a fundamental or non-fundamental character, the qualification of the individual contractual obligation in question remains an important issue for the construction of the contract. Having in mind that an avoidance of the contract is a "remedy of last resort", a careful assessment (in the absence of an explicit agreement) is required in each individual case in order to determine whether the respective breach has caused the substantial deprivation of the innocent party's expectations.

---

[60] According to one opinion, however, costs incurred by way of a "cover transaction" can already be claimed under Art 74 (1) CISG and hence do not necessarily always depend on a fundamental breach, see n 129 below for further reference.
[61] F Ferrari, "Wesentliche Vertragsverletzung nach UN-Kaufrecht" [2003] IHR 1, 3.
[62] See Ferrari (n 61) 3; OLG Koblenz (31 Jan 1997) CISG-online 256.
[63] R Goode et al, *Transnational Commercial Law. International Instruments and Commentary* (2nd edn OUP, Oxford 2012) para 7.82.

A. General Part

28 A better insight into the application of Art 25 CISG by courts and arbitral tribunals can be derived from the existing international case law: More than thirty years after the adoption of the CISG, certain categories of breaches have evolved that are internationally recognized as being **"fundamental"** in character.[64] They can be briefly summarized as follows:

29 Fundamental breaches by the Seller:

30 • **Impossibility** of performance[65] or definite refusal to perform.[66]

31 • **Late delivery** if the parties have either explicitly agreed that time shall be of the essence or the circumstances of the transaction in the individual case imply the same: The latter may in particular be assumed in the case of sales of seasonal goods or commodities[67] provided the parties have agreed upon a specific delivery date. Some legal commentaries and a decision rendered by a German Higher Regional Court[68] have also taken the view that the use of the Incoterms clauses CIF and FOB may serve as (rebuttable) evidence that the observance of a fixed delivery date will be of the essence of the contract. Though this seems from the author's point of view[69] hardly convincing in that generality, the draftsman of a sales contract must take this view into account in case Incoterms are (as it is regularly done) used in an international sales transaction.

32 • The delivery of **non-conforming goods** in principle only amounts to a fundamental breach if the non-conformity of the goods is both substantial in character and at the same time either not remediable (by means of repair or delivery of substitute goods) or cannot be remedied within an appropriate additional period of time.[70] However, even in case of an uncurable defect, a multitude of judgments – in particular rendered by Swiss, German and Austrian courts[71] – repeatedly denied the existence of a fundamental breach if the purchaser can reasonably be expected to resell the defective goods in the ordinary course of business, albeit at a lower price.[72] This

---

[64] Some scholars consider Art. 25 CISG due to its vagueness however still as a major disadvantage of the CISG, see in particular M Bridge, "Avoidance for Fundamental Breach of Contract under the UN Convention of Contracts for the International Sales of Goods" [2011] ICLQ 917 ff.

[65] See ICC-Award No 9978/1999 (1 Mar 1999) CISG-online 708. The CISG prevails also over national provisions that render a contract void in the event of an initial impossibility to perform, see F Ferrari, "The Interaction between the United Nations Convention on Contracts for the International Sale of Goods and Domestic Remedies" (2007) 71 RabelsZ 52, 70 who points specifically to Art 68 (3) CISG in that regard.

[66] See OLG München (15 Sep 2004) CISG-online 1013.

[67] However, even in case of a commodity sale, a delay in delivery will not necessarily always amount to a fundamental breach. It should be taken into account that the principles of English law are in that respect still different from the CISG: Whereas contractual stipulations as to the time of performance are generally considered as "conditions" of a contract, allowing the termination of the contract by the innocent party in case of any (even minor) delay, Art 25 CISG requires a substantial detriment of expectations, see D Peacock, "Avoidance and the Notion of Fundamental Breach Under the CISG: An English Perspective" (2003) 8 Int'l Trade & Bus L Ann 94, 117.

[68] OLG Hamburg (28 Feb 1997) CISG-online 261.

[69] Also U Magnus and J Lüsing, "CISG und INCOTERMS, Leistungsverzug und Fixgeschäft" [2007] IHR 1 ff; P Ostendorf, "Noch einmal: Führt die Vereinbarung einer CIF-Klausel zum Fixgeschäft?" [2009] IHR 100, 101.

[70] BG (16 Dec 2009) CISG-online 1900.

[71] BG (28 Oct 1998) CISG-online 413; BGH (3 Apr 1996) CISG-online 135.

[72] P Huber, "CISG – The Structure of Remedies" (2007) 71 RabelsZ 13, 26 f; OLG Düsseldorf (9 Jul 2010) CISG-online 2171.

III. The CISG

approach may however be limited to contract goods that were intended for resale in the first place (eg commodities) – in case of unrecoverable defects of industrial goods, this reasoning is less likely to apply provided that the goods cannot be used for their intended purpose.[73]

Fundamental breaches by the Purchaser: 33

- **Delayed payment** of the contract price does not on a stand-alone basis constitute a fundamental breach.[74] The same holds true with regard to any delay in taking over of the goods.[75] In both cases, a definite refusal regarding either payment and/or taking over does however amount to a fundamental breach.[76] 34
- An **insolvency** of the purchaser will in principle also amount to a fundamental breach[77]. 35

b) Obligations of the Seller

aa) **Primary obligations.** The seller's **primary obligation** is to deliver the goods and related documents and to transfer the property in the goods (respectively the documents) to the purchaser, Art 30 CISG. Contrary to some domestic laws (in particular German sales law), an obligation to deliver conforming goods – that is to say goods that are free from defects in title and quality – does not form a part of the *primary* delivery obligation.[78] 36

Art 31 and 33 CISG specify the scope, place of performance and due date of the **delivery obligations** in case the parties have not explicitly agreed on these issues in the contract.[79] In case the parties have not agreed on a specific place of delivery, the seller fulfils his delivery obligations by way of handing over the goods to the first carrier for transmission to the purchaser, Art 31 lit a CISG. This rule applies, however, only if the contract involves a carriage of the goods – that is to say provides for the seller to be responsible for organizing the carriage.[80] Otherwise, the seller is already discharged 37

---

[73] See, eg, OLG Linz (23 Jan 2006) CISG-online 1377: Pursuant to the underlying facts of this case, the buyer, who had purchased a defective car for his own professional use, was not requested to resell the car instead of declaring avoidance of the contract based on a fundamental breach. See also US Court of Appeals for the Second Circuit (6 Dec 1995) CISG-online 140; similarly also A Björklund in Kröll/Mistelis/Perales Viscasillas (n 34) Art 25 CISG para 37 (no fundamental breach if the buyer can resell the goods without going outside his usual market).

[74] Similar to non-delivery, non-payment may however transform into a fundamental breach in case of a considerable delay in payment, see for instance the decision of a Chinese arbitral tribunal, cf. CIETAC (10 May 2005) CISG-online 1022, dealing with a delay of payment arising out of a multitude of contracts and amounting to more than one year.

[75] See Tribunal de Grande Instance de Strasbourg (22 Dec 2006) CISG-online 1629: A delay in the takeover of the contractual goods amounting to one month was not considered as a fundamental breach.

[76] See P Schlechtriem and UG Schroeter in Schlechtriem and Schwenzer (n 34) Art 25 CISG para 39ff with reference to further case-law.

[77] See Federal Court of Australia, South Australian District (28 Apr 1995) CISG-online 218.

[78] Contrary, eg, German domestic sales law: Pursuant to § 433 (2) German Civil Code, the conformity of the goods forms part of the main contractual obligation (*Hauptleistungspflicht*) to deliver the goods.

[79] If the parties do not agree on a delivery date, the contractual goods must be delivered within a reasonable time after the conclusion of the contract, Art 33 lit c CISG.

[80] C Widmer in Schlechtriem and Schwenzer (n 34) Art 31 CISG para 5. Hence, Art 31 lit a CISG does not apply if the purchaser is responsible for the performance of the carriage.

A. General Part

from his obligations once he has placed the goods at the purchaser's disposal at the place indicated by either Art 31 lit b or – if the requirements of this provision are not fulfilled – pursuant to Art 31 lit c CISG at his own place of residence. Given that the parties usually define the scope of the delivery obligations owed by the seller in the contract and expressly agree on either a delivery date or at least a timeframe for the delivery, recourse to either Art 31 and/or Art 33 CISG is rarely necessary.

38 The actual content of the delivery obligations also influences the passage of the risk.[81] The **transfer of risk** provisions in the CISG correspond closely with the respective delivery obligations – as a rule of thumb, the risk shifts to the purchaser once the seller has discharged his delivery obligations pursuant to Art 31 CISG, see Arts 66ff CISG. In reality, however, Arts 66ff CISG are usually replaced by specific contract provisions. In particular, the Incoterms deal explicitly with the transfer of risk and prevail – if used by the parties – over these provisions.

39 **bb) Conformity of the goods.** Besides the timely delivery of the goods, the seller's most important contractual duties are his obligations in relation to the quality of the goods. Art 35 (1) CISG stipulates upfront that it is foremost up to the parties themselves to define the applicable quality standard of the goods. It would accordingly appear that only if the parties have not or *not comprehensively* agreed upon the applicable quality standard must recourse be had to the substitute standards defined in Art 35 (2) CISG. However, the relationship between Art. 35 (1) and (2) CISG – in particular the character of Art. 35 (2) CISG as either a "default rule" or a provision that will in principle apply cumulatively with agreed qualification standards according to Art. 35 (1) CISG is still not entirely settled and should accordingly be clarified by the parties in the contract.

40 According to the quality standards implied by law pursuant to Art. 35 (2) CISG, the goods must be fit for the purpose for which goods of the same description would ordinarily be used (Art 35 (2) lit a CISG). If a particular purpose for the goods have been made known to the seller, the goods must also possess the necessary properties to accomplish that purpose (Art 35 (2) lit b CISG). The latter quality standard will apply regardless of whether the parties expressly or implicitly agreed upon its incorporation into their contract. That is surprising from the viewpoint of contract theory and most likely due to influences from Anglo-American law.[82] Within the existing body of case law, Art 35 (2) lit a and lit b CISG have become in particular important in the event that the contractual goods do not conform with public laws (for instance product or food safety rules and the like) applicable in the purchaser's country, respectively the country of use. But according to the prevailing view, the purchaser can regularly not expect compliance of the goods with public laws applicable in the purchaser's country respectively the country of use under Article 35

---

[81] The transfer of risk does not only shift the risk of payment ("payment risk") but also (subject to Art 70 CISG) the "performance risk": Only if the seller commits a fundamental breach, even the accidental destruction or damage of the goods does not do away with the remedies that are available for the breach, see J Erauw, "CISG Articles 66–70: The Risk of Loss and Passing It" (2005) 25 J L & Commerce 203, 209.

[82] The implied warranty of fitness for a particular purpose contained in both Sec 14 (3) SGA 1979 and § 2-315 UCC have apparently been served as a blueprint for Art 35 (2) CISG, see I Schwenzer in Schlechtriem and Schwenzer (n 34) Art 35 CISG para 18.

III. The CISG

(2) CISG.[83] As this view has not remained undisputed[84], the parties are best advised to address this issue explicitly in the sales contract.[85]

Pursuant to Art 35 (3) CISG, the seller is not liable for a lack of conformity if the purchaser knew or could not have been unaware of the defect. However, this exclusion applies only in relation to the "implied" quality standards provided under Art 35 (2) CISG and the purchaser's knowledge will not endanger his remedies for any breach of an express quality standard agreed on by the parties pursuant to Art 35 (1) CISG.[86] 41

Finally, Art 36 (1) CISG stipulates the point in time when the contract goods must conform to the requirements of Art 35 (1) respectively Art 35 (2) CISG. Similar to a multitude of domestic sales laws[87], the CISG holds the seller liable for a defect (or at least the roots for its later appearance) only if it already existed at the time of the transfer of risk whereas the purchaser bears the burden of proof for this fact once the goods have been handed over to him.[88] It should be noted, however, that any non-suitability of the goods for their intended use for a reasonable time after handover may constitute a defect even if the goods appeared to be in good working order at the time of transfer of risk, as the materialization of a defect at a later stage may often be due to the initial unsuitability of the goods (at the time of transfer of risk) to allow for their intended regular or particular use for a reasonable time thereafter.[89] 42

Different rules apply if the parties have agreed on a "guarantee of durability"[90] pursuant to Art 36 (2) CISG. Under a "**guarantee of durability**", the seller remains 43

---

[83] L DiMatteo et al, *International Sales Law: A Critical Analysis of CISG Jurisprudence* (CUP, Cambridge 2005) 114. See, more recently, High Court of New Zealand (30 July 2010) CISG-online 2113; OGH (19 April 2007) CISG-online 1495 (obiter dicta) both following the leading case BGH (8 March 1995) CISG-online 144 (the well known "mussels case"): The seller is only bound by the public law standards outside his own country of residence if either a) the public laws of the purchaser's state are identical to those enforced in the seller's state b) the purchaser has informed the seller about these rules at the time of conclusion of the contract or c) due to special circumstances, such as the existence of a seller's branch office in the purchaser's state.
[84] Contra in particular Schlechtriem and Butler (n 34) para 139.
[85] Piltz (n 34) para 5-44. The remaining "implied warranties" in Art 35 (2) lit c and lit d CISG are only of limited relevance in commercial reality: Pursuant to Art 35 (2) lit c CISG, the goods must comply with the properties of the sample in the event of a "model sale". Finally, Art 35 (2) lit d CISG provides requirements with regard to the packaging of the goods.
[86] S Kröll in Kröll/Mistelis/Perales Viscasillas (n 34) Art 35 CISG para 152 ff. with references to opposing views that favor an analogous application of Art. 35 (3) CISG also with regard to agreed quality standards pursuant to Art 35 (1) CISG.
[87] England: Time of delivery is decisive though Sec 14 (2B) lit e SGA 1979 refers also to the durability of the goods, see P Atiyah, JN Adams and HL MacQueen, *The Sale of Goods* (11th edn Pearson, Harlow 2005); Germany: § 434 (1) 1 German Civil Code; Switzerland: Art 197 CO, see also H Honsell, *Schweizerisches Obligationenrecht. Besonderer Teil* (9th edn Stämpfli, Bern 2010) 77; USA: § 2-725 (2) UCC: "[...] A breach of warranty occurs when tender of delivery is made."
[88] OLG Karlsruhe (8 Feb 2006) CISG-online 1328; BG (13 Nov 2003) CISG-online 846.
[89] It is more difficult to determine the length of a "reasonable time" in this regard, see U Magnus in Staudinger (n 29) Art 35 CISG para 23. See also LG München I (27 Feb 2002) CISG-online 654: This case concerned the delivery of swivel-mounted globes (intended for the commercial displays of videos) that suffered from malfunctions within a couple of months after their delivery. The court considered the globes as defective pursuant to Art 35 (2) lit a CISG given that the utilized components were due to their construction from the outset not suited for failure-free operation within an assumed period of use of three years.
[90] The legal concept contained in Art 36 (2) CISG appears to be closely connected to the legal concept of a guarantee of durability (*Haltbarkeitsgarantie*) that is acknowledged by German and Swiss law (see § 443 (2) German Civil Code; in relation to Swiss law see Honsell (n 87) 88), but also to a "warranty extending to future performance" stipulated in § 2-725 UCC (2003).

liable for any defects of the goods that occur within the guarantee period unless he can prove that the defect was caused by inappropriate use, operation or maintenance of the contractual goods by the purchaser or by other external factors.[91] A guarantee of durability may also influence the commencement and duration of limitation periods, but this impact must be determined by domestic laws.[92]

44 cc) **Defects of Title.** Defects of title are dealt with by Arts 41 and 42 CISG. The CISG distinguishes between general third-party claims in relation to the contract goods (Art 41 CISG), in particular claims based on property or security rights in the goods, and third-party claims related to **industrial or other intellectual property rights** (Art 42 CISG). Two characteristics of these provisions are worth mentioning even in a brief introduction to the CISG: First, unlike many domestic laws,[93] Arts 41 and 42 CISG cover not only existing rights of third parties with regard to the contract goods: The seller is also liable towards the purchaser in the event of **unfounded claims** raised by third parties and must therefore reimburse the purchaser for costs incurred as a result of a defense against unfounded or even frivolous claims.[94] This result seems to be particularly harsh in case of unfounded claims falling within the ambit of Art 41 CISG given that this provision burdens the seller with strict liability.

45 On the other hand, the specific regime with regard to an (alleged) infringement of intellectual or **industrial property rights**[95] of third parties set forth in Art 42 CISG exposes the seller to a lesser degree of liability than under both Art 41 CISG and many domestic sales laws: While the seller can escape from liability under Art 41 CISG only if the purchaser has agreed to take the goods subject to the respective right or claim, solely actual knowledge or grossly negligent ignorance of the existence of third-party rights or claims based on any (alleged) infringement of industrial or other intellectual property rights ("IP rights") will trigger liability pursuant to Art 42 CISG. Additionally, the seller's responsibility is also geographically restricted: Only the infringement of IP rights acknowledged by the domestic laws of the country in which the goods will be resold or otherwise used are of relevance, provided such resale or use in that country was contemplated by both parties at the time of the formation of the contract. In all other cases, only claims arising under the laws of the state where the purchaser has his place of business may give rise to the seller's liability.[96] The

---

[91] I Schwenzer in Schlechtriem and Schwenzer (n 34) Art 36 CISG para 13.

[92] See ch C.VII below.

[93] I Schwenzer in Schlechtriem and Schwenzer (n 34) Art 41 CISG para 9.

[94] Both Arts 41 and 42 CISG request the seller to deliver goods which are free from any right **or claim** [emphasis added] of a third party; see also S Kröll in Kröll/Mistelis/Perales Viscasillas (n 34) Art 42 CISG para 9 ff; see also BG (17 Apr 2012) CISG-online 2346.

[95] Intellectual property rights include inter alia industrial property rights such as patents (registered rights protecting an invention that can be commercially used on an exclusive basis for a certain period), design rights (registered as well as unregistered rights protecting new designs and shapes), trademarks (registered rights protecting a brand name and/or a logo for goods and services) layout-designs of integrated circuits, commercial names and designations as well as geographical indications, petty patents and copyright (the latter regularly being an unregistered right protecting "creative expressions" as the cornerstone of intellectual property rights in the more narrow meaning of this term), see GG Lettermann, *Basics of International Intellectual Property Law* (Transnational Publishers, Ardsley 2001) 4.

[96] Contrary to the property rights in material goods, intellectual and/or industrial property rights (in particular patents) are territorially restricted to the respective jurisdiction in which they are acknowledged respectively registered (the "territorial principle"), see, eg, J Straus and NS Klunker, "Harmonisation of International Patent Law" [2007] IIC 907, 917. However, requirements for and scope of intellectual property rights have been harmonized both on the European and the international level.

III. The CISG

seller's liability ceases finally if the purchaser either knew or could not have been unaware of the right or claim or paved the way for these claims by submitting technical drawings, designs or other specifications to the seller that caused the infringement, see Art 42 (2) CISG.

Though the seller's responsibility under Art 42 CISG has for that reason sometimes been characterized as rather modest,[97] the prevailing opinion imposes a duty on the seller to investigate the existence of IP rights in the relevant countries: In particular, whenever IP rights have been published in public registers of the relevant jurisdiction(s) at the time of the conclusion of the contract, the exemption provided by Art 42 (2) CISG generally does not apply.[98]

dd) Examination of the contract goods and notification of defects. The seller's liability for both quality defects and defects in title[99] is subject to a timely notification of the defect by the purchaser.[100]

In case of quality defects, the notice must be given within a reasonable time after the purchaser has discovered or ought to have discovered the defect, Art 39 (1) CISG. Art 38 (1) CISG requires the purchaser to examine the goods within as short a period as is practicable in the circumstances and thereby clarifies by when the purchaser ought to have discovered the defect. As a result, the purchaser must observe two different time periods – one period for the **examination of** the goods and the other one for the **notification**. The acceptable length of these periods remains one of the most controversial legal issues in the international jurisprudence. However, it would appear that a general tendency has evolved granting the purchaser (subject to the particularities of the individual case) a maximum time frame of one month for the notification pursuant to Art 39 (1) CISG.[101] In specific cases (e.g. perishable goods), the period can however be much shorter. It must also be taken into account that some national courts – most notably the Austrian

---

[97] See HM Flechtner, "Conformity of Goods, Third Party Claims, and Purchaser's Notice of Breach under the United Nations Sales Convention ('CISG'), with Comments on the 'Mussels Case', the 'Stolen Automobile Case' and the Ugandan Used Shoes Case'", University of Pittsburgh School of Law Working Paper Series, Paper 64 (2007) 11. Flechtner expresses in particular doubts whether Art 42 CISG can offer reasonable safeguards for the purchaser in the event that the contractual goods appear to infringe third party's IP-rights.

[98] See for an in-depth discussion of this problem RM Janal, "The Seller's Responsibility for Third Party Intellectual Property Rights under the Vienna Sales Convention" in CB Andersen and UG Schroeter (eds), *Sharing International Commercial Law across National Boundaries: Festschrift for Albert H. Kritzer on the Occasion of his Eightieth Birthday* (Wildy, Simmonds & Hill Publishing, London 2008) 203, 212 ff.

[99] Whereas many domestic legal systems stipulate a similar requirement to notify quality defects, remedies for defects in title are pursuant to the majority of domestic laws not subject to a notification requirement of the purchaser. See for instance Germany: § 377 German Commercial Code (contra however CW Canaris, *Handelsrecht* (24th edn C.H. Beck, München 2006) 441 according to whom defects in title fall within the ambit of § 377 HGB as well; in the same direction more recently OLG Düsseldorf (4 Dec 2012) BeckRS 06665); Russia: Art 484 Civil Code; Switzerland: Art 201 CO; similar as the CISG however the position under US law: § 2-607 (3) lit b UCC.

[100] One US decision has applied Art 39 CISG by analogy also to cases of late delivery, see US District Court, Eastern District of Kentucky (18 Mar 2008) CISG-online 1652. It is respectfully submitted that this view is not convincing – inter alia, because a seller is (contrary to the regular situation in case of a quality defect) regularly fully aware of a delay with delivery.

[101] See in particular I Schwenzer, "The Noble Month (Articles 38, 39 CISG) – The Story Behind the Scenery" [2005] EJLR 353 ff.

A. General Part

Supreme Court – still hold the view that both the examination period and the notification period should as a matter of principle be much shorter.[102]

49 Finally, Art 39 (2) CISG stipulates a **long stop date** for the notification that becomes important in particular in case of hidden quality defects: A defect must be reported at the latest within a period of two years after handover – whether or not it has or could have been discovered within this time period.

50 Defects in title must be reported within a reasonable period of time after they have or ought to have been discovered by the purchaser, Art 43 CISG. A long stop period that would bar the purchaser's remedies based on hidden defects in title does (contrary to claims based on quality defects) not exist.

51 Non-compliance with the notice periods does not constitute a breach of contract. But in this event the purchaser loses any rights and remedies with regard to the defect[103], subject to a claim for a reduction of the price or damages (excluding lost profits) if he has a reasonable excuse for his failure to submit a timely notice, Art 44 CISG.

c) Remedies of the purchaser in case of breach

52 Art 45 CISG introduces the following four **remedies** that are – subject to certain additional prerequisites – available to the purchaser in case of a breach of contract by the seller:
- Specific performance (Art 46 (1) CISG); in case of non-conforming goods[104] either by means of delivery of substitute goods or by repair (Art 46 (2), (3) CISG)
- Reduction of the contract price, Art 50 CISG (in case of non-conforming goods only)
- Avoidance of the contract, Art 49 CISG
- Claim for damages, Arts 74ff CISG

53 The CISG generally does not distinguish between different breaches of contract. Therefore, to the exclusion of the remedies of price reduction, substitute performance and repair of the goods that apply only in case of a quality defect, all remedies provided by the CISG are available regardless whether a breach of contract is committed by means of delivery of non-conforming goods, non- or delayed delivery or any other breach of existing obligations arising from the sales contract.

54 Art 45 (2) CISG follows – in line with many domestic sales laws[105] – a "**cumulative remedies**" **approach**. That means in particular that the purchaser can generally claim damages in addition to other remedies[106] provided the cumulative exercise would not lead

---

[102] The Austrian Supreme Court applies a combined period of 14 days for both examination and notification, see OGH (31 Aug 2010) IHR 2011, 85, 88; in the same direction OLG Hamburg (25 Jan 2008) CISG-online 1681.

[103] Arts 39 (1) and 43 (1) CISG. An exception to this rule is – with respect to quality defects – stipulated in Art 40 CISG: If the seller knew or should have known that the goods were defective, the purchaser is still entitled to all remedies provided by the CISG. In case of defects in title, only actual knowledge of the seller will do away with the legal consequences stipulated in Art 43 (1) CISG, see Art 43 (2) CISG.

[104] It should be noted that the term "non-conformity" is a specific technical term of the CISG that refers only to quality defects to the exclusion of defects in title.

[105] See for instance Germany: § 325 German Civil Code; USA: § 2–711 UCC; Switzerland (in the event of defective goods): Art 208 (2), (3) CO.

[106] The purchaser can however not combine other remedies than damages: Hence, a reduction of the contract price cannot be combined with a declaration of avoidance. By the same token, the purchaser cannot claim a reduction of the contract price or declare the avoidance of the contract in addition to a claim for specific performance.

III. The CISG

to inconsistent results. If, for instance, the purchaser requests specific performance, declares the avoidance of the contract or demands a reduction of the contract price, an additional claim for damages is still available. To avoid overcompensation, however, those claims cover only losses that are not already compensated by the other remedies.[107]

aa) Specific Performance. Art 46 (1) CISG stipulates the purchaser's right to request **performance** of the contract. But some restrictions of this right do apply: First, in case of an actual delivery of non-conforming goods, the purchaser can only demand the delivery of substitute goods if the lack of conformity amounts to a fundamental breach of the contract (Art 46 (2) CISG). The CISG hence clearly prefers a repair of the delivered goods over the delivery of substitute goods, given that the latter may cause additional transportation costs (incurred for example through the backhaul of the defective goods by the seller) and is hence deemed to be economically inefficient. A request to repair the defective goods is also subject to certain restrictions: The seller can refuse the repair in case a corresponding demand of the purchaser would be "unreasonable having regard to all relevant circumstances", see Art 46 (3) CISG.[108] Furthermore, it follows from Art 48 (1) CISG that it is initially up to the seller to determine whether to make good the defect by repair or the delivery of substitute goods, provided he cures the defect in one way or the other without undue delay.[109] However, substitute delivery or repair must be performed at the seller's cost and risk and at the place where the defective goods are located pursuant to the contract.[110] According to another opinion, the place of performance (at least) for substitute delivery must be located at the place of performance of the original obligation.[111] 55

Secondly, a court rooted in a legal system that does not acknowledge claims for specific performance is allowed pursuant to **Art 28 CISG** to ignore Art 46 CISG. Art 28 CISG was specifically tailored for common law jurisdictions that traditionally grant specific performance only under rather limited circumstances.[112] How- 56

---

[107] M Müller-Chen in Schlechtriem and Schwenzer (n 34) Art 45 CISG para 25.

[108] The restrictions set forth in Art 46 (2) and (3) CISG apply pursuant to the prevailing view only in case of quality defects pursuant to Art 35 CISG. In case of a defect in title, the buyer can claim specific performance in accordance with Art 46 (1) CISG without further restrictions, see M Müller-Chen in Schlechtriem and Schwenzer (n 34) Art 46 CISG para 21; P Huber in Kröll/Mistelis/Perales Viscasillas (n 34) Art 46 para 7.

[109] M Müller-Chen in Schlechtriem and Schwenzer (n 34) Art 46 CISG para 35.

[110] M Müller-Chen in Schlechtriem and Schwenzer (n 34) Art 46 CISG para 45.

[111] P Huber in Kröll/Mistelis/Perales Viscasillas (n 34) Art 46 CISG para 41. Pursuant to German domestic sales law (as recently reinterpreted by the German Federal Court of Justice), the place of performance for making good defects will in the absence of a party agreement respectively the individual circumstances of the case indicating otherwise be determined pursuant to § 269 German Civil Code and hence be at the Seller's place of business, BGH (13 Apr 2011) NJW 2011, 2278, 2281.

[112] US law applies compared to English law lower thresholds for granting specific performance. Pursuant to § 2–716 (1) UCC, a court may grant specific performance either in case that the goods are unique or in "other proper circumstances". The new version of the UCC (2003) that has not yet been enacted by the states permits a claim for specific performance (in case of a commercial contract) also if the parties have agreed on the availability of this remedy. Sec 52 (1) SGA 1979 on the other hand allows a court to order specific performance at the court's discretion only in case of specific or ascertained goods.

ever, it seems that neither Art 46 CISG nor Art 28 CISG have played any significant role in the existing case law – most likely due to the fact that the parties usually prefer other remedies instead of specific performance anyway.[113]

57   bb) **Reduction of the contract price (Art 50 CISG).** It is generally agreed that the **price reduction remedy** is only available in case of an infringement of Art 35 CISG and does not apply in case of a defect of title.[114] In the event of a quality defect, the purchaser is entitled to a price reduction in the same proportion as the value of non-conforming goods has to conforming goods on the delivery date[115], Art 50 CISG. The reduction is subject to a corresponding declaration by the purchaser to the seller to that effect but remains available even if the contract price has already been paid.[116] In order to safeguard the seller's right to cure the defect, Art 50 CISG does not apply if the seller has remedied the defect pursuant to Art 37 or 48 CISG or if the purchaser has refused to accept performance by the seller.[117] At first glance, a reduction of the contract price seems to offer no additional benefit compared to a claim for damages based on compensation for the reduced value of the defective goods. However, the remedy of reduction offers an attractive option for the purchaser if the market price for the contractual goods has decreased since the conclusion of the contract and delivery of the goods[118] or a claim for damages is not available at all in the individual case.[119]

---

[113] HD Gabriel, *Contracts for the Sale of Goods: A Comparison of Domestic and International Law* (Oceana, New York 2004) 148.

[114] See I Saenger in F Ferrari et al (eds), *Internationales Vertragsrecht: Kommentar* (2nd edn C.H. Beck, München 2012) Art 50 CISG para 2 with further references. Given that the CISG distinguishes between conformity of the goods and third party claims (see the heading of Part III, Chapter II, Section II) and Art 50 CISG refers exclusively to non-conformity, this view seems convincing. For the application of Art 50 CISG in the event of defects in title however C Brunner, *UN-Kaufrecht – CISG: Kommentar zum Übereinkommen der Vereinten Nationen über Verträge über den internationalen Warenkauf von 1980* (Stämpfli Verlag AG, Bern 2004) Art 50 CISG para 12.

[115] The price reduction remedy of the CISG deviates for this reason (in particular in case of falling or increasing market prices of the contractual goods) from the price reduction remedy provided by the German Civil Code: Pursuant to § 441 German Civil Code, the time of conclusion of the contract rather than the delivery date will be decisive for the calculation of the price reduction.

[116] If the contract price has already been paid, the purchaser may claim a refund directly under Art 50 CISG, see U Magnus in Staudinger (n 29) Art 50 CISG para 26; OLG Köln (14 Aug 2006) CISG-online 1405.

[117] See Art 50 CISG 2nd sentence.

[118] See the example submitted by M Müller-Chen in Schlechtriem and Schwenzer (n 34) Art 50 CISG para 18: Suppose the contract price for the contract goods is EUR 100 whereas the true value of the goods amounts (due to a defect) to only EUR 80 at the time of contract conclusion. If the market price for the goods in question drops by 50 % until delivery, the purchaser can either claim damages in the amount of EUR 10 (value of non-defective goods minus value of delivered goods at the time of delivery) or request a reduction amounting to EUR 20 (100 : 80 = 50 : 40).

[119] Once the requirements for the price reduction remedy are fulfilled, however, a claim for damages is regularly also available given that the reduced value of defective goods is generally foreseeable, see 74 (1) CISG. Furthermore, though Art 79 (1) CISG may in principle also apply in the event of defective goods, these cases will be extremely rare, see CISG-AC Opinion No 7 (12 Oct 2007), Exemption of Liability for Damages Under Article 79 of the CISG (Rapporteur: Professor AM Garro) para 25.

III. The CISG

cc) **Damages.** A breach of contract entitles the purchaser[120] to **claim damages**[121] 58
pursuant to Arts 45 (1) lit b, 74ff CISG in order to cover all his losses (including lost
profits) incurred due[122] to the breach. Similarly as in many domestic laws, Art 74
CISG follows the principle of **full compensation**.[123] Hence, the injured party cannot
only claim damages "in lieu of performance" (eg, in the case of defective goods, a
compensation for the reduced value of the goods, costs of repair or expenses incurred
for a "cover transaction"). Art 74 CISG covers also the "indemnity interest" as well as
the "reliance interest" of the injured party[124] and generally both direct as well as
indirect respectively consequential losses.[125] Accordingly, the purchaser may also
claim compensation for losses incurred in relation to his other legally protected rights
(inter alia property damage external to the goods, bodily injury; the "indemnity
interest") as well as compensation for expenses incurred in reliance on the proper
performance of the contract ("the reliance interest", respectively "negative contract
interest"). It goes without saying that damages "in lieu of performance" (covering the
"expectation interest") cannot be combined with compensation based on the "reliance interest"[126]: The reliance interest places the innocent party in the same position
in which it would have been if it had not relied on the conclusion respectively the
performance of the contract. This calculation inevitably collides with the calculation
of the "expectation interest" that intends to put the innocent party in the same
position in which it would have been if the contract had been properly performed.

---

[120] In particular US law acknowledges third party beneficiaries of warranties assumed under a sales contract (for the benefit of third parties that may reasonably expected to use or otherwise be affected by the goods), see (the further extended) § 2–318 UCC (2003). French and Belgian laws have developed the doctrine of the "action directe" based on Art 1615 Code Civil that enables a sub-purchaser to assert (contractual) remedies against the original seller though no direct contractual relationship exists between these parties, see N Carette, "Direct Contractual Claim of the Sub-purchaser and International Sale of Goods: Applicable Law and Applicability of the CISG" [2008] ERPL 583, 586 f. The German legal concept of a "contract with protective effects for third parties" (*Verträge mit Schutzwirkung zugunsten Dritter*) does on the other hand not apply in case of sales transactions, see BGH (26 Nov 1968) [1969] NJW 269. Third parties are in principle not entitled to claim damages based on a sales contract governed by the CISG: Pursuant to the prevailing view, the CISG does also take precedence over domestic laws that acknowledge contractual rights of third parties even in the context of a sales transaction, see Piltz (n 34) para 2–138; contra however with regard to the action directe (based on the alleged qualification of the action directe as a non-contractual claim) S Jungemeyer, "Haftungsrisiko für Exporteure: die französische 'action directe' als Fallbeispiel für ein kaufvertragliches Durchgriffsrecht" [2009] RIW 701, 705.

[121] Art 74 CISG does only provide a claim for damages. Hence, pursuant to Art 74 CISG, the injured party can neither claim restitution in kind nor an indemnity against third party claims, see Piltz (n 34) para 5–563.

[122] Art 74 CISG requires a causal link between the contractual breach and the damages incurred by the injured party, see D Saidov, *The Law of Damages in International Sales: The CISG and other International Instruments* (Hart Publishing, Oxford and Portland 2008) 79. Pursuant to the prevailing opinion, it will however suffice that the breach was a condition for the occurrence of the damages (so called "but for rule") and no further restrictions developed by some domestic laws with regard to causality apply (see for instance in German and Swiss law the theory of adequate causation), see O Lando, "Foreseeability and Remoteness of Damages in Contract in the DCFR" [2009] ERPL 619, 623 f.

[123] Saidov (n 122) 25.

[124] I Schwenzer in Schlechtriem and Schwenzer (n 34) Art 74 CISG para 3; Piltz (n 34) para 5–515.

[125] OGH (15 Jan 2013) CISG-online 2398.

[126] See B Zeller, *Damages under the Convention on Contracts for the International Sale of Goods* (Oceana, New York 2005) 40.

59   Without prejudice to Art 74 CISG, Arts 75 and 76 CISG permit a specific calculation of a damage claim in the event of the **avoidance of the contract**: Pursuant to Art 75 CISG, the purchaser can claim the difference between the contract price and the price for a (reasonable) substitute transaction (i. e. a cover sale) effected by him within a reasonable time after the termination of the contract. Art 76 CISG provides a basis for a similar claim if the purchaser has not performed a cover sale: In this case, the claimable damages amount to the difference between the contract price and the current market price at the time of the termination of the contract.

60   Arts 75, 76 CISG have given rise to the general controversy about whether a claim for the **"performance interest"** presupposes in principle the termination (i. e. the avoidance of the contract). It would appear, however, that this question is not appropriate: The legal terms of "performance interest" respectively of damages "in lieu of performance" are ambiguous. A closer assessment reveals that some damages falling within the ambit of the "performance interest" can without doubt be claimed if the contract is upheld whereas other damages belonging to the general category of performance interest explicitly presuppose the termination of the contract. For instance, the purchaser can undoubtedly claim damages based on the reduced value of defective goods if he wishes to uphold the contract. The same holds true with regard to lost profits that can be claimed regardless of whether or not the contract has been terminated. On the other hand, the purchaser cannot demand repayment of the contract price (as part of a damage claim) without avoidance as the restrictions set forth by 49 CISG would otherwise be circumvented.[127]

61   To put it in a nutshell, whenever damages are calculated on the basis of the rejection of the non-conforming goods, the termination of the contract becomes a necessary precondition for their recovery. Vice versa, in the event that damages are calculated against the assumption of the purchaser to keep the goods, the avoidance of the contract is not a precondition for these claims.[128] The problem remains whether the purchaser can claim costs incurred with regard to a "cover purchase" not only on the basis of Arts 75, 76 CISG but also under Art 74 CISG – and accordingly even in the absence of a termination of the contract. According to the still prevailing opinion, this is not possible.[129]

62   Contrary to German law as well as other legal systems[130] that belong to the civil law family, a damage claim does not presuppose fault, as the CISG follows a **strict liability** approach in line with Anglo-American law. Hence, a mere breach of the contract suffices even in the absence of any negligence on the part of the seller. It is most likely mainly for that reason that exporters residing in civil law countries have in the past regularly excluded the CISG in their sales terms. This approach neglects, however, not only the fact that the parties are free to introduce fault as a precondition for a damage claim in their contract (Art 6 CISG), but also that differences between legal systems containing a fault

---

[127] M Müller-Chen in Schlechtriem and Schwenzer (n 34) Art 45 CISG para 27; similarly OLG Stuttgart (31 Mar 2008) CISG-online 1658 para 28.

[128] P Huber, "CISG – The Structure of Remedies" (2007) 71 RabelsZ 12, 29.

[129] The prevailing view does however accept a claim for damages resulting from a "cover transaction" if the purchaser has not actually declared the avoidance but the requirements for an avoidance were clearly fulfilled (eg, in the event of a definite refusal to perform), see in particular OLG München (15 Sep 2004) CISG-online 1013. For an option to claim damages incurred by a cover transaction even in the absence of the requirements of an avoidance of the contract apparently OLG Graz (29 Jul 2004) CISG-online 1627; also in particular P Schlechtriem, "Schadensersatz und Erfüllungsinteresse" in M Stathopoulos et al (eds), *Festschrift Apostolos Georgiades* (C.H. Beck, Athens 2005) 383, 387.

[130] See for instance with regard to German domestic law § 280 (1) 2 German Civil Code.

III. The CISG

requirement with regard to contractual liability and systems of strict liability have often been exaggerated. Many civil law systems adhering to a "principle of fault" (*Verschuldensprinzip*) use an objective standard to determine the existence of negligence and have shifted the burden of proof with regard to the (non-)existence of fault to the party in breach of contract.

The CISG itself provides (at least to a certain extent) various tools in order to limit the scope of liability of the breaching party. Though fault is not a precondition, Art 79 CISG excludes either party's liability where non-performance of a contractual obligation is due to **impediments** beyond its control that could not reasonably be expected to have been taken into account at the time of the conclusion of the contract. But the wording of Art 79 (1) CISG does reveal its rather limited effect: Art 79 (1) CISG essentially covers "force majeure" events that could not have been foreseen by the breaching party and therefore rarely applies.

Secondly, the defaulting party's liability depends on a "**foreseeability test**": Pursuant to Art 74 CISG, the amount of damages awarded must not exceed the loss which the party in breach foresaw or – from a reasonable person's point of view[131] – ought to have foreseen as a possible consequence of the breach. In that way, Art 74 CISG adopts a concept that is at first glance similar to the "contemplation rule" respectively the "remoteness test" applied by Anglo-American case law since the famous decision Hadley v Baxendale rendered by the Court of Exeter in 1854, according to which the contemplation of the parties is the decisive factor with regard to damage that did not naturally flow from the breach.[132] However, it is submitted that the contemplation rule adopts – from a claimant's point of view – a stricter standard than a mere "foreseeability test" maintained by the CISG given that the occurrence of damage as a *possible* consequence of a breach may (contrary to Anglo-American law) already be sufficient under the CISG.[133] A recent decision of the English House of Lords in the "Achilleas case" applying the contemplation rule appears to further confirm that view.[134]

63

64

---

[131] Contra Saidov (n 122) 104.

[132] *Hadley v Baxendale* (1854) 9 Ex 341. This decision created the two famous limbs according to which damages are recoverable under common law if they may either 1) fairly and reasonably be considered arising naturally, i.e., according to the usual course of things, from such breach of contract itself, or 2) reasonably be supposed to have been in the contemplation of both parties (at the time they made the contract) as the probable result of the breach.

[133] I Schwenzer in Schlechtriem and Schwenzer (n 34) Art 74 CISG para 48. Stricter apparently Art 7.4.4 UPICC 2010 that refers to harm that "likely" results from a contract breach.

[134] See *Transfield Shipping Inc v Mercator Shipping Inc* [2008] UKHL 48. This case concerned the delayed return of a chartered vessel (the "Achilleas") by the charterers to the owners. Due to the delay, the owners had to renegotiate charter rates with the new charterer in order to postpone a cancellation date that allowed the new charterer to terminate the contract in case of delay with handover of the vessel upon a fixed date. The owners did not only claim the difference between the contract and market rate for the time of delay from the charterer (in this case the market rates for 8 days, amounting to round about USD 160,000) but also loss of profit over the period of the next fixture agreed upon with the new charterers, being the difference between the original hire rate and the renegotiated lower market hire rate throughout the entire period of the new charter (amounting to roughly USD 1,4 million). Though the arbitral tribunal as well as the Court of Appeal reached both the conclusion that the failure to redeliver the Achilleas in time for its next fixture directly caused the lost profits in relation to the new charter contract and were hence within the contemplation of the parties, the House of Lords took the view that these damages were not recoverable. The majority of the Law Lords argued that the contemplation rule does also contain an assumption of responsibility by the breaching party that would be "determined by more than what at the time of the contract was reasonably foreseeable" (see in particular paras 29, 31 of the opinion of Lord Hope of Craighead).

65 It remains doubtful whether the **foreseeability rule** can effectively limit the risk exposure of the breaching party. In a commercial context, a great variety of damage is in principle foreseeable. Though this has been disputed by some authors, even a loss of production and downtime costs are generally recoverable under the CISG at least if the contract goods were specifically intended for commercial production.[135] The latter was explicitly confirmed in the often cited decision of the US Court of Appeals of the Second Circuit in *Delchi Carrier S.p.A. v. Rotorex Corp*[136] where it was held that a supplier of defective compressors for air conditioners could foresee lost profits due to a temporary shutdown of the purchaser's manufacturing operations (an Italian manufacturer of air conditioners).

66 A second problem with the foreseeability rule is the still unsolved question of whether it also covers the *extent* or only – as seems to be the case in Anglo-American law according to the contemplation rule[137] – the *type* of a particular loss. Though there is widespread agreement that the foreseeability of a specific amount of damages is not required given that liability would otherwise only rarely exist, it remains unclear whether the breaching party is released from liability if the amount of damage actually incurred differs fundamentally from the reasonable expectation of the breaching party or whether already any deviation from a rough estimation of the damage amount should be sufficient to escape liability.[138]

67 The third mechanism limiting the scope of liability of the breaching party already by operation of law is the doctrine of **mitigation**. The injured party is obliged to take reasonable measures to mitigate its loss, including loss of profit, resulting from the breach. Any failure to mitigate may entitle the breaching party to request a reduction of the claim in the amount by which the loss should have been mitigated, see Art 77 CISG. Case law with regard to Art 77 CISG has stated that damage caused by further use of defective goods was not recoverable if its occurrence was foreseeable.[139] The duty to mitigate may also cause the injured party to repair defective goods or to undertake a cover sale[140] if and when further substantial damage can only be avoided by that means.

---

[135] U Magnus in Staudinger (n 29) Art 74 CISG para 40.

[136] US Court of Appeals of the Second Circuit (6 Dec 1995) CISG-online 140. See also the decision of the US District Court, Southern District of New York (23 Aug 2006) CISG-online 1272, where the purchaser was pursuant to the court inter alia entitled to recover lost profits from sales and licensing due to the seller's failure to deliver a satisfactory production system. Interestingly enough, the judgment also notes that the foreseeability requirement of the CISG "is identical to the well-known rule of *Hadley v. Baxendale* such that the relevant interpretations of that rule can guide the […] reasoning regarding proper damages" and (quite contrary to the view of the House of Lords in the Achilleas case, see n 134 above) "according to Article 74, only 'the loss' – and not whether a defendant would be *liable* for the loss – need be foreseeable".

[137] With regard to English Law see for instance *Parsons (Livestock) Ltd v Uttley Ingham & Co* [1978] QB 791 and the critical assessment of this decision by Atiyah et al (n 87) 550 as well as *Wroth v Tyler* [1973] 1 All ER 897. French Law has apparently taken a different view, see A Fofaria, "Excluding the Recovery of Consequential and Indirect Losses in English and French Laws" [1995] IBLR 597, 606 with references to relevant French case law that has interpreted Art 1150 of the French Civil Code from the perspective of the breaching party in a more generous manner.

[138] See Saidov (n 122) 114.

[139] U Magnus in Staudinger (n 29) Art 77 CISG para 11; BGH (24 Mar 1999) CISG-online 396.

[140] A duty to perform a cover transaction can however from the viewpoint of the author only arise once the contract has been terminated.

III. The CISG

dd) Avoidance of the contract. The declaration of **avoidance**[141] is the so-called remedy of last resort.[142] As the legal consequences of that remedy go beyond a mere release of the parties from their primary obligations under the contract and allow claims for restitution with regard to anything that has already been supplied or paid under the contract (see below)[143], the CISG sets a high threshold in order to prevent a waste of economic resources caused by the unwinding of contracts in an international context. A contract can in principle only be declared avoided if the seller has committed a fundamental breach, Art 49 (1) lit a CISG. According to Art 49 (1) lit b CISG, this requirement is only dispensable in case of non-delivery of the goods[144] and the lapse of an additional respite set by the purchaser in accordance with Art 47 (1) CISG to no avail. Art 49 (1) lit b CISG does not apply in relation to any other breach – in particular, the purchaser cannot trigger the termination of the contract through this machinery in case of the delivery of defective goods. 68

Further restrictions are provided by Art 49 (2) CISG in the event that the seller has already delivered the goods: In case of **late delivery**, the purchaser must declare the avoidance within a reasonable time after he becomes aware of the delivery. In respect of all other breaches, similar restrictions apply, see Art 49 (2) lit b CISG.[145] But one exceptional provision does permit avoidance even before a fundamental breach has been committed: Pursuant to Art 72 CISG (i.e. based upon the concept of "**anticipatory repudiation**" originally developed by Anglo-American law[146]), either party may declare the contract avoided[147] even prior to the date of contract performance if it is clear that the other party will commit a fundamental breach.[148] In the seller's case, this may for instance involve the refusal to deliver the goods, even if such refusal is combined with an offer to renegotiate (increase) the agreed contract price. Special rules are set forth in Art 73 CISG with regard to a contract for delivery of goods by installments. 69

A declaration of avoidance must be made by notice to the other party in order to become effective, Art 26 CISG. Arts 81–84 CISG govern the legal consequences: Avoidance does not render the contract void with retroactive effect but rather trans- 70

---

[141] The term "avoidance" may sound unfamiliar to both lawyers with a civil and a common law origin. Given that it is the official term of the CISG, it is used both in the suggested International Sales Terms as well as the related annotations.

[142] See U Magnus, "The Remedy of Avoidance of Contract under CISG – General Remarks and Special Cases" (2005-06) 25 J L & Commerce 423, 424.

[143] Art 81 (2) CISG.

[144] It should be kept in mind that non-delivery means physical non-delivery of the goods. Delivery of defective goods (including the delivery of an "aliud") does under the CISG not amount to "non-delivery".

[145] It depends on the circumstances of the individual case to determine the length of a period of "reasonable time" referred to in Art 49 (2) CISG. 2 ½ months have been considered as too late in case of the delivery of a defective car, see OLG Stuttgart (31 Mar 2008) CISG-online 1658.

[146] See in particular § 2–610 UCC et seq.

[147] As an alternative, Art 71 CISG provides the innocent party with a right to suspend its own contractual obligations in case that it becomes apparent that the other party will not perform a substantial part of its obligations. The suspension right is subject to an immediate notice given to the other party and will cease once the other party provides adequate assurance of its performance, Art 71 (3) CISG.

[148] If the other party has not outright declared its unwillingness or inability to perform, the injured party must however (if time allows it) give a reasonable notice before it declares the avoidance of the contract in order to enable the other party to provide adequate assurance of its performance, see Art 72 (2) CISG.

forms the existing contract with prospective effect into a restitutionary relationship.[149] However, each party is (subject to due claims for damages owed to the other party) discharged of its primary contractual obligations as per the effective termination date and may claim **restitution** from the other party – in the purchaser's case a refund of the payment of the contract price, Art 81 (2) CISG (plus interest upon receipt of the price, Art 84 (1) CISG). The impossibility for the purchaser to make restitution of the goods substantially in the condition in which they were received does away with his right to declare avoidance, Art 82 (1) CISG. However, a number of exceptions to this rule limit the scope of this provision so substantially that it will hardly ever apply, see Art 82 (2) CISG.[150] In any event, the purchaser must account to the seller for the benefits which he has derived from the goods or parts of them, Art 84 (2) CISG.[151]

d) Obligations of the purchaser and remedies of the seller

71   The most important contractual obligations of the purchaser consist of (timely) payment[152] of the purchase price as well as the taking over of the contractual goods, see Arts 53 and 54 CISG. In case of a breach of either obligation, the seller may pursuant to Art 61 (1) lit a, b CISG demand performance (Art 62 CISG),[153] declare avoidance (Art 64 (1) CISG) or claim damages pursuant to Art 74ff CISG. In accordance with the "cumulative remedy approach" referred to above, the seller can in principle claim damages regardless of whether or not avoidance has been declared, Art 61 (1) 1 lit b, (2) CISG. Other remedies can, however, not be combined: In particular, the seller cannot demand performance and declare avoidance or claim damages in lieu of performance plus performance.

72   The **seller's remedies** under the CISG essentially mirror the purchaser's remedies – hence, avoidance of the contract presupposes either a fundamental breach (that is regularly not committed simply by reason of a delay with payment) or the lapse of an additional respite set by the seller to no avail, Art 64 (1) lit b CISG.[154] During an additional respite set by the seller, the right to terminate (i. e. declare avoidance) is suspended even if the breach is fundamental in nature, Art 63 CISG. The calculation of damages is the same as in the case of the purchaser (see above).

73   The seller is in case of delay in payment also entitled to interest without further requirements as foreseen by some domestic laws (such as a prior reminder by the

---

[149] That is at least the prevailing view, see R Hornung and C Fountoulakis in Schlechtriem and Schwenzer (n 34) Art 81 CISG paras 6, 10 with further references; M Bridge in Kröll/Mistelis/Perales Viscasillas (n 34) Art 81 CISG para 10 ff.

[150] Brunner (n 114) Art 82 CISG para 8.

[151] This provision applies contrary to its wording also if the seller has declared the avoidance of the contract and the purchaser cannot return the goods, see OLG Karlsruhe (2 Feb 2008) CISG-online 1649.

[152] Subject to a contractual agreement stipulating otherwise, the contract price becomes due upon placement of either goods or transport documents at the purchaser's disposal, Art 58 (1) CISG. However, the purchaser may pursuant to Art 58 (3) CISG withhold payment until he had an opportunity to examine the goods – provided the payment and delivery terms of the contract allow such a prior examination. The examination referred to in Art 58 (3) CISG is to be understood as a superficial check and must not be mixed up with the more comprehensive examination required under Art 38 CISG, see G Hager and F Maultzsch in Schlechtriem and (n 34) Art 58 CISG para 11.

[153] Art 28 CISG may however also in this case prevent a (common law) court to permit an action for the price.

[154] An avoidance of the contract is restricted once the purchaser has rendered payment, see Art 64 (2) CISG.

IV. Swiss law as the supplementary governing law of choice

seller), Art 78 CISG. Though Art 78 explicitly provides for the obligation to pay interest, the actual amount claimable cannot be derived from the CISG. Hence, the prevailing view is that the supplementary governing law (determined by the applicable private international laws) determines the applicable rates.[155]

IV. Swiss law as the supplementary governing law of choice

1. Overview on the relevant issues

Pursuant to Art 4, the CISG governs only the formation of the sales contract and the rights and obligations of the parties arising from it. Legal questions regarding – among other issues – the **validity** of the contract and the effect of the contract on property rights in the goods sold as well as the seller's liability in case of bodily injury caused by faulty products are expressly excluded from the scope of application, see Arts 4 and 5 CISG. Some other legal issues that may arise in the course of a sales transaction are also not addressed by the CISG. Art 7 (2) CISG stipulates that questions concerning matters governed by the CISG which are not expressly settled by it are to be settled in conformity with the general principles on which the CISG is based (so called "internal gaps"). However, where those general principles cannot be derived from the CISG with regard to a specific legal issue, the domestic law applicable by virtue of the rules of private international law of the forum will apply.[156] 74

Whether legal issues that are not expressly governed by the CISG constitute "external" gaps respectively "internal" gaps that cannot be solved on the basis of its general principles is not always clear. However, besides some controversial issues such as the availability of concurring tort claims under domestic law in the event of defective contractual goods in addition to the remedies of the CISG or the scope of rights of retention under the CISG, there is rather widespread agreement that the legal issues indicated in the following must be resolved by the "supplementary" domestic law. 75

If the parties choose **Swiss law** as the governing law for these issues (as suggested in this present book both in relation to contractual claims as well as with regard to concurring claims under tort), Swiss law may accordingly become important in relation to the following legal issues: 76
– Validity of the contract[157], in particular policing of unfair general contract terms and conditions,
– Statute of limitations,

---

[155] HG Kanton Aargau (21 Jun 2011) CISG-online 2432; OLG Hamburg (15 Jan 2008) CISG-online 1681; US District Court Kansas (28 Apr 2008) CISG-online 1682. Some arbitral tribunals have based the applicable rate on Art 7.4.9 (2) UPICC (as an expression of general principles on which the CISG is based pursuant to Art 7 (2) CISG) that stipulates the average short-term lending rate to prime borrowers prevailing for the currency of payment at the place of payment as the relevant rate, see inter alia ICC arbitral award No 8769 (Dez 1996) CISG-online 775.

[156] J Dalhuisen, "Domestic Contract Laws, Uniform International Contract and International Contract Law Principles. International Sales and Contractual Agency" (2000) 11 EBLR 200, 283 f.

[157] The concept of "validity" must be autonomously interpreted. Accordingly, it would appear that the purchaser cannot rescind the contract by means of a "fundamental mistake" (*Grundlagenirrtum*) as to the quality of the goods though this option exists pursuant to Art 24 (1) 4 CO under domestic Swiss sales law even after the transfer of risk, see n 435 below for further reference. The same holds true with regard to the invalidity of a contract under Art 20 (1) CO in case of an initial and objective impossibility to perform the main contractual obligation, see Ferrari (n 65) 70.

- Set-off,
- Assignment of claims,
- Contractual penalties and liquidated damages clauses, though it remains controversial whether the relationship between agreed damages clauses and other available remedies for contract breach (general damages, specific performance and the right to declare the avoidance of the contract) falls within the ambit of the CISG (respectively the "general principles" on which is it based) or domestic laws as well,
- Amount of the interest rate in case of default of payment,
- Concurring liability under tort (in particular product liability) as well as contractual liability in case of death or personal injury caused by defective products.

2. Relevant Swiss contract and tort laws

77   Swiss contract and tort laws that are relevant in relation to a sales transaction are contained in the **Swiss Code of Obligations** (*Obligationenrecht*). The CO, though adopted in 1912, influenced the German Civil Code of 1898 through its predecessor, the old CO of 1881, and vice versa, which may explain some of the rather obvious similarities between the two legal systems.[158] The articles contained in the first and general part of the CO (Arts 1-183 CO) are of particular importance: In addition to the formation and termination of contracts, remedies in the case of non-performance etc, they deal in particular with legal issues that are not addressed by the CISG, inter alia with the transfer of contractual rights, set-off, limitation periods (and their suspension or discontinuation), penalty clauses but also with tort liability and unjust enrichment.

78   The **second part of the CO** (Art 184-529 CO) contains rules for specific contracts such as sales contracts, contracts for work and labor, lease agreements etc that are (besides the statute of limitations) generally superseded by the CISG and hence not discussed in any detail in the following chapter. Also of limited importance for the present purpose and international sales transactions in general is the Swiss Civil Code (*Zivilgesetzbuch*), which deals among other areas of the law with property, inheritance and family law.[159]

79   A variety of **information** sources on Swiss law can be found online. The official website of the Swiss federal administration contains all federal Swiss statutes that are relevant against the background of an international sales transaction, in particular the Code of Obligations as well as the Private International Law Act (PILA), and provides also an English (unofficial) translation of the CO.[160] Case law of the highest Swiss court (also) in matters of private law, the Swiss Federal Supreme Court (*Schweizer Bundesgericht*), is also available online.[161]

---

[158] See E Bucher, "Law of Contracts" in F Dessemontet (ed), *Introduction to Swiss Law* (3rd edn Kluwer Law International, The Hague 2004) 103, 106 f.

[159] Swiss property law will pursuant to the "lex situs" rule in principle only be of relevance in an international sales contract (regardless of the applicable governing law of the contract) if the goods are delivered to Switzerland.

[160] The Code of Obligations can be found online under <http://www.admin.ch/opc/de/classified-compilation/22.html>.

[161] See <www.bger.ch>.

3. Validity of the contract

Questions regarding the **validity** of a contract cover a wide area of different legal issues such as the legal capacity of the parties to enter into the contractual relationship, statutory prohibitions under domestic or international law or infringements against public policy[162] as well as other provisions that may trigger the full or partial invalidity of the contract with initial or retroactive effect. 80

a) Unfair contract terms

Among the most important legal issues in relation to the validity of contracts are in all likelihood the existence, scope and effect of domestic statutes dealing with so-called **unfair contract terms**, in particular but not limited to their use in general terms and conditions that were not negotiated by the parties in the individual case. Contract clauses that either exclude or limit the liability for breach of contract or under tort are the most prominent example though other contract terms and conditions deviating from statutory law may also be disregarded by the courts or arbitral tribunals for similar reasons. 81

The **policing** of contractual terms by Swiss law is still a "light touch regulation". However, some provisions in the Code of Obligations as well as in other statutes lay down certain outer limits of the parties' contractual freedom. Mainly Art 19 (2), 20, 100, 101 and 199 CO and Arts 2, 27 (2) CC must be taken into consideration if a contract is governed by Swiss law. By means of a legislative amendment of Art 8 of the Federal Unfair Competition Act (UWG), which has become effective as of 1 July 2012, the Swiss legislator has also considerably tightened the policing of general terms and conditions. However, the amended § 8 UWG will solely apply in relation to **consumer contracts**.[163] 82

Pursuant to Art 19 (2) and 20 CO, illegal contractual provisions or terms that infringe either public policy, personal rights or morality are invalid. Besides the critical question whether Swiss law applies a stricter standard with regard to the control of general terms and conditions (see below), Art 19 (2), 20 CO become in this context primarily relevant in relation to any contractual exclusion or limitation of either party's contractual or tortuous liability based on **bodily injury**: There is widespread agreement that any contractual exclusion or limitation of liability in case of bodily injury infringes morality and is not enforceable pursuant to Art 20 (1) CO.[164] 83

Articles 100 and 101 CO stipulate specific statutory barriers in relation to limitation of liability clauses. Pursuant to Art 100 (1) CO, a contractual clause that attempts (already before the occurrence of the damaging event) to exclude or limit the **liability**[165] of either party in case of gross negligence or intent is not enforceable. Though the parties are from the outset liable for damage caused by auxiliary persons acting on their behalf (Art 101 (1) CO), they remain however entitled to contractually exclude their liability based on negligent (and even intentional) acts of auxiliary 84

---

[162] See F Ferrari in Schlechtriem and Schwenzer (n 34) Art 4 CISG paras 16–19.

[163] I Wildhaber, "Inhaltskontrolle von Allgemeinen Geschäftsbedingungen im unternehmerischen Geschäftsverkehr" [2011] SJZ 537, 541.

[164] W Wiegand in H Honsell, NP Vogt and W Wiegand (eds), *Basler Kommentar: Obligationenrecht I* (5th edn Helbing Lichtenhahn, Basel 2012) Art 100 CO para 4.

[165] BG (14 Sep 1976) BGE 102 II 256, 264.

personnel, Art 101 (2) CO.¹⁶⁶ It should be taken into consideration though that directors and officers of a company are in accordance with Art 55 (2) CC not regarded as auxiliary personnel and their acts or omissions are accordingly treated as acts or omissions of the company itself. The latter applies not only to the directors and officers who legally represent the company but also to other executive staff.¹⁶⁷

85   With regard to seller's liability based on the delivery of **defective contractual goods**, Art 199 CO appears to provide the seller with more leeway. Pursuant to this provision, the seller can exclude all remedies available to the purchaser in case of quality defects, except only for remedies based on defects that have intentionally been hidden. But the relationship between Art 100 CO and Art 199 CO is still controversial: Whereas some authors and apparently the Swiss Federal Supreme Court have interpreted Art 199 CO as *lex specialis* and accordingly permitted the exclusion of liability in case of defective goods even in the event of gross negligence,¹⁶⁸ other scholars have rejected the view that Art 199 CO supersedes Art 100 CO.¹⁶⁹ Furthermore, it also remains doubtful whether Art 199 CO takes precedence with regard to concurring claims in tort or claims of damages based on the general provision for contractual malperformance (Art 97 CO). The Federal Supreme Court has in the past also taken recourse to "good faith principles" when considering the construction and interpretation of exemption clauses pursuant to Art 199 CO: In a decision rendered in 2004, the Federal Supreme Court held that a quality defect that could not reasonably be expected at the time of the conclusion of the contract did not fall within the ambit of an exemption clause given that the defect substantially "affected the economic purpose" of the contract.¹⁷⁰

b) The grip of control of Swiss law in relation to general terms and conditions

86   Whereas particular statutes have been enacted in many European jurisdictions that entitle courts or administrative bodies to carry out a **material control** (*offene Inhaltskontrolle*) of general terms and conditions,¹⁷¹ Swiss law has so far addressed this issue only to a very limited extent. Art 8 UWG as well as Art 256 (2) lit a CO and Art 288 (2) lit a CO are the only statutory provisions that deal explicitly with the policing of general terms and conditions.¹⁷²

---

¹⁶⁶ However, an employer can as a matter of principle not limit his liability (either incurred due to his own or any of his employees' wrongdoings) towards his own employees, see Art 100 (2), 101 (3) CO.

¹⁶⁷ C Huguenin in H Honsell, NP Vogt and T Geiser (eds), *Basler Kommentar: Zivilgesetzbuch I* (3ʳᵈ edn Helbing Lichtenhahn, Basel 2006) Art 54/55 CC para 13.

¹⁶⁸ BG (7 Dec 1999) BGE 126 III 59, 67; H Honsell in Honsell et al (n 164) Art 199 CO para 1.

¹⁶⁹ See RH Weber, *Berner Kommentar. Allgemeine Bestimmungen: Die Folgen der Nichterfüllung. Kommentar zu Art 97-109 OR, Band VI, 1. Abt.* (Stämpfli, Bern 2000) Art 100 CO para 39. Some scholars argue that Art 100 CO should in any event prevail if a sales contract is predominantly governed by the CISG given that the delivery of conforming goods is (contrary to Swiss domestic law) pursuant to the CISG part of the performance obligation of the Seller, see for this view N Voser and C Boog, "Die Wahl Schweizer Rechts – was man wissen sollte" [2009] RIW 126, 139.

¹⁷⁰ BG (6 Oct 2004) BGE 130 III 686.

¹⁷¹ European law has partially harmonized the control of unfair terms contained in consumer contracts, see Council Directive 93/13/EEC of 5 April 1993 on unfair terms in consumer contracts [1993] OJ L95/29. In some European jurisdictions, however, the relevant statutory provisions apply explicitly to commercial contracts as well, see inter alia Germany: §§ 307 ff, 310 German Civil Code; Austria: § 879 (3) ABGB; England: UCTA 1977; The Netherlands: Art 6:233 BW.

¹⁷² A lessor can pursuant to Art 256 (2) lit a CO und Art 288 (2) lit a CO not exclude his liability in general terms and conditions with regard to his obligation to maintain the rental property in good shape throughout the term of the lease. Both articles have no impact on sales contracts.

IV. Swiss law as the supplementary governing law of choice

Pursuant to the recently amended Art 8 UWG, the use of general terms and conditions will amount to an abusive trade practice (and must hence be deemed invalid[173]) if these contractual terms *"provide, in a manner that is contrary to the principles of good faith, for a significant and unjustified imbalance between the contractual rights and the contractual duties to the detriment of consumers"*. However, though the amended version of § 8 UWG does now bite regardless of a deception of the other party, its scope of application has expressly been limited to consumer contracts. Given that the inclusion of commercial contracts within the scope of application has been discussed within the legislative proceedings, but finally ruled out[174], it would also appear that § 8 UWG cannot be applied by way of analogy to commercial contracts.[175] Articles 256, 288 CO on the other hand apply solely in relation to exemption clauses in lease agreements and play no further role in sales transactions. 87

The Federal Supreme Court has so far refused to carry out an **open control** of general terms and conditions based on Art 19 (2) CO or any other statutory basis. Alternatively, Swiss jurisprudence has developed certain rules of interpretation and construction of general terms and conditions that can also affect their validity. Besides the general rule that any deviations from statutory law in general terms and conditions must be restrictively construed, the Swiss Federal Supreme Court has repeatedly applied the "uncertainty rule" (*Unklarheitenregel*), according to which (similar to the "contra proferentem" doctrine used in other jurisdictions) remaining doubts regarding the interpretation of standard terms are resolved to the benefit of the other party.[176] Additionally, Swiss courts have resorted to the so-called "unusual terms rule" (*Ungewöhnlichkeitsregel*), according to which terms and conditions that are from an objective point of view unusual or untypical in the specific context of the transaction in question and could therefore not reasonably be expected by the other party do not become part of the contract.[177] But under Swiss case law, the user of general terms and conditions can prevent the application of this rule by clearly drawing the other party's attention to the clause in question, for instance by way of bold print.[178] As it is generally agreed that a similar rule is also rooted in the CISG, it would appear that the unusual terms rule is superseded by Art 8 CISG whenever the CISG is primarily governing the contract.[179] 88

Nevertheless, contrary to the case law of the Swiss Federal Supreme Court, an open substantial review, in particular based on requirements of public policy pursuant to Art 19 (2) CO respectively the good faith obligation imposed by Art 2 89

---

[173] J Schmid, "Die Inhaltskontrolle Allgemeiner Geschäftsbedingungen: Überlegungen zum neuen Art. 8 UWG" [2012] ZBJV 2012, 1, 16.
[174] See H Stöckli, "Der neue Art. 8 UWG – offene Inhaltskontrolle, aber nicht für alle" [2011] BR/DC 184, 187.
[175] B Ehle and A Brunschweiler, "Schweizer AGB-Recht im Umbruch" [2012] RIW 262, 271 take however the view that Swiss courts may potentially utilize § 8 UWG as a "guideline" also in relation to the review of general terms and conditions used in commercial contracts.
[176] Weber (n 169) Art 100 CO para 80; BG (17 Jul 1989) BGE 115 II 264, 268.
[177] BG (6 Dec 1983) BGE 109 II 452, 456 ff.
[178] BG (5 Aug 1993) BGE 119 II 443, 446.
[179] Brunner (n 114) Art 8 CISG para 45.

A. General Part

(2) CC, has been promoted by a variety of legal scholars.[180] Practical consequences – in particular the applicable standard for such a review – have, however, not been clarified yet.[181]

4. Limitation of actions
a) Limitation periods for warranty claims and product liability

90 The most relevant **limitation period** related to claims arising from a sales contract is stipulated in Art 210 (1) CO. This provision sets out the limitation period for all of the purchaser's warranty claims in case of delivery of defective goods, in particular the purchaser's claims for damages, a reduction of the contract price, avoidance of the contract as well as a demand to deliver substitute goods or otherwise making good any defect.[182] Two exceptions apply: Claims based on defects in title are subject to the general limitation period set forth in Art 127 CO (see below).[183] Furthermore, the general limitation period stipulated in Art 127 CO also applies if the seller willfully deceived the purchaser with regard to a defect, Art 210 (6) CO.[184]

91 According to recent legislative amendments of Art. 210 CO[185], claims falling within the ambit of **Art 210 (1) CO** must be formally asserted (in particular either by bringing an action before a court or arbitral tribunal or making an application in bankruptcy proceedings) within two years (formerly one year) after the handover of the goods and regardless of whether the purchaser has or ought to have detected the defect before the lapse of that period.[186] Pursuant to Art 210 (5) CO, however, the purchaser may defend himself against a payment claim asserted after the lapse of the limitation period if the required notice has been submitted to the seller within two years after delivery.

92 Certain problems that were caused by the interaction of Art 39 (2) CISG and the former version of Art 210 (1) CO are due to the legislative amendments not longer relevant: Given that the purchaser may pursuant to Art 39 (2) CISG give notice of a defect to the seller (at the latest) within two years after the handover of the goods, the limitation period of one year contained in the former Art 210 (1) CO could pursuant to the prevailing view not literally apply to a sales contracts governed by the CISG given that warranty claims would otherwise always be time barred pursuant to Art 210 (1) CO before the lapse of the **"cut-off" period** set forth in Art 39 (2) CISG. The Swiss Federal Supreme Court had acceded to this view but not determined how the problem should be resolved.[187] Due to the alignment of both

---

[180] See A Schnyder in M Amstutz et al (eds), *Handkommentar zum Schweizer Privatrecht* (2nd edn Schulthess, Zurich 2012) Art 1 CO para 6; T Koller, "Einmal mehr: Das Bundesgericht und seine verdeckte AGB-Inhaltskontrolle" [2008] AJP 943, 950.

[181] I Schwenzer, *Schweizerisches Obligationenrecht: Allgemeiner Teil* (6th edn Stämpfli, Bern 2012) para 45.13.

[182] See Brunner (n 114) Art 4 CISG para 20.

[183] S Hrubesch-Millauer in Amstutz et al (n 180) Art 193 CO para 5.

[184] BG (23 Jun 1981) BGE 107 II 231.

[185] See P Gauch, "Die revidierten Art. 210 und 371 OR – Änderungen des Obligationenrechts vom 16. März 2012" [2012] recht 124 ff.

[186] The limitation period will however amount to five years where "defects in an object that has been incorporated in an immovable work in a manner consistent with its nature and purpose have caused the work to be defective", Art. 210 (2) CO.

[187] See BG (18 May 2009) CISG-online 1900.

IV. Swiss law as the supplementary governing law of choice

periods, Art. 210 (1) CO can in the future be literally applied even if the sales contract is predominantly governed by the CISG.

Art 210 (1) CO does not apply in relation to concurring **claims under tort** based on defective products (Art 41 CO). The prevailing view amongst Swiss legal scholars favors the application of the regular limitation period for claims under tort stipulated in Art 60 (1) CO in this event.[188] Though this provision states merely a one-year period, this limitation period commences only once the claimant becomes aware of the damage that gave rise to the claim.[189] 93

b) Limitation periods for other claims arising from a sales contract

Other relevant contractual claims are subject to the **general limitation period** stipulated in Art 127 CO. In the case of a sales contract, Art 127 CO comes into play in relation to claims of specific performance of either party (delivery of the goods and payment of the contract price), but also with regard to warranty claims based on defects in title (see above). The general limitation period applies also to restitution claims that may arise in case of the avoidance of a sales contract (see Art 84 CISG).[190] Claims falling within the scope of Art 127 CO are time barred ten years after the claim becomes due, Art 130 (1) CO. According to Art 129 CO, the duration of the general limitation period set forth in Art 127 CO is mandatory and cannot be amended by the parties. 94

It can be inferred from the wording of 129 CO that the parties remain entitled to either extend or shorten the applicable limitation periods besides those stipulated in Articles 128 and 129 CO.[191] Contractual amendments must, however, neither extend a maximum length of ten years[192] nor unduly burden the legal assertion of the corresponding claims.[193] 95

c) Suspension and Discontinuation of Limitation Periods

Compared to other jurisdictions[194], Swiss law considerably limits the number of events that may trigger either the suspension (*Hemmung*) or the **discontinuation** (*Unterbrechung*) of a limitation period. A limitation period discontinues pursuant to Art 135 CO only if the defendant has either expressly or impliedly acknowledged the claim (for instance by way of a partial payment, the payment of interest or the performance of remedial measures) or the claimant has taken formal legal steps to assert his claims in particular before a court or an arbitral tribunal. 96

The provisions on **suspension** do not play an important role in the context of international commercial transactions. Although Art 134 No 6 CO indicates that the 97

---

[188] M Müller-Chen in Amstutz et al (n 180) Art 197 CO para 3.
[189] Claims under tort become however regardless of the knowledge of the claimant at the latest time barred after ten years from the event causing the damage, see Art 60 (1) CO.
[190] However, in case of a contract that is void ab initio, Art 67 (1) CO applies instead and restitution must be claimed within one year after the claimant has become aware of his claim for restitution.
[191] RK Däppen in Honsell et al (n 164) Art 129 CO para 2. Restrictions apply in relation to consumer contracts, see in particular Art. 210 (4) CO.
[192] BG (8 Mar 1973) BGE 99 II 185, 189.
[193] BG (21 Sep 1982) BGE 108 II 194, 196.
[194] For instance, according to Dutch law a claim letter according to which the claimant expressly declares the reservation of its claims towards the other party may already trigger the suspension of the limitation period, s. Art. 3:317 *Burgerlijk Wetboek*.

A. General Part

limitation period is to be suspended as long as the claimant has not been able to proceed with a lawsuit before a Swiss court, this provision does not apply if the parties to an international contract have either intentionally excluded the jurisdiction of Swiss courts upfront or Swiss courts do not – in the absence of any explicit contractual agreement on jurisdiction – have jurisdiction for the matter in the first place.[195]

5. Set-off

98 It is the prevailing view that issues of **set-off** are outside of the scope of application of the CISG.[196] This view is convincing as the relevant details of set-off (for instance the question whether a set-off operates automatically or requires an express declaration) can hardly be derived from general principles on which the CISG is based.[197]

99 The provisions of the Swiss Code of Obligations regarding set-off (*Verrechnung*) are almost identical with the relevant provisions in the German Civil Code, namely §§ 389 BGB et seq. A set-off requires the existence of a valid and due claim of a similar nature as the main claim and, contrary to legal systems such as French law where a set-off operates automatically, a declaration of set-off[198] towards the other party. Once that declaration has been made, the mutual amounts owing are extinguished with retroactive effect.

100 However, with regard to the required "similar nature" of the claims, one important distinction compared to German law does exist: Swiss law permits a set-off also in case the corresponding claim is owed in another **currency** than the main claim.[199] The parties can prevent set off in this case if they agree on a "currency clause" that permits only a set-off with claims owed in the same currency. Additionally, the parties are free to agree on a complete exclusion of set-off rights, Art 126 CO.[200]

6. Assignment

101 Swiss law in principle permits the transfer of any kind of claim to a third party by way of an **assignment** without prior approval by the debtor of the claim, Art 164 (1) CO.[201] Whereas the underlying contract containing the cause in law for the assignment and its further conditions needs no further formal requirements for its effectiveness (Art 165 (2) CO), the assignment as such (*Verfügung*) must be performed by way of a document signed by the assignor (see Art 165 (1) CO and Art 13 CO).

---

[195] RK Däppen in Honsell et al (n 164) Art 134 CO para 7.

[196] That applies at least with regard to claims that arise from different contracts and not from the same contractual relationship, see BG (20 Dez 2006) CISG-online 1496.

[197] Pursuant to some courts, however, set-off falls within the scope of the CISG at least if both claims arose from the same sales transaction, see for that view and further references also M Djordjevic in Kröll/Mistelis/Perales Viscasillas (n 34) Art. 4 CISG para 40 f.; see for further particulars and an analysis of the current case law S Kröll, "Selected problems concerning the CISG's scope of application" (2005-06) 25 J L & Commerce 39, 51.

[198] See for instance Art 1290 of the French Civil Code.

[199] See BG (2 Mar 2004) BGE 130 III 312, 318.

[200] That applies in principle also for corresponding exclusions contained in general terms and conditions, BG (21 Jun 1983) BGE 109 II 213.

[201] The Swiss Federal Supreme Court has however not accepted the assignment of the rights of a purchaser to alter the terms of a sales contract respectively bring the contract to an end (*Gestaltungsrecht*) in particular by means of a declaration of termination or reduction of the contract price in case of defective products, see BG (11 Oct 1988) BGE 114 II 239, 247.

IV. Swiss law as the supplementary governing law of choice

Swiss law does, however, also allow the exclusion of an assignment by way of a contractual agreement (i. e. an **anti-assignment clause**) between the owner and the debtor of the claim. The effect of an anti-assignment clause under Swiss law is not limited to a contractual duty of the claim owner to refrain from the assignment of the claim to any third party (with the potential consequence of a claim for damages if this obligation is breached). Rather, an anti-assignment clause has erga omnes effects and thus prevents the acquisition of the claim by the assignee.[202]

102

7. Contractual penalties and liquidated damages

The CISG is silent in relation to **penalty and liquidated damages** clauses. Hence, in case of its application as the (supplementary) governing law of the contract, Swiss domestic law determines according to the prevailing view[203] also whether and to what extent the parties may agree on and subsequently enforce a contractual penalty respectively a liquidated damages clause. It is less clear whether domestic law or, in the alternative, general principles on which the CISG is based are in charge of determining the relationship between a penalty respectively a liquidated damages clause and general damages, respectively other remedies available in case of breach. Given that general principles of the CISG in relation to this problem can hardly be derived from the CISG (and domestic laws are rather divergent on this issue as well), the former view seems more convincing.[204] In a sales contract, both penalty and liquidated damages clauses are predominantly used in relation to delays in delivery given that actual damages are particularly difficult to quantify in this area. Compared to a claim for general damages (as already provided for by Art 45 (1) lit b, 64 (1), 74 CISG), penalty respectively liquidated damages clauses offer one essential benefit: In case of a penalized breach, the injured party can claim the penalty or, as the case may be the liquidated damages without the burden of having to prove corresponding losses.

103

Though liquidated damages and penalties serve a similar purpose, they must be carefully distinguished. This is of particular importance given that contractual penalties are not enforceable in some jurisdictions whereas liquidated damages clauses give less rise to concerns. In line with the majority of other legal systems,

104

---

[202] Other domestic legal systems as well as international instruments follow a more restrictive approach regarding the effect of an anti-assignment clause towards third parties, see M Armgardt, "Die Wirkung vertraglicher Abtretungsverbote im deutschen und ausländischen Privatrecht" (2009) 73 RabelsZ 314 ff. For instance, pursuant to § 354 a (1) of the German Commercial Code, an anti-assignment clause cannot prevent the assignment of a monetary claim based on a transaction between merchants. Anti-assignment clauses governed by Anglo-American law are generally not enforceable towards third parties, see Armgardt, 327 ff. See also Art 9.1.9 UPICC 2010: An assignment of a monetary claim is effective notwithstanding the existence of an anti-assignment clause between assignor and debtor. The United Nations Convention on the Assignment of Receivables (that has due to a lack of the necessary minimum amount of ratifications not yet been enacted) follows a similar approach in its Art 9 (1), see for the text and current status of this Convention http://www.uncitral.org/uncitral/en/uncitral_texts/payments/2001Convention_ receivables.html.

[203] J Graves, "Penalty Clauses and the CISG" [2012] J L & Commerce 153, 163 with further references. Contra B Zeller, "Penalty Clauses: Are They Governed by the CISG?" [2011] Pace Int'l L Rev 1, 3.

[204] Contra Saidov (n 122) 49 and more recently CISG-AC Opinion No 10 (3 Aug 2012), Agreed Sums Payable upon Breach of an Obligation in CISG Contracts (Rapporteur: P Hachem) para 8.1.2 according to which this question is not one of validity and "should therefore not be dealt with under domestic law".

Swiss jurisprudence takes recourse to the **parties' intention** rather than the "label" used in the contract in order to distinguish between the two instruments. Whereas courts usually assume the existence of a "liquidated damages clause" if the parties aimed to reasonably pre-estimate the damages incurred for the respective breach, the parties are regularly deemed to have agreed on a penalty if the purpose of the clause was not limited to compensating the innocent party but to preventing the breach of the contract in the first place.[205]

a) Contractual penalties

105   Contrary to Anglo-American law,[206] but in line with other civil law systems,[207] **penalty clauses** (*Konventionalstrafen*) are enforceable under Swiss law and the parties are in principle free to determine the amount of the penalty that shall become due for a given breach, Art 163 (1) CO. Some restrictions do, however, apply: A contractual penalty that either intends to enforce an illegal or immoral obligation or was triggered by the impossibility of the breaching party to perform its obligations cannot be claimed if the impossibility was not culpably caused (and the parties did not agree otherwise), Art 163 (2) CO. Finally, an excessive penalty is subject to a **reduction** in the discretion of a court (respectively an arbitral tribunal), Art 163 (3) CO.

106   Unless the parties agree otherwise, it would appear that a claim for a contractual penalty due in case of a delay in delivery does not (contrary to penalties for non-performance) require fault[208] on the seller's part and will neither release the seller from the obligation to continuously deliver the contractual goods nor prevent the purchaser from claiming additional general damages, Art 161 (2) CO.[209]

107   From the claimant's point of view, a contractual penalty is generally speaking more favorable than a "liquidated damages clause" or a "lump sum" payment agreement: A

---

[205] BG (13 Dez 1983) BGE 109 II 462, 468.

[206] Penalty clauses are invalid respectively unenforceable under both US and English law (amongst other common law jurisdictions) whereas "liquidated damages clauses" are permitted. Pursuant to the traditional view of English law, a liquidated damages clause must reflect a "genuine pre-estimate of loss"; see G McMeel, *The Construction of Contracts* (2nd OUP, Oxford 2011) 494. However, more recent decisions have upheld liquidated damages provisions as long as they were not predominantly aimed at deterring a contract breach in the first place, s. *Azimut-Benetti Spa (Benetti Division) v Healey* [2010] EWHC 2234 (Comm) para 21: "On the other hand, (as the claimant points out) this does not imply that if the comparison between the amount payable on breach and the loss that might be sustained on breach discloses a discrepancy, it follows that the clause is a penalty. A particular clause might be commercially justifiable provided that its dominant purpose was not to deter the other party from breach." Pursuant to the amended § 2-718 (1) UCC (2003) – that has not yet been adopted by the US states – a liquidated damages clause in a commercial contract is already upheld if the stipulated amount is "reasonable in the light of the anticipated or actual harm caused by the breach".

[207] The enforceability of a penalty clause is, inter alia, in principle acknowledged by German law (§§ 339 ff German Civil Code), French law (Art 1152 ff Code Civil) as well as pursuant to Russian Law (Art 330ff Civil Code). Some domestic contract laws do not strictly distinguish between liquidated damages and penalties, see for instance Art 114 of the Chinese Contract Law 1999; see also Art 7.4.13 UPICC 2010.

[208] P Gauch et al, *Schweizerisches Obligationenrecht Allgemeiner Teil. Band II* (9th edn Schulthess, Zurich 2008) paras 3791, 3841. Contrary however FR Ehrat in Honsell et al (n 164) Art 160 CO para 14.

[209] In the event of a penalty for non-performance, however, the innocent party can (in the absence of an agreement stipulating otherwise) claim the penalty only in lieu of specific performance, Art 160 (1) CO.

IV. Swiss law as the supplementary governing law of choice

penalty can be collected even when it is apparent that no damage has been suffered at all as a result of the penalized breach[210] whereas general damage incurred in excess of the penalty remains claimable. However, one substantial legal trap is solely associated with penalty clauses: Claims for penalties that have become due by reason of a delay in performance or non-compliance with the place of performance must be expressly reserved by the claimant at the very moment of acceptance of performance as they will otherwise perish in their entirety, Art 160 (2) CO.[211]

b) Liquidated damages

108 The Swiss Code of Obligations does not contain any statutory provisions in relation to liquidated damages clauses. However, the concept has long been recognized and developed further by case law. Under Swiss law a "**lump sum damages clause**" (*pauschalierter Schadensersatz*) relieves the injured party from the burden to prove the precise amount of actual damage incurred as a result of the breach. Contrary to the common law understanding of liquidated damages, however, the injured party must apparently at least prove the existence of some damage.[212] If the agreed lump sum amount is grossly excessive in relation to the actual harm caused by the contract breach, a court may apply Art 163 (3) CO by way of analogy and appropriately reduce the amount awarded.[213]

109 The use of the term "liquidated damages" in an international sales contract governed by Swiss law may cause ambiguities: Though the legal concept of liquidated damages as construed and interpreted under the common law shares many features with "**lump sum damages clauses**" acknowledged by Swiss law, some important differences remain.[214] The parties are therefore well advised to address this problem

---

[210] BG (30 Nov 1976) BGE 102 II 420, 425 with reference to Art 161 (1) CO.

[211] BG (26 Oct 1971) BGE 97 II 350; similarly German law, see § 341 (3) German Civil Code.

[212] See M Schneider and M Scherer, "Switzerland" in R Knutson (ed), *FIDIC. An Analysis of International Construction Contracts* (Kluwer Law International, The Hague 2005) 313, 324; FR Ehrat in Honsell et al (n 164) Art 160 CO para 12. In particular English law takes a different view and allows a claim for liquidated damages even if the innocent party has suffered no damages at all – provided the stipulated amount of liquidated damages reflects a reasonable pre-estimation (made at the time of contract conclusion) of potential damages for the breach, see *BFI Group of Companies Ltd v DCB Integration Systems Ltd.* [1987] CILL 328.

[213] Schwenzer (n 181) para 71.16.

[214] The concept of "liquidated damages" under common law is similar though by no means identical with a "lump sum damages" clause (*pauschalierter Schadensersatz*) pursuant to Swiss and German law. In particular, once the amount of liquidated damages agreed by the parties fulfils the test of a "genuine pre-estimate of loss", the parties are in principle excluded from arguing that actual damages incurred are either higher or lower than the set amount of liquidated damages. Accordingly, a liquidated damages clause must with regard to the respective contract breach regularly (and even in the absence of an explicit agreement to that effect) be construed as a cap on liability though an unreasonably low amount may be considered as unreasonable and hence not enforceable. This principle is in particular deeply rooted in English law, cf. *Biffa Waste Services Ltd & Anor v Maschinenfabrik Ernst Hese GmbH & Ors* [2008] EWHC 6 (TCC) para 108; according to US law (respectively the laws of individual states), an LD clause allowing the recovery of additional general damages may even trigger the invalidity of the LD clause due to an assumed lack of a reasonable attempt to estimate expected losses ("Have Cake and Eat it"), see JM Perillo, Calamari and Perillo on Contracts (6th edn Thomson Reuters, St. Paul 2009) 534. It seems that this restriction does not apply with regard to the concept of *pauschalierter Schadensersatz* under Swiss and German law and the innocent party may claim (proven) higher general damages incurred due to the respective breach, see, eg, BGH [1982] NJW 2316, 2317.

A. General Part

either by replacing the term "liquidated damages" with a neutral term or by clarifying the precise meaning of the liquidated damages clause in the individual contractual context.

8. Concurring claims under tort (product liability)

110 The seller's liability for bodily injury or death caused by (defective) goods is explicitly excluded from the scope of application of the CISG (Art 5 CISG) and therefore governed by national contract and tort law. In addition, concurring claims under domestic tort law may also come into play in case of property damage external to the goods (caused by defective products or other breaches of contract), though this is still disputed.[215]

a) Liability under general tort law and the Product Liability Act

111 Swiss tort law provides for fault-based liability of anyone who unlawfully causes damage to another person, see Arts 41ff CO. Although Art 41 (1) CO was drafted as a "blanket clause", its scope of application has been substantially narrowed down by Swiss jurisprudence. As a result of this development, liability under Swiss tort law arises only in the event of an infringement of **"absolute rights"** such as property and physical integrity whereas pure economic loss as well as compensation for damage to the delivered products due to a defect are generally not recoverable.[216]

112 Finally, strict liability of a manufacturer of defective goods has also found its way into Swiss law by means of the **Product Liability Act**.[217] Pursuant to the Act, which is based essentially on the European Directive on Product Liability[218], a manufacturer is liable for personal injury as well as property damage (provided the damaged property was used for private purposes) caused by defective goods.

113 It should be taken into consideration, however, that tort and contract law apply **different standards** when assessing the question of whether a product is defective and the seller should be held liable for damages resulting from the defect. Whereas a defect in the context of contract law presupposes preliminary a deviation from the quality standard defined in the contract, tort law utilizes an objective standard: Pursuant to both Art 4 of the Swiss Product Liability Act and Art 41 CO, a product is defective for the purposes of tort law if it does not fulfill an average user's legitimate expectation at the time it was put into circulation.[219]

b) Contractual liability under domestic sales law

114 Given that liability for death or personal injury is completely carved out of the scope of application of the CISG (Art 5), Swiss domestic sales law plays also a limited role for claims based on **bodily injury** or death. A claim of this kind can either be based on Art 97

---

[215] See in particular Ferrari (n 65) 74ff with further references.

[216] Schwenzer (n 181) paras 50.06, 50.17 with further references; for a different view see Rusch, "Weiterfresserschaden auch in der Schweiz?" [2012] HAVE 269 ff.

[217] Bundesgesetz über die Produktehaftpflicht (*Produktehaftpflichtgesetz*).

[218] Council Directive 85/374/EEC of 25 July 1985 on the approximation of the laws, regulations and administrative provisions of the Member States concerning liability for defective products [1985] OJ L 210/29.

[219] D Hoffmann and J Hoffmann, "Switzerland" in HL Kaplan and GL Fowler (eds), *Product Liability in 36 jurisdictions worldwide* (IBA/ABA 2008) 182.

(1) CO or Art 208 CO (whereas the latter provision deals specifically with claims for damages in case of defective goods supplied under sales contracts). Though a defect of the goods as well as fault is, generally speaking, a condition precedent for a damage claim, the seller may pursuant to Art 208 (2) CO even face strict liability if the recovery of "direct damages" are sought and the purchaser has rescinded the contract upfront (*Wandlung*).[220] Against the background of the definition of "direct damages" developed by Swiss jurisprudence (as confirmed by a recent decision of the Swiss Federal Supreme Court), damage caused by death or personal injury as a consequence of defective products may indeed constitute "direct damage" in the individual case.[221]

V. Outlook: The Proposal for a Common European Sales Law (CESL) – a potential alternative for the CISG?

On 11 October 2011, the European Commission has published the proposal for a Common European Sales Law (CESL).[222] The official objective of the proposal is the provision of a uniform set of contractual rules in order to improve the conditions for the establishment and the functioning of the internal market.[223] The envisaged scope of application covers cross border contracts concerning the sale of movable goods[224], related service contracts as well as the supply of "digital content".[225] In principle, both commercial as well as consumer contracts fall within the ambit of the CESL subject to one rather bizarre and already heavily criticized exception: According to Art. 7 CESL-Regulation, the CESL can only be chosen by the parties for B2B contracts if at least one trading party is a so called small or midsize undertaking (SMU).[226] Contrary to the CISG, the application of the CESL requires also an express agreement of the parties in this regard ("opt in" instead of "opt-out"), Art. 3, 8 CESL-Regulation. Furthermore, the CESL will not prevail over private international laws: Rather, the parties may only choose this instrument as a so called "2nd national regime" if and when the contract is (in accordance with the determination by private international laws, in particular the Rome I Regulation) governed by the laws of a member state of the EU in the first place.[227]

114a

---

[220] A claim of damages under Art 208 CO requires pursuant to the literal construction of this provision (as applied by the Federal Supreme Court) the rescission (*Wandelung*) of the contract, see BG (19 Feb 2007) BGE 133 III 335, 339. Accordingly, it would appear that the purchaser must declare the avoidance of the contract pursuant to Art 49 CISG before he can claim damages due to bodily injury on the basis of Art 208 CO.

[221] BG (28 Nov 2006) BGE 133 III 257, 271.

[222] COM (2011) 635 final. The Proposal consists of a draft Regulation whereas the substantial part of the CESL constitutes Annex I of the Regulation.

[223] See Art. 1 (1) CESL-Regulation.

[224] According to Art. 2 lit h CESL-Regulation "goods" within the meaning of the CESL are "tangible movable items to the exclusion of electricity, natural gas as well as water and other gas unless they are put up for sale in a limited volume or set quantity."

[225] Art. 4 CESL-Regulation (cross border requirement), Art. 5 CESL-Regulation (material scope of application).

[226] C Wendehorst in R Schulze (ed), *Common European Sales Law (CESL) – Commentary* (C.H. Beck in cooperation with Hart Publishing and Nomos, München 2012) Art. 8 CESL-Regulation para 22 rightly points out that large enterprises will due to this fact rarely risk the use of the CESL in contractual relations with other traders as they would otherwise have to determine whether the respective other party fulfills the requirement of a SMU.

[227] M Fornasier, "28. versus 2. Regime – Kollisionsrechtliche Aspekte eines optionalen europäischen Vertragsrechts" (2012) 76 RabelsZ 401, 405.

A. General Part

114b Given that the Commission has intended to create an instrument that covers "matters of contract law that are of practical relevance during the life cycle" of a sales contract (s. Recital 26 CESL-Regulation), the CESL contains contrary to the CISG also inter alia provisions on defects in consent (Art. 48 through 57 CESL), the incorporation of general terms and conditions into a contract (Art. 70 CESL) to the inclusion of an express provision resolving the battle of forms problem[228], the policing of unfair general terms and conditions (Art. 86 (1) CESL), limitation periods (Arts 178-186 CESL) and the applicable interest rate in case of late payment (Art. 168 CESL). Apart from that, the material provisions (in particular regarding the obligations of the parties as well as applicable remedies in case of breach) of both CISG and CESL (the latter as regards B2B contracts) are rather similar in substance[229]: For instance, both instruments provide for a similar scope of remedies (i.e. specific performance, termination, price reduction and damages)[230], acknowledge a "right to cure" of the seller[231] and require in principle a fundamental breach as a precondition for a termination of the contract.[232] Both instruments adhere in relation to damage claims (that are in either case subject to a foreseeability test) also to the principle of strict rather than fault based liability.[233] In line with the CISG (but more specifically), the CESL requires the buyer also to examine the contractual goods within as short a period as is reasonable not exceeding 14 days from the date of delivery (Art. 121 CESL) and to notify defects to the seller within a reasonable time when the buyer discovered or could be expected to discover the lack of conformity (Art. 122 CESL) in order to preserve applicable remedies based on non-conforming goods.

114c The future relevance of the CESL (once enacted) is currently hard to predict.[234] For the time being, it cannot even be excluded that both scope as well as content of the instrument will be substantially altered due to harsh criticism of the legal community. For instance, the European Law Institute has in 2012 published a comprehensive statement on the proposal that both identifies a multitude of alleged shortcomings and makes practical recommendations for potential alterations of the instrument in order to increase its utility in practice.[235] The Committee on Legal Affairs of the European Parliament has in the meantime proposed to reduce the scope of application to

---

[228] See Art. 39 (1) CESL that explicitly adopts the "knock out rule" (subject to certain exceptions contained in Art. 39 (2) CESL).

[229] See in more detail U Magnus, "CISG and CESL" in P A Nielsen et al (ed), *Liber Amicorum Ole Lando* (Djoef Forlag, Copenhagen 2012) 225, 241 ff.; M Loos and H Schelhaas, "Commercial Sales: The Common European Sales Law Compared to the Vienna Sales Convention" [2013] ERPL 105, 120 ff.

[230] See from the perspective of the buyer Art. 106 CESL in combination with Art. 110 CESL (specific performance); Art. 114 ff. CESL (termination); Art. 120 CESL (price reduction); Art. 159 ff. CESL (damages). In addition, the CESL provides expressly for a right to withhold performance, Art. 113 CESL.

[231] Arts. 106 (2) lit a, 109 CESL.

[232] See from the perspective of the buyer Arts 114, 87 (2) CESL. Likewise, in case of delay in delivery a fundamental breach is not required if a reasonable grace period set by the buyer has lapsed to no avail, Art. 115 (1) CESL (comp. Art. 49 (1) lit b CISG).

[233] Art 159 CESL. Damages may not be claimed in the event of circumstances that are beyond the control of the party in breach, Art. 88 CESL (comp. Art. 79 CISG).

[234] For a pessimistic view inter alia P Mankowski, "CESL – who needs it?" [2012] IHR 45 ff.

[235] Statement of the European Law Institute on the Proposal for a Regulation on a Common European Sales Law COM (2011) 635 final. The statement can be downloaded under http://www.europeanlawinstitute.eu/projects/publications/.

VI. Relevant laws beyond the governing law of the contract

"distance contracts" – meaning in the essence, that the CESL may only apply in relation to sales via the internet.[236] This having said and besides justified criticism, from the viewpoint of the author the CESL may however offer at least some, though not essential, advantages compared to the CISG: On the one hand, the role of the supplementary (domestic) governing law will become less important given that the CESL closes many (though not all) gaps of the CISG. On the other hand, some provisions of the CESL enhance legal certainty in comparison with similar provisions in the CISG – for instance, by providing a specific maximum length of the period of examination (Art 121 (1) CESL) and an express right to withhold performance (Arts 113, 133 CESL). Other examples may include the clarification of the relationship of the right to cure with other remedies of the buyer such as termination, damages and price reduction (Art. 106 (2) lit a, Art. 109 CESL) as well as leqal consequences triggered by a merger clause contained in the contract (Art. 72 CESL).[237]

VI. Relevant laws beyond the governing law of the contract

The law governing a sales contract (the "lex contractus") is not the only legal source that may become relevant in relation to the execution of a sales transaction. Laws of other jurisdictions can also play an essential role, in particular with regard to proprietary aspects of a sales contract that do not fall within the ambit of the "lex contractus". Besides proprietary aspects, it is also widely accepted that **mandatory laws** of jurisdictions other than the (chosen) governing law may in exceptional cases apply to a contractual dispute, either in addition or even in lieu of the governing law. The most important examples of those overriding mandatory laws are competition laws as well as export and exchange control regulations.

Finally, sales transactions can also impose liability on the seller to third parties that are not bound by the contract. Though **tort liability for defective products** (in particular to third parties) on the international level is outside the scope of this book, the last subparagraph of this chapter contains a brief discussion of European private international law that determines specifically which legal order should apply in relation to claims based on product liability – at least if a court based in the EU is called upon to resolve the third party dispute (see ch A.V.6 below).

1. Mandatory rules: General issues

Mandatory laws are traditionally divided into two groups: "Regular" or "domestic" mandatory rules are intended to be applicable only if they form part of the governing law of the contract or (regardless of the chosen governing law) in the event that all relevant elements of the contract are linked exclusively to the country that has established these mandatory rules. "Internationally mandatory" respectively overriding mandatory laws on the other hand require observance regardless

---

[236] Draft Report on the proposal for a regulation of the European Parliament and of the Council on a Common European Sales Law, 2011/0284 (COD) as of 6 March 2013.
[237] Some added value of the CESL compared to the CISG has also been identified by M Loos and H Schelhaas (n 229) 127 f. Contra inter alia S Balthasar, "The draft common European sales law – overview and analysis" [2013] I.C.C.L.R. 43 ff.

of the (diverging) governing law of a contract[238] and may accordingly play a role even in case of a commercial contract with genuine international elements.

a) Domestic mandatory laws

118 Pursuant to the private international law regimes of many jurisdictions, regular or **domestic mandatory laws** apply either as a part of the governing law of the contract or – regardless of a contradicting choice of law by the parties – in the event that a contract is **solely linked** to the jurisdiction to which these mandatory rules belong. Therefore, in case of a domestic sales contract, "domestic" mandatory laws of this jurisdiction must be applied even if the parties have chosen a different governing law.[239] The policing of general terms and conditions maintained by some legal systems in order to prevent the use of unfair contractual terms may serve as a good example in this respect: For instance, a German seller who contracts on the basis of his general sales terms with a purchaser based in Germany as well can in the absence of any other genuine "international link" and regardless of a deviating governing law provision not prevent that his standard sales terms are scrutinized in the light of the relevant provisions of the German Civil Code.

119 European private international law has adopted the principle of an **"internal situation"** also at the European level and thereby created a new restriction for international contracts that have no genuine links outside the EU: Pursuant to Art 3 (4) Rome I Regulation, the contracting parties cannot escape mandatory European law if, apart from the choice of (a foreign) law, all elements characterizing the contractual relationship (eg, residence of the parties, place of performance) relate solely to one or more EU member states. According to its wording, Art 3 (4) Rome I Regulation refers (similarly as Art 3 (3) Rome I Regulation) to all mandatory laws of the European Union (respectively, in the case of EU Directives, their implementation by domestic laws of the forum) and not only overriding mandatory laws[240]. Accordingly, even the choice of the law of a jurisdiction outside the EU by the parties (eg, Swiss law) does not prevent the application of mandatory EU law in this case whenever a party turns to a court based in the EU in order to resolve a contractual dispute.[241]

120 It is another question whether an arbitral tribunal with a seat inside the EU may be affected by the aforementioned restrictions of European private international law

---

[238] For this distinction see E McKendrick, *Goode on Commercial Law* (4th edn Penguin, London 2010) 1218 ff.

[239] Pursuant to European private international law (in particular the Rome I Regulation, see n 3), in case that all relevant elements (besides the choice of law provision of the parties) of the dispute are located in one country, a court located in the EU must apply all mandatory laws of this country, see Art 3 (3) Rome I Regulation. Even though Swiss private international law does not explicitly contain a similar provision, it is widely acknowledged that mandatory Swiss law must be applied in case that all relevant elements of a given contract are solely connected to Switzerland. Similarly also the proposed new amendments to US private international law: § 1-301 UCC (2003) permits the choice of law in a "business to business" transaction without the precondition of a reasonable relationship of the contract with the chosen law (as it is still required by the currently enacted versions of the UCC); however, the chosen law must be that of a US state in the event that the contract does not bear a reasonable relation with any country other than the USA and hence constitutes a mere "domestic transaction", see SC Symeonides, *American Private International Law* (Wolters Kluwer, New York 2008) para 470.

[240] V Behr, "Rome I Regulation" [2010] J L & Commerce 233, 257.

[241] See also O Lando and PA Nielsen, "The Rome I Regulation" (2008) 45 CML Rev 1687, 1718.

VI. Relevant laws beyond the governing law of the contract

as well. According to the author's opinion, neither **Art 3 (3) nor Art. 3 (4) Rome I Regulation** are in this event directly relevant given that only state courts within the EU are under an obligation to apply the Rome I Regulation.[242] However, even based on this view, it remains controversial whether (domestic) conflict of laws statutes in place for arbitral tribunals with a seat in the corresponding member state provide for similar restrictions.[243]

For the time being, however, (either simple or "overriding") **mandatory EU law** regulating commercial contract law (in particular with the aim of protecting the weaker party of a contract) is still "at the embryonic stage".[244] Accordingly, Art 3 (4) Rome I Regulation plays currently only a rather limited role in this area of law. It remains to be seen whether EU law will increase its regulatory touch towards B2B contracts in the future.[245]

121

b) "Overriding-mandatory" rules

Some mandatory domestic laws demand their application even in relation to international commercial contracts that are governed by the laws of another jurisdiction. Hence, the parties to an international commercial contract may not always be able to escape certain mandatory rules by way of a choice of law clause. Whether **"overriding-mandatory"** rules are applied and prevail over contractual terms in that event depends amongst other things on whether a court of law or an arbitral tribunal is called upon to resolve the individual contractual dispute. Courts of law are obliged to apply the private international laws of the forum state.[246] These rules generally provide for the application of "overriding-mandatory" rules of the forum state[247] but may also permit the courts to apply "overriding-mandatory" rules that belong neither to the "lex contractus" nor to the "lex fori" but to other legal systems.[248]

122

---

[242] However, this still prevailing view has met with increasing doubts, s. eg P Mankowski, "Rom I und Schiedsverfahren" [2011] RIW 30 ff. with further references.

[243] See for a discussion of this problem with regard to § 1051 German Civil Code as well as Art 187 PILA J Kondring, "Flucht vor dem deutschen AGB-Recht bei Inlandsverträgen" [2010] RIW 184, 187 ff.; P Ostendorf, "Wirksame Wahl ausländischen Rechts auch bei fehlendem Auslandsbezug im Fall einer Schiedsgerichtsvereinbarung und ausländischem Schiedsort?" [2011] SchiedsVZ 234 ff. Even further T Pfeiffer, "Die Abwahl des deutschen Rechts in Inlandsfällen bei Vereinbarung eines Schiedsverfahrens" [2012] NJW 1169, 1171 who takes the view that domestic mandatory substantial laws can in this event be derogated even by way of a partial choice of the corresponding domestic law.

[244] V Roppo, "From Consumer Contracts to Asymmetric Contracts: A Trend in European Contract Law?" [2009] ERCL 304, 311.

[245] See Roppo (n 244) 311 ff, who takes the view that EU law is already more and more focusing on "asymmetric contracts" in general (including also B2B contracts between parties with unequal bargaining power).

[246] That was the prevailing view even before the enactment of the Rome I Regulation, see with regard to German private international law for instance BGH (21 Sep 1995) [1996] NJW 54.

[247] See Art 9 (2) Rome I Regulation (n 3): "Nothing in this Regulation shall restrict the application of the overriding mandatory provisions of the law of the forum." Similarly Art 18 PILA: "This Code does not prevent the application of those mandatory provisions of Swiss law which, by reason of their particular purpose, are applicable regardless of the law designated by this Code."

[248] See for instance Art 9 (3) Rome I Regulation (n 3): "Effect may be given to the overriding mandatory provisions of the law of the country where the obligations arising out of the contract have to be or have been performed, in so far as those overriding mandatory provisions render the performance of the contract unlawful. In considering whether to give effect to those provisions, regard shall be had to their nature and purpose and to the consequences of their application or non-application."

123 It should be noted that only few mandatory laws qualify as "overriding-mandatory" rules. For instance, Art 9 (1) of the Rome I Regulation defines "overriding-mandatory" rules on the basis of the definition created in a judgment of the European Court of Justice[249] as those provisions *the respect for which is regarded as crucial by a country for safeguarding its public interests, such as its political, social or economic organisation, to such an extent that they are applicable to any situation falling within their scope, irrespective of the law otherwise applicable to the contract under this Regulation.* (Mandatory) private laws that preliminarily seek to protect the interests of the weaker party to a contract accordingly fall only in exceptional cases within the ambit of this definition.[250]

124 **Art 18 of the Swiss PILA** has been interpreted in a similar manner. Though this article does not contain a comparable restriction with regard to scope and content of "overriding-mandatory laws", there is general agreement that only mandatory (Swiss) laws that have a "fundamental meaning for state and society against the background of an international dimension"[251] are covered.

125 Both Rome I Regulation and Swiss private international laws permit courts under narrow circumstances to apply (at their discretion) "overriding-mandatory rules" of **foreign jurisdictions**. According to Art 19 PILA, a Swiss court may, instead of the law that would otherwise be applicable, take recourse to mandatory foreign laws provided that overwhelming interests of one party justify (from the viewpoint of Swiss jurisprudence) that approach and the dispute is closely connected to the mandatory laws in question.[252] Art 9 (3) of the Rome I Regulation is even more restrictive: Courts may (at their discretion) solely give effect to foreign super mandatory laws of the place where the contractual obligations must be performed – provided these provisions would render the performance unlawful.[253]

c) Application of overriding mandatory rules by arbitral tribunals

126 The picture is less clear with regard to **arbitration** given that arbitral tribunals are not bound (or not to the same extent as the courts of law) by domestic private international law (see above). Besides mandatory substantive rules of the governing law of the contract, an arbitral tribunal must observe the mandatory procedural rules of the lex arbitri (i. e. those mandatory rules for arbitral proceedings that have been put in place by the seat state of the tribunal) in order to avoid that an award will be set aside by courts of the seat state. However, an arbitral tribunal is not under a general obligation to observe material "overriding-mandatory" rules of

---

[249] See the judgment of the ECJ, Joined Cases C-369/96 and C-376/96 *Arblade and Others* [1999] ECR I-8453 para 30.

[250] R Freitag, "Die kollisionsrechtliche Behandlung ausländischer Eingriffsnormen" (2009) 29 IPRax 109, 112; A Bonomi, "Overriding Mandatory Provisions in the Rome I Regulation on the Law Applicable to Contracts" in A Bonomi and P Volken (eds), *Yearbook of Private International Law: Vol. X 2008* (Sellier, München 2009) 285, 293.

[251] See W Wenger and C Müller in H Honsell et al (eds), *Basler Kommentar: Internationales Privatrecht* (2nd edn Helbing Lichtenhahn, Zürich 2007) Art 18 PILA para 10.

[252] The Swiss Federal Supreme Court has stressed the rather exceptional character of Art 19 PILA as well, see BG (7 May 2004) BGE 130 III 620, 630.

[253] A narrow construction of Art 9 (3) Rome I Regulation with regard to the scope of overriding mandatory rules that render the performance unlawful may however cause unjust results: That holds in particular true with regard to mandatory laws that aim to establish mandatory contractual claims but do not intend to prevent performance of the contract, see in particular Freitag (n 250) 113.

VI. Relevant laws beyond the governing law of the contract

states (including those of the "seat state") even if a link to the dispute in question exists – for instance, because the place of performance is located in the state concerned or one party in the arbitral proceedings intends to enforce the award in that specific state. A general obligation to apply overriding mandatory laws has only been assumed in case of those "overriding mandatory rules" that are acknowledged on an international level and form part of the "transnational public policy".[254]

Nevertheless, observance of "overriding mandatory rules" of jurisdictions in which the enforcement of the award may be sought has some practical relevance given that courts of law may otherwise refuse to recognize and enforce the award in accordance with Art V (2) of the New York Convention on the recognition and enforcement of international arbitration awards. 127

Another potential impact of overriding mandatory laws is the potential **invalidation** of arbitration agreements by a court.[255] This risk is clearly illustrated by a judgment of a German Higher Regional Court rendered in 2006: In that case, the claimant, a sales representative with a contractual territory in Germany, had lodged a claim for compensation as a consequence of the termination of the agency agreement in accordance with the EC Directive on Commercial Agents.[256] Though the sales representative agreement provided for arbitration as the exclusive means of dispute resolution and opted for the laws of the State of California as the law governing the contract, the representative nevertheless filed the lawsuit with a German court. Contrary to the court of first instance, the Higher Regional Court München affirmed its international jurisdiction and invalidated the arbitration agreement: According to the reasoning of the decision, the combination of the arbitration agreement and the choice of law infringed Arts 17, 18 of the European Directive on Commercial Agents (respectively § 89 b German Commercial Code, the transformation provision of German law), which have since the famous Ingmar decision been considered as "overriding mandatory rules".[257] In the essence, the Higher Regional Court München considered the risk that an arbitral tribunal would decide the case solely in accordance with the laws of California (without giving due consideration to the European Directive) as a sufficient justification to displace the arbitration agreement.[258] This 128

---

[254] See N Horn, "Zwingendes Recht in der internationalen Schiedsgerichtsbarkeit" [2008] SchiedsVZ 210 f. Only a core of fundamental legal principles such as the principle of pacta sunt servanda and the prohibition of corruption belong to the "transnational ordre public". An arbitral tribunal with a legal seat in Switzerland is not bound by Art 18 PILA and the prevailing view rejects also an analogous application of Art 19 PILA; see PA Karrer in H Honsell et al (n 251) Art 187 PILA para 255, 262 with further references. That view corresponds also to the interpretation of Art 190 (2) lit e PILA that permits an annulment of an arbitral award only in the event of an infringement of the (narrowly interpreted) "ordre public", see SV Berti and AK Schnyder in Honsell et al (n 251) Art 190 PILA para 73.

[255] See OLG München (17 May 2006) [2007] IPRax 322.

[256] See Art 17 and 18 of Council Directive 86/653/EEC of 18 December 1986 on the coordination of the laws of the Member States relating to self-employed commercial agents [1986] OJ L382/17. Pursuant to these Articles, that had to be transformed into domestic laws of all Member States of the EU, a commercial agent is entitled to a compensation if the agency contract has been terminated by the principal.

[257] Case C-381/98 *Ingmar GB Ltd v Eaton Leonard Technologies Inc* [2000] ECR I-9305.

[258] For a critical review of this decision see D Quinke, "Schiedsvereinbarungen und Eingriffsnormen – Zugleich Anmerkung zu OLG München, 17. 5. 2006" [2007] SchiedsVZ 246 ff.

view has recently been confirmed (in relation to a jurisdiction agreement in a rather similar scenario) by a judgment of the German Federal Court of Justice.[259]

129   As already stated above, international commercial contracts should however generally not raise many substantial concerns in that regard. Besides competition laws, export control and currency exchange regulations that may in the individual case directly interfere with the validity of the sales contract or of individual contractual provisions, mainly the transfer of property in the contractual goods is still a relevant legal issue resolved by laws other than the law governing the contract.

2. Proprietary aspects: The transfer of property in the goods sold

130   According to a widely accepted view shared by almost all domestic private international laws,[260] the **transfer of property** in the contract goods is not dealt with by the governing law of the contract but the (property) laws of the state where the contract goods are located (the "**lex situs**"). In cases where the property has already been transferred to the purchaser before delivery pursuant to the laws of the country of origin, a subsequent carriage of the goods into another jurisdiction does not affect the acquisition of property.[261] If, on the other hand, the property has not yet been transferred at that point of time, the laws of the country of destination as the new, "second" *lex situs* determine whether and when title passes to the purchaser.[262] It follows that the parties are not entitled to choose the applicable law for the transfer of property themselves though the availability of that option has recently gained popularity:[263] Notably, Swiss and Chinese private international laws permit a (restricted) choice of law also in relation to the applicable lex situs in relation to movable property.[264]

131   The decisiveness of the *lex situs* can have a detrimental effect on the impact of a **retention of title clause**: If the property laws of the country of destination do not acknowledge the retention of title[265], either as a matter of principle or because

---

[259] BGH (5 Sep 2012) [2013] IHR 35 f. A similar decision has been rendered by the English High Court in *Accentuate Limited v ASIGRA Inc* [2009] EWHC 2655 (QB).

[260] Germany: Art 42 EGBGB; Switzerland: Art 100 (2) PILA; England: *Air Foyle Ltd. & Anor v Center Capital Ltd* [2002] EWHC 2535 para 42.

[261] McKendrick in Goode (n 238) 1235.

[262] Laws of potential transit countries are pursuant to the prevailing opinion irrelevant, see D Martiny in C Reithmann and D Martiny (eds), *Internationales Vertragsrecht* (7th edn Dr. Otto Schmidt, Köln 2010) para 996.

[263] J Fawcett, J Harris and M Bridge, *International Sales of Goods in the Conflict of Laws* (OUP, Oxford 2005) para 18.39 ff.

[264] Swiss private international law permits a (limited) choice of law of the parties: Pursuant to Art 104 (1) PILA, the parties may submit both acquisition and loss of interest in movable property to the law of the state of shipment, the state of destination or the governing law of the contract. Pursuant to Art 104 (2) PILA, however, such choice will have no effect towards third parties – this restriction renders the choice of law option almost nugatory, see P Fisch in Honsell et al (n 251) Art 104 PILA para 17; more far reaching apparently § 37 Act on the Application of Laws to Foreign-related Civil Relationships of the People's Republic of China.

[265] A simple retention of title clause contained in a sales contract is inter alia acknowledged in Germany (§ 449 BGB); England (Sec 19 (1) SGA 1979); France (Art L 621-122 Code de Commerce), China (Art 134 Contract Law 1999) and Russia (Art 491 Civil Code). A formal registration (filing) of the reservation of title is inter alia required in Switzerland (Art 715, 716 CC) and the USA (§§ 9–302, 9–305 UCC). Attempts to harmonize the substantive property laws on the international level have so far not been a huge success. The Convention on International Interests in Mobile Equipment (16 Nov 2001) prepared by Unidroit has however been acceded by some 57 states (status 31 July 2013); for the current status see <http://www.unidroit.org/english/implement/i-2001-convention.pdf>. The scope of

certain formalities such as, eg, a registration requirement have not been complied with, property rights of the seller based on the retention of title are regular lost upon arrival of the goods in the country of destination and regardless of whether or not the contract price has already been paid in full.[266]

3. Competition and antitrust laws

Competition and antitrust laws[267] belong to the realm of public law. Though the vast majority of states have enacted their own antitrust laws, both EU competition and US antitrust laws have clearly become the most influential sets of rules on the global level.[268] Besides their mandatory character, both EU competition law and US antitrust laws have extended their scope of application also by means of the so called **"effects doctrine"**: Based on this theory, (also) an international sales contract restraining competition may fall within the ambit of the relevant statutes regardless of the parties' place of residence or the place where the contract has been implemented – the creation of economic effects inside the respective jurisdiction (i. e. either the EU or the US) already suffices.[269] Other domestic competition laws have taken a similar view.[270]

132

An infringement of competition laws may besides the significant risk of fines imposed by domestic or supranational competition authorities (in case of EU competition law the European Commission, respectively the national competition authorities of the EU member states) or damages claims by third parties result in the **invalidity** of individual contractual clauses.[271] EU law imposes a duty on the courts of the EU member states to apply EU competition law (as part of the "ordre public") on their own initiative and regardless of the governing law of the

133

---

the Convention is limited to security rights in airframes, aircraft engines and helicopters, railway rolling stock and space assets, see Art 2 (3) Convention.

[266] See for instance the decisions of the Swiss Federal Supreme Court, BG (6 Jul 1967) BGE 93 III 96, as well as BG (2 Jun 2005) BGE 131 III 595. The seller was in both cases not entitled to demand the separation of contract goods delivered under a retention of title clause from the bankruptcy estate of the insolvent Swiss purchaser given that applicable Swiss property laws require the registration of a retention of title in a public register (that was not effected in either case) as a condition precedent for its enforceability.

[267] In North America, the term "antitrust law" refers roughly to the same rules that are labeled "competition law" in England and elsewhere (i. e. laws promoting free competition in the marketplace holding illegal agreements that restrain trade – to be distinguished from statutes dealing with unfair commercial practices), see EW Daigneault, *Drafting International Agreements in Legal English* (Manz, Wien 2005) 66.

[268] EU competition law prevails over domestic competition law of EU member states with regard to agreements that are capable of affecting trade between the member states. In relation to anticompetitive unilateral conduct of (dominant) undertakings, the member states can sustain their own stricter competition laws; see Art 3 (1), (2) Council Regulation (EC) No 1/2003 of 16 December 2002 on the implementation of the rules on competition laid down in Articles 81 and 82 of the Treaty [2003] OJ L1/1.

[269] For the application of the "effects doctrine" by EU competition law see J Faull and A Nikpay (eds), *The EC Law of Competition* (2nd edn OUP, Oxford 2008) para 3.389. Pursuant to the Foreign Trade Antitrust Improvement Act of 1982, US antitrust laws willl not apply to conduct involving trade or commerce with foreign nations to the explicit exception of conduct having a "substantial and reasonably foreseeable effect" on domestic commerce (see 15 USC § 6a).

[270] See for instance § 130 (2) of the German Act against Restraints of Competition (GWB).

[271] See with regard to EU competition law Art 101 (2) TFEU. The effect of an invalid clause on the remainder of the contract is however determined by the governing law of the contract.

A. General Part

contract.²⁷² It is, however, still controversial whether competition laws also form part of the "transnational ordre public" and may on that basis become relevant for courts and arbitral tribunals abroad as well. The Swiss Federal Supreme Court has for instance taken the view that EU competition law does not constitute a matter of public policy pursuant to Art 190 lit e PILA and, based on that view, upheld an arbitral award notwithstanding its non-compliance with EU competition laws.²⁷³ But it should be kept in mind that this view does not do away with problems related to the enforcement stage: Pursuant to the view of the European Court of Justice, all courts based in the EU must refuse to enforce arbitral awards that are contrary to EU competition law. This directive has placed an indirect burden on arbitrators to take EU competition law duly into account – in particular when enforcement of the award is likely to be sought in the EU.²⁷⁴

134   The basic provisions of the relevant EU competition law and US antitrust laws are contained in the Treaty on the Functioning of the European Union as well as in the Sherman Act and other US statutes.²⁷⁵ Whereas Art 101 (1) TFEU prohibits agreements that are restrictive of competition, Section 1 of the Sherman Act declares agreements in restraint of trade and commerce illegal.²⁷⁶ Both EU competition law and US antitrust laws do however acknowledge (though to a different extent) that vertical agreements (that is to say agreements concluded between undertakings on a different level in the production and distribution chain) generally constitute a less severe potential threat to competition than horizontal agreements between competitors. Based on that reasoning, vertical restraints are nowadays generally regarded as not being "per se" illegal under US law. Rather, they are subject to a "rule of reason" test that takes market shares and the parties' position, the duration of the restraint and other factors into account.²⁷⁷ EU competition law has on the other hand adopted block exemption regulations that provide a "safe harbor" for commercial parties who

---

²⁷² See for instance with regard to EU competition law Art 3 Council Regulation (EC) No 1/2003 (n 239).

²⁷³ BG (8 Mar 2006) BGE 132 III 389, 398; see for a thorough review of this decision M Meinhard and JM Ahrens, "Wettbewerbsrecht und Schiedsgerichtsbarkeit in der Schweiz – Eine Würdigung des Entscheids des Bundesgerichts vom 8. März 2006" [2006] SchiedsVZ 182.

²⁷⁴ Case C-126/97 *Eco Swiss China Time Ltd. v. Benetton International NV* [1999] ECR I-3055. See also SI Dempegiotis, "EC Competition Law and International Arbitration in the Light of EC Regulation 1/2003" (2008) 25 Journal of International Arbitration 365, 385. According to a more recent tendency (in particular applied by French jurisprudence), courts must however only refuse the enforcement of an arbitral award if the arbitrators have infringed EU competition law in a direct and obvious manner, see B Kasolowsky, "Ordre public-Widrigkeit kartellrechtlicher Schiedssprüche – der flagrante, effective et concrète-Test der französischen Cour de cassation" [2009] IPrax 268 with further references.

²⁷⁵ 15 USC §§ 1-7 (Sherman Act). The Sherman Act and other federal antitrust legislation can be found on the official website of the US government under <http://www.gpoaccess.gov/uscode/browse.html>.

²⁷⁶ The unilateral abuse of a dominant market position is dealt with under EU law by Art 102 TFEU. Similar provisions exist in the USA: In particular § 2 of the Sherman Act (15 USC § 2) prohibits monopolization respectively attempts to monopolize. Restrictions imposed by these provisions are not further subjected in this book.

²⁷⁷ See the landmark decision of the US Supreme Court in *Continental T.V. v GTE Sylvania* 433 US 36 (1977) that has established the "rule of reason" test for all non-price vertical restraints. Pursuant to a more recent decision by the US Supreme Court, the rule of reason test has for the first time also been applied to vertical price restraints (i.e. resale price maintenance) that are accordingly no longer considered being "per-se" illegal, see US Supreme *Leegin Creative Leather Products, Inc v PSKS*, Inc, 551 US 877 (2007).

VI. Relevant laws beyond the governing law of the contract

agree on (vertical) restraints once their requirements are fulfilled. The most important block exemption regulation for vertical restraints in sales and distribution agreements – Council Regulation (EU) 330/2010[278] – explicitly permits vertical restraints that are not explicitly excluded ("black listed") from the exemption provided that both supplier and purchaser have a market share on the relevant market of no more than 30 %.[279] The non-fulfillment of the requirements of a block exemption regulation does not automatically trigger the illegality of the contractual provision in question. However, if a black-listed clause is used, there is generally a strong assumption that the clause in question falls foul of Art 101 (1) TFEU and can also not be exempted under Art 101 (3) TFEU.[280]

Though standard sales and supply contracts generally do not raise any antitrust concerns, some contractual arrangements made in the context of sales transactions (usually contained in framework agreements such as dealership, franchise and framework supply agreements rather than individual sales contracts) may infringe competition laws. Given that sales contracts are in general not entered into between competitors, the following brief overview of typical antitrust pitfalls is limited to restraints entered into between companies that are active on different levels in the production or distribution chain. Further restrictions imposed by competition laws on dominant undertakings will also not be discussed. 135

- **Resale Price Maintenance**: A seller is generally not permitted (neither directly nor indirectly) to set binding (minimum) prices that have to be charged by the purchaser to his own customers.[281] A mere recommendation of retail prices as well as a binding agreement as to *maximum* resale prices are in principle permitted provided these measures do not amount to a factual setting of a minimum price level. Resale price maintenance is still considered as a "hardcore" restriction by EU competition law and fines have regularly been imposed on non-complying manufacturers. US law on the other hand takes a more lenient approach: According to a more recent judgment of the US Supreme Court, resale price maintenance is no longer considered as being illegal "per se" but subject to a rule of reason test.[282] 136
- **Territorial and customer sales restrictions**: Under EU competition law, the seller must generally not (neither directly nor indirectly) restrict the geographic areas or the range of customers to whom the purchaser can resell the contractual goods. Restraints with regard to "active" sales by the purchaser are permitted in certain circumstances[283] whereas a total "export ban" that also includes a prohibition of passive (unsolicited) 137

---

[278] Commission Regulation (EU) No 330/2010 of 22 April 2010 on the application of Article 101 (3) of the Treaty on the Functioning of the European Union to categories of vertical agreements and concerted practices [2010] OJ L 102/1.

[279] Art 3 (1) Council Regulation (EU) No 330/2010 (n 278). From the perspective of the seller, the relevant market is the market on which the seller sells the contract goods whereas the market on which the buyer purchases the contract goods is the relevant market from the buyer's perspective.

[280] Faull and Nikpay (n 269) para 9.207.

[281] Accordingly, a block exemption is categorically denied by Art 4 lit a Council Regulation No 330/2010 (n 278).

[282] With regard to US law see the decision of the US Supreme Court in *Leegin Creative Leather Products, Inc v PSKS*, Inc, 551 US 877 (2007) pursuant to which resale price maintenance is now subject to the "rule of reason test" and may hence be upheld in an individual case.

[283] A supplier may restrict active sales into territories or to a customer group which the seller has either reserved for himself and/or allocated to another distributor on an exclusive basis, see Art 4 lit b Council Regulation (EU) No 330/2010 (n 278).

sales of the contractual goods to certain areas or customers represents a "hard-core" restriction.²⁸⁴ US law does not make a similar distinction between "active" and "passive" sales and thus permits more far reaching restrictions.²⁸⁵

138 • **Non-compete obligations**: EU competition law restricts the use of non-compete obligations that prohibit the purchase of competing products by the purchaser: Non-compete obligations are (subject to the general market share threshold) only block-exempted under Regulation (EU) 330/2010 if they are limited to the contractual term of the agreement and have a maximum duration of five years.²⁸⁶ US law once again treats non-compete obligations (referred to as "exclusive dealing") in a more liberal manner: Contractual clauses on "exclusive dealing" (this term contains both non-compete obligations and exclusive supply obligations) are regularly upheld unless this restraint causes a substantial elimination of market forces.²⁸⁷

139 • **Tying**: Tying occurs when the seller makes the sale of a certain product (the "tying product") conditional on the purchase of another distinct product (the "tied" product).²⁸⁸ Tying falls within the ambit of the block exemption regulation (EU) No 330/2010 (and is not blacklisted) provided the seller's market share does not exceed 30 %. Similarly, US antitrust law renders tying illegal only if the seller enjoys sufficient market power in the market for the tying products and the tying forecloses a substantial part of the market.²⁸⁹

4. Export control regulations

140　A seller must, regardless of the law governing the contract, strictly comply with all export regulations that apply to the intended sales transaction. From the perspective of a European seller, it is foremost the foreign trade legislation enacted by the EU that must be observed. However, national legislation may lay down even stricter rules in the individual case. Additionally, US export regulations have become notorious for their extraterritorial effect: As a consequence, a basic understanding of the scope of application of US export control laws is mandatory even from the perspective of a seller residing in the EU or elsewhere. An infringement of either US or EU export control laws may include administrative fines but can also trigger criminal prosecution. Furthermore, an infringement may pursuant to some domestic statutes also invalidate the contract as a whole.²⁹⁰

---

²⁸⁴ See in relation to EU competition Law Art 4 lit a Council Regulation (EU) No 330/2010 (n 278).
²⁸⁵ For US law see the decision of the US Supreme Court in *Continental T.V. v. GTE Sylvania*, 433 US 36 (1977) applying the rule of reason to any form of territorial and customer sales restrictions.
²⁸⁶ Art 5 (1) Council Regulation (EU) No 330/2010 (n 278). Post-contractual non-compete obligations are only exempted under particular narrow circumstances, see Art 5 (3) Council Regulation (EU) No 330/2010 (n 278).
²⁸⁷ B Klein and AV Lerner, "The expanded economics of free riding: How exclusive dealing prevents free-riding and creates undivided loyalty" (2007) 74 Antitrust L J 473: Exclusive dealing regularly permitted in case of foreclosure levels of 40 % or less; similarly TA Baker, "Thoughts on Exclusive Dealing & Related Practices" (2006) 7 The Sedona Conference Journal 43, 44.
²⁸⁸ See Faull and Nikpay (n 269) para 9.359.
²⁸⁹ F Alese, *Federal Antitrust and EC Competition Law Analysis* (Ashgate, Aldershot 2008) 259 f.
²⁹⁰ See with regard to German law for instance § 31 (1) AWG. Domestic respectively supranational export control regulations are regularly considered as "overriding-mandatory" rules that apply in principle regardless of the governing law of the contract, see N Voser, "Mandatory Rules of

VI. Relevant laws beyond the governing law of the contract

The following section only provides a rather basic overview of the relevant European and US regulations on export control and cannot replace a detailed assessment in each individual case.   141

a) European export laws

EU Regulation No 428/2009[291] (the "Dual-Use Regulation") is the centerpiece of EU export control laws. Pursuant to Art 3 (1) Dual-Use Regulation, an export of goods to a destination outside the EU[292] requires an export authorization if the goods are listed in Annex I of the Regulation ("dual use items"). The export of **non-listed goods** also requires an authorization if the exporter has been informed by the competent authority in his home jurisdiction or is otherwise aware of the fact[293] that the goods are or may be intended either a) for use in connection, inter alia, with the development, production, operation, maintenance, storage, detection, identification or dissemination of ABC-weapons or related carrier missiles (Art 4 (1) Regulation), b) for a military end-use (by means of incorporation into military items or use for development, production or maintenance of those items) provided the purchasing country is subject to an arms embargo decided by the EC Council, the OSCE or the Security Council of the United Nations (see Art 4 (2) Dual-Use Regulation) or c) for use as parts or components of military items that have been illegally exported from the territory of a member state (Art 4 (3) Dual-Use Regulation).   142

The competent national authorities of the member states (and not the European Commission) are responsible for the implementation of the Dual-Use Regulation.[294] Accordingly, the exporter must obtain necessary **export authorizations** (in form of individual, global or general export authorizations) from the competent authority of the EU member state where he is established.[295] One exception to this rule is the Community General Export Control Authorization contained in Annex II of the Dual-Use Regulation: Exports of listed goods to Australia, Canada, Japan, New Zealand, Norway, Switzerland and the USA (with the exception of particularly sensitive goods listed either in Annex 4 or Annex 2, Part 2 of the Dual-Use Regulation as well as goods that are intended for any of the uses referred to in Art 4 (1),(2) Dual-Regulation) are exempted from further authorization requirements though the exporter must notify the competent authority within 30 days once he first uses the Community General Export Control Authorization.   143

Law as a Limitation on the Law applicable in International Commercial Arbitration" (1996) 7 Am Rev Int' Arb 319, 326.

[291] Council Regulation (EC) No 428/2009 of 5 May 2009 setting up a Community regime for the control of exports, transfer, brokering and transit of dual-use items (Recast) [2009] OJ L134/1 ("Dual-Use Regulation").

[292] An "export" of goods must be distinguished from a mere intra-community "transfer" according to which the goods are merely delivered from one member state into another member state of the EU. Intra-community transfers of dual use goods are in principle not subject to authorization requirements provided these goods are not listed in Annex IV of the Regulation, see Art 22 Dual-Use Regulation. The member states may however impose additional authorization requirements.

[293] Pursuant to Art 4 (4) Dual-Use Regulation, awareness of the exporter of any of the uses referred to in Art 4 (1), (2) and (3) triggers the obligation to notify this fact to the relevant export control authority that will subsequently decide whether an authorization is needed for the intended transaction.

[294] See http://trade.ec.europa.eu/doclib/docs/2006/december/tradoc_114154.pdf.

[295] P Bentley and E Kostadinova in A Kritzer et al (eds), *International Contract Manual* (Thomson Reuters West 2008) Volume 2 § 37:15.

A. General Part

144   It is unfortunate that the Dual-Use Regulation is not a self-contained export control regime: According to Art 8 Dual-Use Regulation, all EU member states are expressly entitled to impose their own **additional authorization requirements** on the export of dual-use items that are not listed in Annex I for reasons of public security or for human rights considerations. It follows that mere compliance with EU law does not suffice from the exporter's point of view – further restrictions imposed by the relevant domestic export control laws must be taken into account as well.[296] Furthermore, export control of **military items** is generally a matter of the national law of the member states.[297]

145   Besides the regular export control regime contained in the Dual-Use Regulation, EU export control laws include also **sanctions** and other restrictive measures against certain countries and individual persons (in particular terrorist groups and terrorists). Of particular importance is Council Regulation (EU) No 267/2012 of 23 March 2012 concerning restrictive measures against Iran.[298] Given that these measures are subject to permanent updates and amendments, no further summary on the existing instruments will be submitted here.

b) US Export Laws

146   Export control laws of the USA consist predominantly of the **Export Administration Regulations** (EAR) administered[299] by the Bureau of Industry and Security of the United States Department of Commerce (BIS).[300] From the perspective of a non US exporter, it is important to keep in mind that goods are subject to the EAR not only in relation to exports from US territory but cover also the re-export[301] of goods that are of US origin respectively incorporate U.S. content or are directly based on US technology and software, § 743.3 EAR.[302] According to a "de minimis" rule contained in § 734.4 (c), (d) EAR, however, goods containing less than 25 % (respectively 10 % in relation to supplies to the "designated terrorist supporting" states Cuba, Iran, North Korea, Sudan and Syria) of parts and components of US origin (based on the value of the goods) generally do not fall within the ambit of the EAR.[303]

---

[296] See with regard to German export control laws for instance §§ 5 c and 5 d AWV.

[297] Bentley and Kostadinova (n 295) § 37:3.

[298] Council Regulation (EU) No 267/2012 of 23 March 2012 concerning restrictive measures against Iran and repealing Regulation (EU) No 961/2010 [2012] OJ L 88/1.

[299] The Obama administration is currently in the process of reforming US export control laws. The reform plan provides also for the creation of a single list of controlled goods as well as one single licensing agency, see G Husisian "United States: export control reforms" [2012] Int. T.L.R. 18 ff.

[300] The most recent versions of the EAR and the Commerce Control List can be found on the website of the Bureau of Industry and Security, see <http://www.bis.doc.gov>. A special regime (Arms Export Control Act and the International Traffic in Arms Regulations) applies in relation to an intended export of arms and ammunition (see P Luther in Kritzer et al (n 295) § 36:4) that is not further subjected in this book.

[301] From the perspective of US law, the term re-export comprehends both actual shipment of goods from a foreign country to another but also the release of technology to a foreign national outside the US, see EL Hirschhorn, *The Export Control and Embargo Handbook* (2nd edn Oceana Publications, New York 2005) 179.

[302] In exceptional cases, the EAR may even apply in case of foreign products that do not contain any parts or components of US origin but are (partially) based on US technology, see P Luther in Kritzer et al (n 295) § 36:3.

[303] The de-minimis rule does however not apply (respectively apply with a lower threshold) with regard to some specifically sensitive items, see § 734.4 EAR (a) and (b) for further particulars.

VI. Relevant laws beyond the governing law of the contract

The **Commerce Control List** (CCL) as an integral part of the EAR lists the types of goods (i. e. dual-use goods) that may in certain cases require (dependent on the type of the goods and the country of final destination[304]) an individual export license. The (re-)export of goods that are not listed in the CCL (so called "EAR 99" goods) is in principle exempted from license requirements. However, the "General Prohibitions" 4 through 10 contained in § 736 EAR lay down further restrictions (also) in case of EAR 99 goods. These prohibitions contain inter alia restrictions with regard to listed "Denied Persons", (General Prohibition 4), unauthorized exports and re-exports to prohibited end-users and end-uses, in particular regarding nuclear, missile technology, chemical and biological weapons as well as certain items for aircraft and vessel (all as further defined in § 744 EAR) provided the supplier is aware of the same (General Prohibition 5), unauthorized exports and re-exports to embargoed or otherwise sanctioned countries, in particular Cuba, Sudan, Syria, North Korea, Iran, Iraq and Rwanda (General Prohibition 6). General Prohibition 7 contains a prohibition for US persons against knowingly supporting specified proliferation activities even if the products in question are otherwise not subject to the EAR. Furthermore, the export of EAR 99 goods may also be subject to specific sanctioning regimes against certain states or persons (see below). 147

In addition to the regular export control regime based on the EAR, **economic sanctions** (based inter alia on the Trading with the Enemy Act (TWEA) and the International Emergency Economic Powers Act)[305] have been imposed against certain countries and individuals by the US government, acting through the Office of Foreign Assets Control (OFAC) at the US Department of the Treasury. Far-reaching sanctions are currently in place against Cuba, Iran, Syria and Sudan, among other countries, as well as in relation to individuals and entities identified on Specially Designated Nationals and Blocked Persons Lists (SDN's). These embargos generally prohibit the export of almost any goods (whether listed on the CCL or not) but also restrict the import of goods from and financial transactions with these countries.[306] Generally speaking, only US citizens, entities and permanent residents of the USA need to observe the restrictions imposed by a sanctions program. As one important exception, however, the Cuba Assets Control Regulations cover also **foreign entities** that are owned or controlled by US companies or citizens – though this far-reaching extraterritorial effect has consistently caused criticism about its alleged non-compliance with principles of international public law.[307] The extraterritorial reach of US-sanctions has recently even further been expanded by legislation targeting Iran, in particular the Comprehensive Iran Sanctions, Accountability, and Divestment Act of 2010 (CISADA) as well as the Iran Freedom and Counter-Proliferation Act of 2012 (IFCA). Both acts impose sanctions also on non US-persons (and with regard to Non-US origin goods) that inter alia supply to Iran significant goods or services used in 148

---

[304] The relevant countries are listed in the Commerce Country Chart in Supplement No 1 to § 738 EAR.

[305] See Hirschhorn (n 301) 179.

[306] Further information of the sanctions programs can be found online on the website of the United States Department of the Treasury, see <http://www.treas.gov/offices/enforcement/ofac/programs/index.shtml>. Economic sanctions are also in place with regard to a multitude of other countries though these measures are more limited in scope.

[307] H Wolff, "Unilateral Economic Sanctions: Necessary Foreign Policy Tool or Ineffective Hindrance on American Businesses?" (2006) 6 Hous Bus & Tax L J 239, 336.

connection with the petroleum industry as well as the automotive, energy, shipping, or shipbuilding sectors.

149 In summary, US export laws apply inter alia also to exports of a seller not based in the USA if either the contractual goods contain more than 25 % (respectively 10 % with regard to designated terrorist supporting states) of materials, components etc. of **US origin** or (with regard to US sanction programs and regardless of the origin of the goods) the exporter must be considered as a US person. The seller should be aware of the fact that US export laws define the term "US person" differently with regard to the respective sanction regulations (for instance, in relation to exports to Cuba, even a company based and legally established outside the USA will qualify as a "US person" if it is owned or controlled by US citizens or companies) and that some US-sanctions, in particular **targeting Iran**, will apply also in relation to non US-persons and Non-US origin goods.

5. Exchange control regulations

150 In particular due to international conventions,[308] domestic exchange control regulations (even if they do not belong to the governing law of the contract) may have an impact on the enforceability of sales contracts. Notably Art VIII (2) lit b of the **IMF Treaty** (the Articles of Agreement of the International Monetary Fund)[309], which has been ratified by some 186 member states, renders **"exchange contracts"** which involve the currency of any member state of the agreement and which are contrary to the exchange control regulations of this state unenforceable provided the regulations in question are maintained or imposed consistently with the provisions of the IMF Treaty. VIII (2) lit b (respectively its adoption by domestic laws) constitutes both a mandatory conflict of laws provision as well as substantive law whereas foreign domestic exchange control regulations falling within the ambit of this Article prevail over the governing law of the contract.[310]

151 International case law has interpreted the legal term "exchange contracts" rather differently: According to Anglo-American courts, the term exchange contracts must be narrowly construed.[311] German courts, on the other hand, have given this term a much broader meaning and international sales contracts were explicitly included in the definition of exchange contracts pursuant to VIII (2) lit b IMF Treaty.[312] As a

---

[308] Even if international conventions do not dictate this result, courts of law may also apply mandatory exchange control laws of the forum or foreign laws in accordance with the applicable domestic private international law.

[309] The Articles of Agreement of the IMF can be found online on the website of the International Monetary Fund under <http://www.imf.org/external/pubs/ft/aa/index.htm>.

[310] W Ebke, *Internationales Devisenrecht* (Verlag Recht und Wirtschaft, Heidelberg 1991) 159. Arbitral tribunals are bound by Art VIII Section 2 (b) IMF as well, see O Sandrock, "Are Disputes Over the Application of Article VIII, Section 2 (b) of the IMF Treaty Arbitrable?" (1989) 23 Int'l Law 933, 939.

[311] See inter alia RA Brandt, "Non-Conventional Issues in the Preparation of Transnational Sales Contracts" [1988] J L & Commerce 145, 176.

[312] See W Ebke, "Article VIII, Section 2 (b), International Monetary Cooperation, and the Courts" (1989) 23 Int'l Law 677, 688 with further references to German court decisions. The disadvantages of the latter view (that is still applied by German courts though subject to mounting criticism) are twofold: On the one hand, the burden of proof that the requirements of Art VIII (2) lit b IMF-Treaty are not fulfilled rests on the claimant. On the other hand, due to the characterization as a "procedural requirement", a later amendment of exchange control regulations that did

consequence, VIII (2) lit b may in principle restrict the **enforceability of** a claim for the contract price (or a secondary claim for damages in lieu of specific performance) at least in those jurisdictions that interpret this Article more broadly. This risk (though remote) is often hardly foreseeable given that the IMF does not maintain comprehensive and updated lists on domestic exchange control regulations that have been enacted in compliance with the IMF Treaty.[313]

Though the characterization of **Art VIII (2) lit b IMF Treaty** as either a defense 152 (the existence of which must be expressly claimed and proven by the defendant in the proceedings) against a contractual claim or a procedural requirement which the claimant must comply with as a condition precedent to initiating legal proceedings is still controversial, the contract as such does in any event remain valid.[314] Accordingly, the purchaser has no restitution claims based on unjust enrichment once payment has been made to the seller. It follows that receipt of payment before delivery will once again substantially decrease the risks for the seller.

6. Product liability towards third parties

Not only the purchaser, but also **third parties** may assert claims against a seller 153 if defective goods cause either property damage or bodily injury. Under some domestic tort laws, a third party may even claim compensation for pure economic loss notwithstanding the fact that a contractual relationship with the seller does not exist.[315] (Non-contractual) claims of third parties cannot be restricted in a sales contract given that contract law permits (at best) only contracts for the benefit[316] but not to the detriment of a third party.[317]

A court in charge of handling a third-party product liability claim will determine 154 the applicable tort laws governing the claims by recourse to the private international

---

originally allow the transaction may affect the enforceability of the claim until the end of the last hearing of the court. The ongoing controversy with regard to legal character and scope of VIII (2) lit b has apparently so far not been addressed by Swiss jurisprudence, see F Dasser in Honsell et al (n 251) Art 147 PILA para 28, who is however in favor of a restrictive interpretation.

[313] See W Ebke in J v Staudinger (ed), *Kommentar zum Bürgerlichen Gesetzbuch. EGBGB/IPR* (13th edn Sellier de Gruyter, Berlin 2002) Anh zu Art 34 para 44.

[314] Ebke (n 312) 694.

[315] The author has personally been involved in the defense of such a claim. Pursuant to the underlying facts of this case, a Dutch (end) customer claimed compensation for pure economic loss (i.e. costs incurred for the lease of substitute equipment) as a result of allegedly defective construction equipment against the manufacturer though the sales contract had been entered into with an independent distributor (who had successfully excluded his liability for these heads of damages towards the end customer).

[316] Pursuant to the common law rule of "privity", Anglo-American law has traditionally not acknowledged contracts for the benefit of third parties. This position has however been largely undermined by statutory law. See with regard to English law in particular the Contracts (Rights of Third Parties) Act 1997. Under the UCC, third parties may benefit from (contractual) warranties even to a greater extent than pursuant to many civil law jurisdictions, see in particular § 2–318 UCC (2003). German and Swiss law acknowledge (besides contracts for the benefit of third parties) contracts with protective effects for third parties though sales contracts do not fall within the ambit of this instrument, see K Zweigert and H Kötz, *An Introduction to Comparative Law* (3rd edn OUP, Oxford 1998) 461.

[317] The parties may however agree on an indemnity clause pursuant to which the purchaser must indemnify and hold the seller harmless for third party claims based on alleged defects of the delivered goods, see ch C.VI below for further review of such a clause.

A. General Part

law of the forum. The recently enacted **Rome II Regulation** of the EU[318] has at least harmonized conflict of laws rules with regard to (non-contractual) product liability claims – all courts located in the EU must apply this Regulation in relation to all harmful events that have occurred after 11 January 2009. Pursuant to Art 5 Rom II Regulation, the country of the injured party's habitual residence, alternatively the country in which the product was acquired or the country in which the injury took place, will govern the claim (in this order of priority) provided that the contractual goods were in each case marketed in the respective jurisdiction. If the contractual goods were not marketed in either of the indicated jurisdictions,[319] the material tort laws of the seller's country of residence will be decisive.

---

[318] Regulation (EC) No 864/2007 of the European Parliament and of the Council of 11 July 2007 on the law applicable to non-contractual obligations (Rome II) [2007] OJ L199/40.

[319] Pursuant to the prevailing opinion, the "marketing" requirement is already fulfilled if products of the same type (and not necessarily the individual product that has given rise to the claim) have been marketed in the respective jurisdiction, see M Illmer, "The New European Private International Law of Product Liability – Steering Through Troubled Waters" (2009) 73 RabelsZ 269, 292.

B. The Main Contract Document

SALES CONTRACT
between
1. [...] (hereinafter "Seller")
2. [...] (hereinafter "Purchaser")
   Seller and Purchaser hereinafter also individually referred to as "Party" and collectively referred to as "Parties"
Seller agrees to deliver and Purchaser agrees to purchase the following contractual products including the scope of supply as further described in the enclosed Specifications pursuant to the terms and conditions below.

Contractual Products:	[...]
Contract Price:	EUR [...] plus VAT (if applicable). The Parties agree that the Purchaser is not entitled to pay the contract price in any other currency. Place of performance for the payment is the Seller's place of business.
Payment Terms:	Payment shall become due upon delivery of the Contractual Products in accordance with the Delivery Terms set forth below.
	Payment shall be effected via letter of credit against the following documents pursuant to § 2 (3) of the International Sales Terms:
	1. Commercial Invoice
	2. [...]
Delivery Terms:	[...] (INCOTERMS © 2010) subject to any amendments set forth in the International Sales Terms (see below).
Delivery Period:	[...]
Country of Use:	[...]
Terms & Conditions:	The attached International Sales Terms (including in particular the arbitration agreement stipulated in Art 14 of the International Sales Terms) [*alternatively: including the forum selection clause stipulated in Art 14 of the International Sales Terms*] shall apply to this sales transaction to the exclusion of any other terms and conditions.

_____   _____
Seller   Purchaser

_____   _____
Place, Date   Place, Date

I. The benefit of a countersigned main contract document

155 Even the most perfectly drafted general terms and conditions of sale are worthless if they are not effectively incorporated into the individual sales contract. In commercial reality, an **incorporation** of general terms often fails because the parties do not comply with the general requirements that exist in relation to the incorporation of general terms into international contracts and/or do not cope appropriately with the notorious "battle of forms" problem.

156 Whereas compliance with general requirements for the incorporation of general terms into international contracts should not cause any major problem, no easy solution exists for the **"battle of forms"** problem. From a legal point of view, the seller can rely on the (exclusive) application of his sales terms with sufficient legal certainty only if the purchaser has explicitly accepted the same in writing. For that reason, it is clearly advisable (whenever possible) to make use of a written document that contains an explicit reference to the general sales terms and is signed by both parties. This main contract document can also contain contractual terms that are usually individually tailored for each sales transaction, such as the contract price, delivery and payment terms.

1. Requirements for the incorporation of general terms into international contracts

157 Compared to domestic sales transactions, an effective incorporation of general terms and conditions into an international contract is subject to **additional prerequisites**. These requirements apply even if the general terms are intended to exclude the CISG altogether, as the validity of such an exclusion is a matter of contract formation falling within the ambit of the CISG.[320]

158 The parties to a sales contract are, however, often not aware of the necessary general steps that have to be taken in order to achieve the **effective incorporation** of their general terms and conditions into the sales contract. In case of both oral and written contractual negotiations that may last for several weeks or even months and regularly contain the exchange of a plethora of e-mails, facsimiles and other means of communication, the picture can become even more blurred with regard to the fundamental question of whether, when and with what particular content a sales contract has been concluded.

159 The seller should therefore make sure to take three basic steps in order to incorporate his general terms in the first place:

160 • The seller must firstly clearly state in his correspondence forming part of the intended contract conclusion (that is to say in an offer or acknowledgment of an order) that his offer or, as the case may be, the acceptance is **subject to** specified general sales terms.[321]

---

[320] B Piltz, "AGB in UN-Kaufverträgen" [2004] IHR 133, 136; see also U.S. District Court, S.D. of New York (18 Jan 2011) CISG-online 2178.

[321] See U Magnus, "Incorporation of Standard Contract Terms under the CISG" in CB Andersen and UG Schroeter (eds), *Sharing International Commercial Law across National Boundaries: Festschrift for Albert H Kritzer on the Occasion of his Eightieth Birthday* (Wildy Simmonds & Hill Publishing, London 2008) 303, with reference to a decision of the Cour d'appel de Paris (13 Dec

I. The benefit of a countersigned main contract document

- The general sales terms must be submitted to the purchaser *before* the sales contract is concluded. As opposed, for instance, to German domestic law regarding purely domestic commercial contracts, a mere **reference** to general terms and conditions in either offer or acceptance is predominantly considered here to be insufficient.[322] 161
- The general sales terms must finally be formulated in the **contractual language** (i. e. the language that was used by the parties throughout the negotiation of the contract) or – in the alternative – in a language that is comprehensible for the purchaser.[323] 162

2. The "battle of forms" problem

Even when the seller is in compliance with the prerequisites indicated above, the substantial risk that his general terms will collide with the purchaser's general purchase terms does remain. Accordingly, the "battle of forms" problem must be appropriately resolved. 163

From the outset, usually both the seller and the purchaser aim to incorporate their respective general terms and conditions into the contract. In the vast majority of these cases, both parties also use so-called **"rejection clauses"** that contain explicit language to the effect that the other party's general terms should not apply.[324] In that event, offer and acceptance fail at first sight to comply with the "mirror image rule" as the basis of a valid contract formation as set forth in Art 19 (1) CISG. But if the parties execute the sales transaction thereafter, a contract is nevertheless deemed concluded.[325] The question remains, however, what terms control the contract. In a nutshell, mainly two solutions have been suggested in 164

1995) CISG-online 312: Mere submission of standard terms in a separate document without an express reference that they should form part of the contract is (in the absence of special circumstances such as a trade practice between the parties, international usage etc) insufficient for their incorporation into the contract.

[322] See in particular BGH (31 Oct 2001) CISG-online 617; OLG Naumburg (13 Feb 2013) CISG-online 2455 and OLG Celle (24 Jul 2009) CISG-online 1906. For a more lenient approach inter alia PP Viscasillas, "CISG Articles 14 Through 24" in HM Flechtner, RA Brand and MS Walter (eds), *Drafting Contracts under the CISG* (OUP, New York 2008) 295, 316, who considers a mere reference to a website as sufficient; similarly M Schmidt-Kessel in Schlechtriem and Schwenzer (n 34) Art 8 CISG para 53.

[323] See for instance OLG Düsseldorf (21 Apr 2004) CISG-online 913: General terms submitted only in German were pursuant to the court not effectively incorporated given that English was the contractual language; see also U Magnus (n 321) 325 with further references. But see also OLG München (14 Jan 2009) CISG-online 2011, with a more lenient view: Pursuant to this decision, formulation of the terms in the contractual language is not a mandatory requirement for their incorporation – the submission in the English language was considered as sufficient regardless whether or not the other contractual party did understand this language.

[324] For the potential impact of such a clause see however OLG Frankfurt (26 Jun 2006) CISG-online 1385: A "rejection clause" used by one party of a sales contract governed by the CISG prevented pursuant to the court not only contradicting but also supplementing terms of the other party.

[325] See K Wildner, "The German Approach to the Battle of the Forms in International Contract Law: The Decision of the Federal Supreme Court of Germany of 9 January 2002" (2008) 20 Pace Int'l L Rev 1, 16. See however also A Corterier, "A Peace Plan for the Battle of Forms" (2006) 10 Int'l Trade & Bus L Rev 195 ff, according to whom a contract may come into effect in case of deviating standard terms even before any act of performance of either party.

B. The Main Contract Document

order to resolve the problem, known as the "last shot rule" on the one hand and the "knock out doctrine" on the other.[326]

165   The approach of the "last shot rule" is often (though not necessarily always) more beneficial for the seller: According to this theory, the party that last referred to its general terms (which is often the seller by means of an "order confirmation") before the assumed contract conclusion wins the battle of forms and therefore its terms prevail. The last shot rule is – at least at first glance – well founded in general principles of contract theory that are also contained in Art 19 CISG: The reply of the second party referring to its general terms does not constitute acceptance but a counter-offer (Art 19 (1), (3) CISG) whereas subsequent performance of the contract by the first party (for instance the payment of the contract price or the taking of delivery by the purchaser) may be regarded as an acceptance of the counter-offer by way of conduct (Art 18 (3) CISG).

166   Besides its dogmatic merits, the last shot rule involves rather obvious disadvantages given that the outcome of its application not only often depends on mere coincidence but also forces the (well informed) contracting parties to extend the battle until the other party finally gives in. For that reason, the rule has become increasingly unpopular and has been set aside in many jurisdictions.[327]

167   The "knock-out rule" (*Restgültigkeitstheorie*) on the other hand has gained popularity as the solution that may accomplish more just results. According to the "knock-out rule", the parties' general terms are replaced by the law governing the contract to the extent that they conflict with each other. This solution often harms the seller as – for instance – limitation of liability clauses, the most essential part of general sales terms, do in this event regularly not survive. The knock-out rule is applied today by the majority of domestic laws in Europe[328], inter alia in Germany[329], Switzerland[330], Austria[331] and France[332]. The latest revision of the Uniform Commercial Code undertaken in 2003 now opts even more clearly than before for this rule and has overcome former existing ambiguities.

168   The question of whether the last shot rule or the knock-out rule applies to a battle of forms problem is especially difficult to resolve in the case of an international sales transaction, as the answer to this question presupposes the correct determination of

---

[326] In particular Dutch law provides a third solution that is best described as a "first shot rule": According to 6:225 (3) BW, general terms referred to by the offeror will prevail subject only to their explicit rejection by the other party within its declaration of acceptance whereas the mere use of defensive incorporation clauses in general terms will not amount to an explicit denial in this regard.

[327] For a thorough critique of the last shot rule see inter alia M Viscasillas, "Battle of the Forms" Under the 1980 United Nations Convention on Contracts for the International Sale of Goods: A Comparison with Section 2–207 UCC and the UNIDROIT Principles" (1998) 10 Pace Int'l L Rev 97, 98 f. In particular English law adheres still to the "last shot rule", see *Butler Machine Tool Ltd v Ex-Cell-O Corp (England) Ltd* (1979) 1 WLR 401. But see also *Sterling Hydraulics Ltd v. Dichtomatik Ltd* [2007] 1 Lloyd's Rep 8: The statement "Delivery based on our General Terms of Sale" at the foot of the first page of the acknowledgement of an order has been considered as being insufficient to constitute a (deviating) counter-offer under English law.

[328] See also Art 2.1.22 UPICC 2010, opting explicitly for the application of the "knock-out rule" in case of a battle of forms.

[329] BGH (9 Feb 1977) BGHZ 61, 282.

[330] See Schwenzer (n 181) para 45.15.

[331] OGH (7 Jun 1990) CISG-online 13.

[332] See O Lando and H Beale, *Principles of European Contract Law: Part I and II* (Kluwer Law International, The Hague 1999) 183.

the law that governs the **formation of the contract**. This question can for obvious reasons not be answered by mere recourse to the presumably applicable law³³³ if the general terms and conditions of the parties stipulate contradicting choice of law provisions and the respective laws chosen resolve the battle of forms problem in a different manner.³³⁴ If both parties reside in member states of the CISG, the CISG overrides domestic laws and can independently resolve this problem. But one problem remains even in this case: Though there is general agreement that the battle of forms problem falls within the ambit of the CISG, it is still controversial whether the CISG follows the knock-out rule or adheres to the last shot rule. Whereas the German Federal Supreme Court,³³⁵ but also some US courts³³⁶ have applied the knock out rule also in sales contracts governed by the CISG, other courts have relied on a literal interpretation of **Art 19 CISG** and applied the last shot rule instead.³³⁷ It remains to be seen how international case law will tackle this problem in the future and whether the decision by the German Federal Supreme Court apparently in favor of the knock-out rule will in fact become a leading case.³³⁸

As a result, the seller cannot rely on the exclusive application of his general sales terms even if he fires the last shot before the contract is performed (and thereby concluded). Therefore, only one measure can provide sufficient legal certainty: The seller must seek the purchaser's **explicit agreement** that his own sales terms alone will apply to the transaction. The latter is best achieved by means of a document that explicitly refers to the general sales terms and is signed by both parties.

II. Price

The parties should not determine the contract price before they have reviewed the agreed allocation of rights and obligations in the sales contract and their impact moneywise.³³⁹ If the contract fully specifies the allocation of responsibilities and costs

---

³³³ See, eg, Art 10 (1) Rome I Regulation: "The existence and validity of a contract [...] shall be determined by the law which would govern it under this Regulation if the contract or term were valid."

³³⁴ Fawcett et al (n 263) para 13.60 ff: The authors suggest the application of the law of the forum as the most simple solution to this problem. Another potential solution would be the simultaneous application of both putatively applicable laws in order to assess whether a conflict would remain even thereafter. According to the author, it is neither convincing to solve the battle of forms problem in this case pursuant to the (substantive) laws of the forum nor by the simultaneous application of both putatively applicable laws. It seems more appropriate to apply the "lex contractus" (to be determined by means of the conflict of laws provisions of the forum) instead.

³³⁵ BGH (9 Jan 2002) CISG-online 651.

³³⁶ US District Court, S.D. of New York (18 January 2011) CISG-online 2178. The CISG Advisory Council, a private group of leading scholars, has also recently opted for the application of the knock-out rule, s. CISG-AC Opinion No 13 (20 Jan 2013), Inclusion of Standard Terms under the CISG (Rapporteur: S Eiselen), paras 10.1 ff.

³³⁷ See for instance OLG Köln (24 May 2006) CISG-online 1232; US District Court Minnesota (31 Jan 2007) CISG-online 1435. In favor of the application of the last shot rule also F Ferrari in Kröll/Mistelis/Perales Viscasillas/Ferrari Art. 19 CISG para 15.

³³⁸ See P Schlechtriem and UG Schroeter in Schlechtriem and Schwenzer (n 34) Art 19 CISG para 25.

³³⁹ See JM Klotz, *International Sales Agreements* (2ⁿᵈ edn Kluwer Law International, The Hague 2008) 67.

thereby incurred have been included in the contract price, a **price clause** can be kept short and simple.

171   Under the CISG, payment must be made by the seller in the currency that has been contractually agreed between the parties.[340] In that regard, it is clearly in the best interest of the seller to demand payment in his own **currency** to avoid substantial currency exchange risks that exist even in relation to the major currencies.[341] The suggested main contract document provides for payment in Euro under the assumption that the seller resides in a member state of the EU belonging to the Eurozone. If the seller is forced to accept a contract price in a foreign currency, currency exchange risks should be minimized either by way of a currency clause[342] or by currency hedging.

171a   However, the ongoing Euro crisis has triggered concerns that the exit of individual EU member states such as Greece, Cyprus or Portugal out of the Eurozone may pose risks even if the Euro has been contractually agreed by the parties as the (sole) contractual currency. In particular, mandatory rules of the European Union (most likely an EU regulation) that may be adopted in order to regulate legal consequences of such an exit on existing contractual relationships may permit the payment of the contract price by the buyer in the new domestic currency of the residing state of the buyer, respectively the state in which the place of performance for monetary claims is located.[343] This may in particular harm the seller if and when the new currency devaluates compared to the Euro before the maturity date of the claim but after the date on which an official exchange rate between the Euro and a new relevant domestic currency has been fixed. In order to mitigate these risks, some authors have proposed the use of contractual clauses that provide for compensation of the seller or stipulate that monetary claims must be paid in the currency of a state outside the EU once mandatory EU laws allow payment in the new domestic currency.[344] It seems doubtful, however, whether either alternative will be enforceable. Risks may however be reduced if the parties agree on the Seller's principal place of business as the place of performance for monetary claims.

III. Payment Terms

1. The legal position under the CISG

172   Unless otherwise agreed by the parties, the purchaser is not obliged under the CISG to pay the price before the seller has placed the contractual goods or – in the alternative – the documents controlling their disposition (such as a bill of lading or other transport

---

[340] According to the prevailing opinion, the buyer is generally not entitled to replace the agreed currency by another one, cf. P Butler and A Harindranath in Kröll/Mistelis/Perales Viscasillas (n 34) Art. 54 CISG para 13.

[341] For instance, the British Pound has in 2008 lost approximately 40 % of its value against the Euro in roughly one year.

[342] A currency clause fixes in advance the exchange rate between the contractual currency and seller's preferred currency and provides for an adjustment of the contract price in case the fixed exchange rate fluctuates; see for sample clauses Klotz (n 339) 75.

[343] W Ernst, "Privatrechtliche Folgen eines Ausscheidens einzelner Staaten aus der Euro-Währung – ein Problemaufriss" [2012] ZIP 49, 57.

[344] See for different alternatives inter alia P Kindler, "Währungsumstellung, Vertragskontinuität und Vertragsgestaltung" [2012] NJW 1617 ff.

documents) at the purchaser's disposal (Art 58 (1) CISG). Furthermore, the contract price becomes due only once the purchaser had an opportunity to examine the contract goods (Art 58 (3) CISG). Accordingly, due payment of the contract price is not sufficiently secured if the contract involves a carriage of goods.[345] These risks are also not effectively minimized by the fact that the seller may make payment a condition for the handover of the goods, or (in case of a carriage of the goods) may dispatch the goods under the condition precedent that they will only be handed over against receipt of payment (Art 58 (1) 2, (2) CISG): At that point of time, the seller generally no longer has access to the contractual goods as **security** for his monetary claims.

2. The preferred payment method: The letter of credit

The best solution for this problem is a contractual agreement that requires the purchaser to pay **in advance** for the goods. However, as a purchaser will generally not agree (unless the seller has significant bargaining power) on advance payments without also obtaining appropriate securities, payment by means of a letter of credit is the second best option from the seller's perspective and normally an acceptable compromise for both parties.

a) General background of a letter of credit transaction

A **letter of credit** is essentially an assurance by the purchaser's bank[346] (the issuing bank) to the seller that the contract price will be paid upon the presentation of certain documents that are further specified in the letter of credit. In case of an international transaction, the issuing bank regularly advises another bank (the "advising bank") at the locality of the seller to inform the latter about the issuance of the credit for his benefit. The advising bank normally also functions as the nominated bank that is in charge of performing the credit operation on behalf (and for the account) of the issuing bank against receipt of the stipulated documents that are subsequently (via the issuing bank) forwarded to the purchaser. Both the advising bank and the nominated bank act solely as agents of the issuing bank and the seller can accordingly enforce his claims under the credit only against the issuing bank. However, if the advising bank or the nominated bank confirms the letter of credit, the seller can enforce his payment claims against this bank as well. Accordingly, the issuing bank and the confirming bank are in this event jointly and severally liable towards the seller.[347]

A letter of credit provides **security** for both parties: Once an (irrevocable) letter of credit has been issued, the seller avoids the risk of losing access to the goods before receipt of payment is secured. The purchaser, on the other hand, can by means of a letter of credit ensure that payment is made subject to the explicit condition precedent that certain documents are handed over beforehand – usually transport documents such as a bill of lading (in case of a carriage by sea) or rail, air and road transport documents that evidence not only the delivery of (on their face) conforming contractual goods[348] but also entitle the purchaser to claim the goods from the carrier.

---

[345] Brunner (n 114) Art 58 CISG para 4.
[346] Klotz (n 339) 122.
[347] See, eg, from the perspective of German law C v Bernstorff, *Rechtsprobleme im Auslandsgeschäft* (5th edn Fritz Knapp, Frankfurt aM 2006) 223.
[348] In order to comply with the requirements under a letter of credit, transport documents must at least not indicate that the goods are in a defective condition, see below.

B. The Main Contract Document

176 The underlying terms and conditions for letter of credit transactions have been largely harmonized by the Uniform Customs and Practice for Documentary Credits (UCP) published by the International Chamber of Commerce. The latest edition of the **UCP** (UCP 600) is in effect since 1 July 2007. Though the legal character of the UCP is still controversial[349] and Art 1 UCP 600 itself clarifies that the application of the UCP is subject to their express incorporation into the credit by the parties, the UCP do apply to almost all letters of credit transactions given that the vast majority of issuing banks incorporate them by default.[350] The UCP thus function in a similar manner as the governing law of the contract – they fill gaps, define obligations and rights of the different parties involved in a letter of credit transaction and help to interpret ambiguous terms of a letter of credit.[351] The UCP also stipulate the two fundamental principles of letter of credits:[352] A letter of credit is independent of the underlying sales contract ("principle of autonomy"). As a consequence, a bank must honor its payment obligations under the letter of credit regardless of whether the purchaser has any claims or defenses against the seller under the sales contract.[353] Secondly, the bank is only obliged to pay if and when the requested documents are **strictly in compliance** with the terms of the letter of credit ("principle of **strict compliance**"). A survey of the existing international case law reveals that this principle is vigorously applied: The English Court of Appeal has for instance held that payment was rightfully rejected on the ground that the credit demanded the presentation of documents confirming the delivery of "coromandel groundnuts" whereas the tendered bill of lading referred instead to "machine shelled groundnut kernels" – though both terms are used interchangeably in the branch of business concerned.[354] The Swiss Federal Supreme Court reached a similar conclusion in a more recent case concerning the delivery of oil and petrol where a bank rightfully (according to the court) refused to accept a certificate of quality that referred to "existent gum washed" instead of the required specification "gum existent" of the fuels, though both expressions refer according to the applicable industrial standards apparently to one and the same

---

[349] The prevailing view considers the UCP simply as a set of standard rules with no force of law as far as they have not been incorporated into the credit by the parties, see in relation to the traditional position of English law McKendrick in Goode (n 238) 1076; with regard to German law J Nielsen in *Münchener Kommentar zum Handelsgesetzbuch. Band 5* (2nd edn C.H. Beck, München 2009) Anhang I para H 39.

[350] See McKendrick in Goode (n 238) 1055.

[351] Klotz (n 339) 122.

[352] C Murray, D Holloway and D Timson-Hunt, *Schmitthoff's Export Trade: The Law and Practice of International Trade* (12th edn Sweet&Maxwell, London 2012) para 11.06 ff.

[353] See Art 4 lit a UCP 600. Though the UCP deal not explicitly with exceptions of the "autonomy principle", it is widely accepted that the issuing respectively confirming bank is only under rather narrow circumstances entitled to refuse payment once the seller has presented conforming documents. Pursuant to (the particularly restrictive) English law, payment may in this case only be refused in case of fraud, provided the seller or a third party acting on his behalf have been involved in the fraudulent behavior (the "fraud exception"). See also the decision of the Court of Appeal, *Montrod Ltd v Grundkötter Fleischvertriebs GmbH* [2002] 1 WLR 1975, where the court has taken the view that even a "nullity" of the documents alone would not entitle the bank to refuse payment in case the documents were tendered by the seller in good faith. For a critical appraisal of this decision however McKendrick in Goode (n 238) 1106. Fraudulent behavior is also a condition precedent under Swiss and US law, see the decision of the Swiss Federal Supreme Court, BG (11 Jun 1974) BGE 100 II 145, 151. For the position under US law see JF Dolan, *The Law of Letters of Credit* (4th edn A.S. Pratt, Austin 2007) § 7.04. Under German law, it is still not entirely clear whether the doctrine of "legal abuse" presupposes intentional behavior or not, see BGH (16 Apr 1996) WM 1996, 995.

[354] *J H Rayner & Co Ltd v Hambros Bank Ltd* [1943] 1 KB 37.

III. Payment Terms

product.³⁵⁵ The relevant provisions in the UCP 600 have not eliminated the principle of strict compliance.³⁵⁶ That is inter alia confirmed by a more recent judgment of the English Court of Appeal³⁵⁷: In this case, the letter of credit requested the presentation of a certificate issued by the seller, stating that the negotiating bank had dispatched the required shipping documents by air courier to the issuing bank (located in buyer's country) at seller's cost. The certificate tendered stated that the documents were dispatched at "issuing bank's cost" even though the costs were actually borne by the seller. The Court of Appeal has nevertheless rejected the view that this discrepancy should be regarded as trivial and held that the documents did not constitute a complying presentation.

The credit must state whether it is available by sight payment, deferred payment, acceptance or negotiation, Art 6 lit b UCP 600. In case of **availability by sight**, payment becomes due immediately upon the presentation of (complying) documents. In case of acceptance or negotiation, the seller has to submit a draft (time) bill of exchange together with the documents that will be accepted by the bank upon presentation of (complying) documents. Availability by deferred payment amounts essentially to a supplier credit as the bank does not have to pay upon presentation but only on the maturity date stipulated in the credit.³⁵⁸ Payment by sight is therefore from the seller's perspective clearly the best as well as the most commonly used option. 177

b) Essential contractual terms in a letter of credit

From the seller's point of view, the following conditions are essential in order to ensure a smooth performance of a letter of credit transaction: 178

- A letter of credit should always be **irrevocable** in order to prevent a withdrawal of the issuing bank (or, as the case may be, the confirming bank) from its payment commitment under the credit at any time, which would essentially destroy the essential purpose of the credit to guarantee the payment of the contract price. In the light of the last revision of the UCP, an explicit provision to this effect in the letter itself has become less important than before given that a letter of credit is pursuant to Art 3 UCP 600 deemed to be irrevocable even if there is no indication to that effect.³⁵⁹ 179

---

³⁵⁵ BG (3 Jul 2006) BGE 132 III 620 para E 2.3 (relevant part of the decision unpublished).

³⁵⁶ SC Debattista, "The new UCP 600 – Changes to the Tender of the Seller's Shipping Documents under Letter of Credits" [2007] J Bus L 329, 338.

³⁵⁷ *Fortis Bank* v *Indian Overseas Bank* [2011] EWCA Civ 58.

³⁵⁸ It is controversial whether a bank is entitled (in case of a credit available by deferred payment) to render payment even before the maturity date. The latter may become relevant if the purchaser obtains sufficient evidence that the underlying claim under the sales contract is obviously unfounded during the time period between presentation of the documents and maturity date. According to a decision of the Swiss Federal Supreme Court, a bank does not forego its right of recourse against the purchaser in that case given that it is not the intention of a deferred payment clause to provide the purchaser with further opportunities to review the legitimacy of the claim under a credit. English and German courts have taken the contrary view, see BGH [1987] WM 977; *Banco Santander SA* v *Banque Paribas* [2000] Lloyd's Rep Bank 165 (CA). Art 7 lit c and 8 lit c UCP 600 explicitly permit the premature payment of the nominated bank though doubts as to the validity of these clauses under domestic laws have been expressed; see with regard to German law for instance J Nielsen, "ICC Uniform Customs and Practices for Documentary Credits" [2008] TransportR 269, 270.

³⁵⁹ The parties remain however free to explicitly agree upon a revocable letter of credit. In this case, however, it remains doubtful whether the UCP 600 (even if explicitly incorporated) would apply given

B. The Main Contract Document

180 • From the seller's perspective it is highly advisable to insist on a confirmed letter of credit. An unconfirmed credit may force the seller to institute proceedings against the issuing bank abroad.[360] Additional risks of an unconfirmed credit exist if the issuing bank is based in a country with high country specific risks, as restrictive domestic exchange control regulations may prevent the seller from enforcing his claims against the issuing bank.

In some jurisdictions (notably Iran and China), banks are prohibited from seeking a confirmation of their letter of credits by a second bank abroad. In this case, the seller can only try to obtain a **"silent confirmation"** from a bank residing in his home jurisdiction at his own cost. A silent confirmation amounts to an independent commitment of a bank to pay the seller under the credit in the absence of a corresponding instruction by the issuing bank that is outside of the scope of application of the UCP 600.[361]

181 • According to the UCP 600, a letter of credit must stipulate an **expiry date** for the presentation of the documents.[362] For that reason, the seller needs to address the problem that claims under the credit may lapse in case of any substantial delay in delivery for whatsoever reason. Though the issuing bank and the confirming bank (if any) in a letter of credit transaction can agree jointly with the beneficiary on any amendments to the credit (in this case a postponement of the expiry date)[363], a seller should not take it for granted that all necessary approvals will be obtained on time. Risks are minimized in the first place if the expiry date is set at a considerable amount of time after the scheduled delivery date.

182 • The letter of credit should explicitly indicate that it is **transferable**.[364] The transferability of a letter of credit provides the seller with an option to (partially) forward the credit to his own sub-suppliers already before the delivery of the goods in order to finance the sales transaction. The same effect can be achieved by means of a back to back letter of credit if the original credit is not transferable. This option would, however, trigger additional costs for the seller for the provision of the second separate (back to back) credit.

---

that Art 2 UCP 600 defines "credits" as "any arrangement [...] that is irrevocable [...]" and therefore seems to exclude revocable credits from the scope of application of the UCP 600, see Debattista (n 356) 334 f. Pursuant the preceding version of the UCP (UCP 500), a credit could be either revocable or irrevocable whereas a presumption for its irrevocability applied, see Art 6 UCP 500.

[360] See Murray et al (n 352) para 11–027.

[361] Accordingly, a bank providing a "silent confirmation" does not acquire the status of a "confirmation bank" though it may take recourse against the issuing bank under its (potential) status as a nominated bank. See with regard to a "silent confirmation" P Derleder, KO Knops and HG Bamberger (eds), *Handbuch zum deutschen und europäischen Bankrecht* (2nd edn Springer, Berlin 2009) 1865.

[362] Art 6 UCP 600. The expiry date must be distinguished from a further time bar provision set forth in the UCP with regard to the presentation of transport documents. Provided the terms of the credit stipulate nothing to the contrary, the seller must present the requested original transport documents no later than 21 days after the date of actual shipment, see Art Art 14 lit c UCP 600. Though this period is subject to contractual amendments, it seems reasonable to keep it unchanged given that the purchaser regularly needs the documents in order to claim the contractual goods at the place of destination from the carrier.

[363] See Art 10 lit a and lit c UCP 600. An approval of the nominated bank is however not required if the nominated bank has not confirmed the credit, see Nielsen (n 358) 275.

[364] Only a credit that explicitly stipulates that it is transferable may be considered as a transferable credit, see Art 38 lit b UCP 600.

- Particular attention should apply with regard to the selection of the **documents** that must be presented to the bank for payment. A seller should always ensure that he can easily obtain the required documents without any further involvement of the purchaser. Otherwise the purchaser can easily prevent the drawing on the credit.

Arts 18 to 28 UCP 600 lay down specific requirements for the acceptance of documents that are generally used in letter of credit operations. For instance, a commercial invoice must (appear to) have been issued by the beneficiary (generally the seller) and must be made out in the applicant's name (generally the purchaser) in the same currency as the credit. Furthermore, the description of the contractual goods in a commercial invoice must correspond with the description appearing in the credit, see Art 18 lit a and lit c UCP 600. The issuing bank enjoys discretion whether or not to accept an invoice stipulating an amount in excess of the amount permitted by the credit, Art 18 lit b UCP 600.

Requirements for the acceptance of a bill of lading are set out in Art 20 UCP 600: The bill must indicate the carrier and be signed either by the carrier or by an agent or master acting on his behalf. The bill must also indicate that the contractual goods have been shipped on board a named vessel at the port of loading and shipment will be effected from the port of loading to the port of discharge. As it is required of any transport document, the bill of lading must also be a "clean" bill: A bank must not accept a document indicating a defective condition of the goods.[365]

183

The issues discussed above must be directly addressed in the letter of credit as the banks involved will not take any recourse to the terms of the sales contract. That does not, however, mean that the sales contract can be silent on these issues: Quite the contrary, the seller can demand the replacement of an insufficient letter of credit only if the **sales contract** contains the requirements that the credit must fulfill. Hence, the seller should set out the appropriate terms and conditions of the letter of credit in the sales contract and thoroughly check the letter of credit once issued to ensure that it is in compliance with the requirements stipulated in the sales contract.

184

IV. Delivery and Trade Terms

1. The role of standardized trade terms in international sales transactions

Delivery terms and legal issues directly related to delivery are without doubt another cornerstone of a sales contract. The parties to international sales transactions often use abbreviated **trade terms** (regularly three-letter acronyms) that not only specify the scope of the seller's delivery obligations but also cover related issues such as the transfer of risk as well as the allocation of responsibilities and costs between the parties for customs clearance, the issuance of necessary export and import licences as well as other transport documents etc. Trade terms also have an indirect impact on the question of whether the seller is in delay with delivery and must accordingly be held liable for damages incurred by the purchaser. That holds true in particular if the CISG applies to a sales transaction: Art 30 CISG requires the seller to deliver the goods, to hand over related documents and to transfer the property to the purchaser, but does not contain a specific duty to hand over the goods. It follows that a seller is

185

---

[365] It is not necessary that the word "clean" appears on the document (even if the credit requires a document to be "clean on board"), see Art 27 UCP 600.

not liable for any delays occurring after the **delivery** of the goods as provided for by the contract. In particular the use of the "C-terms" of the Incoterms have frequently caused misunderstandings in this regard, as will be illustrated below.

186 Whenever the parties use trade terms, in particular the Incoterms © 2010, they can by that means spare further efforts to draft detailed contract clauses, e.g. with regard to the allocation of responsibilities and costs in relation to transport, loading and unloading of the goods, customs formalities, the issuance of necessary import and export licences, the transfer of risk and transport insurance obligations: Instead, a mere choice of the trade term that best fits the intended transaction will suffice. This having been said, the parties of course remain free to expressly modify the meaning of a specific trade term. Any such alteration should, however, be handled with care in order to avoid ambiguities.

2. The Incoterms © 2010

187 The International Commercial Terms, published by the International Chamber of Commerce (a private international organization representing private business and commerce worldwide) since 1936 together with official rules for their interpretation, are the most commonly used trade terms in international sales transactions. The ICC revises the Incoterms on a regular basis roughly once every decade. Since 2011, the Incoterms © 2010 are the most recent version.[366] Compared to its predecessor, the Incoterms 2000, the Incoterms © 2010 have been reduced to 11 terms.[367] The terms DAF, DEQ, DES and DDU have been replaced by the two new terms DAP (Delivered at Place) and DAT (Delivered at Terminal). Further amendments of the ICC rules[368] include inter alia the express allocation of the parties' obligations with regard to security related clearances and related information as well as terminal handling charges, a more favorable approach towards the use of electronic communication[369] and (with regard to the "sea and waterway" rules FAS, FOB, CFR and CIF) the replacement of the ship's rail as the relevant point of delivery (relevant also for the transfer of risk) with the obligation to place the goods "on board of the vessel.[370] The latter is deemed to reflect more accurately modern commercial reality.[371]

188 If the parties want to use Incoterms in their sales contract (as suggested in this book), they should clearly indicate that the chosen trade term is intended to be governed by the "Incoterms © 2010". By means of this reference, the **ICC rules** for the interpretation of the term concerned are incorporated into the contract as well and ambiguities are avoided as both domestic laws as well as standard trade terms sponsored by other international trade organizations (that can have a different

---

[366] See ICC Rules for the Use of Domestic and International Trade Terms – Incoterms © 2010 by the International Chamber of Commerce.

[367] For an overview of the amendments introduced by the Incoterms © 2010 compared to the Incoterms see B Piltz, "Incoterms © 2010" [2011] EJCCL 1 ff.

[368] ICC Rules, Introduction.

[369] According to Articles A1/B1, electronic means of communication may generally have the same effect as paper based communication provided the parties have either so agreed or the use of electronic communication is customary in the individual case.

[370] Stowage and trimming is not required, J Erauw in Kröll/Mistelis/Perales Viscasillas (n 34) Art. 67 CISG para 30.

[371] The Introduction of the ICC Rules (p. 9) puts it as follows: "This more closely reflects modern commercial reality and avoids the rather dated image of the risk swinging to and from across an imaginary perpendicular line".

meaning in the individual case) often use the same or similar wordings as the Incoterms.[372] Additionally, the parties should be aware that some of the Incoterms are limited to carriage by sea or inland waterway transport. These terms should therefore not be used if the contractual goods are shipped by other means of transportation – otherwise, confusion as to the allocation of risks and responsibilities of the parties in relation to the delivery of the goods may easily arise. In order to prevent an inappropriate use, the ICC has grouped the Incoterms © 2010 into two major subcategories – one category containing rules that are appropriate for any mode of transportation whereas the other subcategory includes clauses that should exclusively used for sea and inland waterway transport.[373]

Though the parties remain at liberty to alter the meaning of the Incoterms pursuant to the ICC rules (and do so in commercial reality, e.g. by use of terms such as EXW *loaded* or CIF *landed*), the ICC rules rightfully point out that potential risks as regards legal certainty may be caused in this event. For instance, if the parties supplement the EXW term with the term "loaded" (indicating that loading on the means of transportation is within the responsibility of the seller), it is not clear which party bears the risk of loss or destruction occurring during the loading procedure.[374] 188a

The 11 existing Incoterms can be divided into **four major groups**: According to the "E-term", the seller fulfils his delivery obligation already by making the goods available for transport at his own premises at the stipulated time of delivery. According to the "F-terms", the seller must deliver the goods to a carrier appointed by the purchaser whereas the purchaser is in charge of both organization and payment of the main transport. The "C-terms" require the seller additionally to organize (and pay for) the main carriage, but the goods are already deemed delivered once they have been handed over to the main carrier. Finally, if the parties utilize "D-terms", the seller is not only responsible for organizing and paying for the main transport but also bears risks related to the transport of the goods to the stipulated place of destination.[375] 189

The allocation of contractual delivery obligations and other legal consequences arising from the use of any of the Incoterms can be briefly summarized as follows: 190

- EXW Ex works [**named place of delivery**]: Under the EXW term, the seller's obligations are limited to placing the goods (packed for transport) at the purchaser's **disposal at his premises** (or at another named place such as a warehouse or the seller's factory), whereas the risk of accidental loss or damage to the goods will already pass to the purchaser upon readiness of the goods at the agreed time for delivery.[376] Further obligations of the seller solely include the submission of a commercial invoice, the provision of assistance (on request and at the purchaser's risk and expense) that the purchaser may need in order to obtain necessary export 191

---

[372] See in particular English law where these terms have a similar though not always an identical meaning.

[373] The terms FAS, FOB, CFR and CIF are tailored for maritime and inland waterway transport. The terms EXW, FCA, CPT, CIP, DAT, DAP and DDP are suitable for any mode of transport.

[374] J Wertenbruch, "Die Incoterms – Vertragsklauseln für den internationalen Kauf" [2005] ZGS 136, 137; with regard to the modification "CIF Landed" also Piltz (n 367) 7. Hence, the ICC Rules (EXW, Guidance Note) suggest that the use of the FCA term is more appropriate if the seller is in a better position to load the goods. In this case, the seller bears costs and risks of the loading procedure.

[375] ICC Rules (n 366) Introduction para 5.

[376] If the purchaser is entitled to stipulate the date of delivery (within an agreed delivery period), the transfer of risk takes also place if the purchaser omits to give due notice on the requested delivery date, see ICC Official Rules (n 366) EXW para B 5.

authorizations as well as information possessed by the Seller that is required for the security clearance of the goods. Accordingly, the purchaser is not only responsible for loading the goods on the proper means of transportation at the seller's premises but must also clear the contract goods for export.

192 • **FCA** Free Carrier [**named place of delivery**]: Pursuant to the FCA term, the seller must deliver the goods to the indicated place of delivery where they are handed over to the carrier nominated by the purchaser. Contrary to the EXW term, the seller is responsible for loading the goods on the means of transport provided by the **nominated carrier**[377], must obtain the necessary export authorizations and carry out the export customs formalities. The seller must also submit a commercial invoice and render assistance (at the purchaser's risk and expense) to the purchaser in obtaining documents which may be required for the transit or the import of the goods into the country of destination. The transfer of risk takes place upon the handover of the goods to the main carrier.

The use of the FCA term has been recommended in particular (eg, in lieu of the terms FOB and FAS) if the contractual goods are carried in **containers**: In this event, the seller must generally hand over the goods already to a container freight station ashore and not to a maritime carrier at the ship's side.[378] Therefore, the transport of the loaded containers from the freight station onto the vessel is regularly completely outside the seller's sphere of control. Contrary to the FOB term, this problem is appropriately dealt with by the FCA term, given that the risk of accidental loss or damage to the goods passes to the purchaser already upon the handover of the goods to the container freight station (handover to the carrier). Accordingly, the buyer must also bear terminal handling charges charged by the terminal operator.

193 • **FAS** Free Alongside Ship [**named port of shipment**]: The seller must clear the goods for export, carry out the necessary customs formalities for export of the goods and submit a commercial invoice to the purchaser. The purchaser is responsible for contracting for the carriage of the goods from the named port of shipment and the submission of necessary import authorizations and other customs formalities related to import, respectively any transit of the goods through any third country. Contrary to the FOB term (see below), the seller is only obliged to place the goods alongside the vessel nominated by the purchaser at the port of shipment whereas the loading of the goods onto the ship is carried out at the purchaser's risk and expense.

194 • **FOB** Free on Board [**named port of shipment**]: The seller must clear the goods for export and place them on board of the vessel (nominated by the purchaser) in the **port of shipment**. Furthermore, the purchaser must submit a commercial invoice, obtain the necessary official authorizations for export and clear the goods through customs at his expense. The risk of any loss or damage to the goods

---

[377] This obligation applies however only if the named place of delivery is the seller's premises; otherwise the seller is not responsible for unloading the goods, see ICC Official Rules (n 366) FCA A 4.

[378] J Ramberg, "CISG and INCOTERMS 2000 in Connection with International Commercial Transactions" in CB Andersen and UG Schroeter (eds), *Sharing International Commercial Law across National Boundaries: Festschrift for Albert H Kritzer on the Occasion of his Eightieth Birthday* (Wildy, Simmonds & Hill Publishing, London 2008) 394, 395 f. The Guidance Note of the ICC Rules also states that "FOB may not be appropriate where goods are handed over to the carrier before they are on board the vessel, for example goods in containers […]".

IV. Delivery and Trade Terms

shifts to the purchaser once the goods have been placed on board on the vessel. Contrary to the CIF term (see below), the purchaser is therefore responsible for the organization and payment of the carriage by sea. Consequently, the purchaser must nominate a vessel within a reasonable time to enable the seller to deliver the goods to the port of shipment on time.

If the contractual goods are transported in containers, the FCA term is more suitable as loaded containers must be handed over already at the container terminal of the seaport, whereas the seller would continue under the FOB clause to bear the risk of any damage or loss that occurs while the goods are stored in the terminal (see also above).[379]

- **CIF** Cost, Insurance and Freight [**named port of destination**]: The CIF term essentially requires the seller to clear the goods for export, to organize and pay for the carriage of the goods to the named **port of destination**, to obtain transport insurance covering at least 110 % of the contract price[380] and to submit (besides the obligatory commercial invoice) transport documents that not only entitle the purchaser to claim the goods from the carrier but also permit the resale of the goods in transit by way of a documentary sale.[381] Contrary to the other Incoterms, the seller must (unless otherwise agreed by the parties) accordingly submit a document of title to the purchaser (such as a negotiable bill of lading) that represents property rights in the goods.

195

According to the general outline of the "C-terms" and notwithstanding the obligation to procure the contract for the main carriage of the contract goods, the seller's delivery obligations are in case of a CIF-delivery already fulfilled once the goods have been placed onto the vessel, and the purchaser must consequently bear all risks of loss or damage to the goods until this very moment. In particular due to the combination of the clause with the indication of the port of destination instead of the port of loading, the use of the CIF-clause often causes **major misunderstandings** with regard to the meaning of delivery dates and the seller's liability in relation to delays in delivery. This may be demonstrated with an older decision of the Austrian Supreme Court rendered in 1986[382]: A sales contract (governed by Swiss domestic sales law) provided for an obligation of the seller to deliver petroleum products on the basis CIF Vienna, outgoing January [1983]. The fuel was loaded onto the transport ship in Novi Sad (port of loading) at the end of January 1983. But the vessel did not leave Novi Sad until the beginning of February. Additionally, further delays occurred during the river transport due to bad weather and the

---

[379] Wertenbruch (n 374) 139.

[380] However, pursuant to the CIF term, the seller is only required to obtain maritime insurance on minimum cover (Clause (C) of the Institute Cargo Clauses (LMA/IUA). Risks outside of major casualties that affect both cargo and ship (eg, fire or explosion, collision or contact of the vessel with any external object other than water, vessel being stranded, grounded, sunk or capsized) are not covered by the basic insurance offered by the Institute of London Underwriters, see J Ramberg, *The Law of Transport Operators* (Norstedts Juridik AB, Stockholm 2005) 160 ff; Piltz (n 367) 4. Clause A 3 of the Rules provides however, that the seller shall at buyer's request (and expense!) provide additional cover, if procurable.

[381] For further requirements of the transport documents see ICC Official Rules (n 366) CIF para A.8. Inter alia, the documents must cover the contract goods and provide for an issuance date within the period agreed for shipment.

[382] OGH (6 Jun1986) File No 8Ob510/86. The judgment can be obtained online under the following link: < http://www.ris.bka.gv.at/Jus>.

contractual goods only arrived in Vienna in the middle of February. Because of a major fall in the price of petroleum products since the end of January, the purchaser refused to take delivery of the goods after their arrival and declared the avoidance of the contract based on an alleged delay of the seller in making delivery. The Austrian Supreme Court rightfully rejected this position, ruling accurately that the seller had fulfilled all delivery obligations existing under the CIF-clause already at the time of loading and within the stipulated time of delivery (end of January 1983). Accordingly, neither the delayed departure from Novi Sad nor the delayed arrival of the goods in Vienna could trigger any liability of the seller for the delay.

196 • **CFR** Cost and Freight [**named port of destination**]: The CFR clause can be used instead of the CIF term if the parties do not wish to impose any transport **insurance responsibilities** upon the seller. Apart from the non-existing obligation of the seller to procure transport insurance, the CFR term is identical with the CIF term.

197 • **CIP** (Carriage and Insurance paid to [**named place of destination**]: Both the CFR and the CIF term are suitable only in case of a carriage of the goods by sea. Otherwise the CIP or CPT term should be used. The CIP term provides essentially for the same allocation of responsibilities, obligations and risks as the CIF term. As the CIP term can be used for **any mode of transportation** (eg, by rail, road, air, sea, inland waterway or any combination of such transport modes), the relevant point of delivery is not on board a vessel but the place where the carrier responsible for the main transport to the named place of destination collects the goods from the seller.

198 • **CPT** Carriage paid to [**named place of destination**]: The CPT term does not provide for any obligations of the seller to procure transport insurance. Otherwise, the term is identical with the CIP term.

199 • **DAP** Delivered at Place [**named place**]: The seller must deliver the goods to the named place, clear them for export (if necessary) and submit the necessary transport documents to the purchaser. The purchaser is responsible for unloading the goods at the named place and (if required) for their further transport to the final place of destination. The purchaser remains responsible for import clearance and bears accordingly the costs incurred for the importation of the goods.

200 • **DAT** Delivered At Terminal [**named terminal at port or place of destination**]: According to the DAT term (which is suitable regardless of the mode of transportation), the seller is responsible for clearing the goods for export (not for import!) and must both organize and pay for the carriage of the goods to the named port of destination. Additional duties of the seller include the obligation to submit the relevant transport documents to the purchaser as well as to inform the purchaser in due time upon the estimated arrival of the ship in order to permit timely collection of the goods. The seller's delivery obligations are fulfilled once the goods are ready for unloading in the named **port of destination** and the purchaser must consequently bear the costs for unloading the goods from the ship as well as all risks of loss or damage to the goods from that time. The purchaser is also responsible for obtaining import authorizations, the payment of import duties (if any) and carrying out any other necessary formalities for importation.

203 • **DDP** Delivered Duty Paid [**named place of destination**]: While the EXW term represents the minimum obligation from the seller's point of view, the DDP term imposes (within the spectrum of the Incoterms © 2010) the **maximum scope** of obligations upon the seller. According to the DDP term, the seller must not only place the (unloaded) goods at the purchaser's disposal at the named place of

destination, but is also responsible for obtaining all necessary export and import licenses and carrying out all customs formalities necessary for both export (plus transit) and import of the contractual goods. As the seller already bears all risks of loss or damage until the goods have reached the place of destination, DDP does not entail any obligation for the seller to procure adequate transport insurance.

Like the EXW term, the DDP term is not among the more popular terms of the Incoterms © 2010, as the purchaser is usually more familiar with the relevant customs regulations and procedures in the country of destination and can generally more easily obtain the necessary authorizations for the import of the goods.

C. The International Sales Terms

I. General Provisions

1. The suggested clause

§ 1 GENERAL PROVISIONS

(1) The following International Sales Terms shall apply to the supply of the contractual goods and related services (if any) by the Seller (hereinafter collectively referred to as the "Products") and shall together with the written Sales Contract signed by both parties and the agreed Technical Specifications of the Products (if any) collectively constitute the entire contract between the parties (hereinafter the "Contract). No other terms and conditions shall apply, including the terms contained in the Purchaser's general terms and conditions or referred to by the Purchaser, whether or not such terms conflict with or supplement these International Sales Terms and regardless of whether or not the Seller has explicitly objected to such terms.

(2) The International Sales Terms shall apply to the present Contract with the Purchaser. They shall by means of a framework agreement also apply to all future contracts concluded with the Purchaser, whose preponderant object is the supply of Products or related spare parts.

(3) The International Sales Terms shall not apply if the Products are intended for personal, family or household use by the Purchaser.

2. Annotations

Subparagraph 1

§ 1 (1) attempts foremost to shield the seller against the application of contractual terms submitted by the purchaser, regardless of whether such purchasing terms contradict the International Sales Terms or merely supplement them.[383] It has already been discussed above that a **"rejection clause"** like the one contained in § 1 (1) does not suffice to win a "battle of forms" in the favor of the seller.[384] General sales terms should nevertheless always contain a "rejection clause" given that this clause may at least help to prevent the application of deviating or supplementing terms of the purchaser[385] if the parties perform the contract though the purchaser has not adhered to the exclusive application of the International Sales Terms by means of a countersigned contract document.

205

---

[383] A separate "rejection clause" in general sales terms is for obvious reasons not necessary if the purchaser signs (as suggested in this book) a main contract document that provides already for the exclusive application of the sales terms. The rejection clause may however become relevant whenever the International Sales Terms are used on a stand-alone basis.

[384] See ch B.I.2 above.

[385] See OLG Frankfurt (26 June 2006) CISG-online 1385.

Subparagraph 2 and 3

206   A second aim of § 1 is to determine the **scope of application** of the International Sales Terms. According to § 1 (2), the International Sales Terms apply not only to the present contract but also to any future sales contracts entered into with the purchaser without the need to expressly incorporate them anew. This clause (that can be found in a multitude of general terms and conditions) is from a legal perspective in principle feasible. However, the seller should not solely rely on the valid incorporation of the International Sales Terms into future sales contracts based on § 1 (2) alone given that some scholars have considered this clause (at least when contained in general terms and conditions) as inoperative due to its "unusual" and "surprising" character.[386]

207   § 1 (3) clarifies finally that the application of the present International Sales Terms is limited in scope to **commercial contracts**. National consumer protection laws restrict deviations from statutory law in a consumer contract to a much greater extent[387]. Consumer contracts are also in principle outside the scope of the CISG[388] though mandatory domestic and supranational laws[389] generally define consumer contracts more broadly than Art 2 lit a CISG and may for that reason cause overlaps between these legal regimes. Although in principle the CISG does (within its scope of application) prevail over both substantive[390] and private international laws aiming to protect consumers,[391] national consumer protection laws may nevertheless trigger the invalidity of individual contract terms, see Art 4 (2) lit a CISG.

208   Though a corresponding exemption is not explicitly stated in § 1, the seller should also not use the present International Sales Terms for the **provision of services** that form not only a minor part of the overall scope of supplies.

---

[386] This is at least the view under German domestic law based on § 305 c (1) BGB, see T Pfeiffer in M Wolf, WF Lindacher and T Pfeiffer (eds), *AGB-Recht* (5th edn C.H. Beck, München 2009) § 305 BGB para 115. Swiss domestic law contains an "unusual terms rule" as well, see BG (6 December 1983) BGE 109 II 452, 456 ff. The existence of a similar rule under the CISG is controversial, in favor apparently OLG Düsseldorf (21 April 2004) CISG-Online 915; contra (based on Art. 4 lit. a) CISG) U Magnus in Staudinger (n 29) Art. 4 CISG para. 25.

[387] See in particular national consumer protection laws in EU member states based on the European Directive 1999/44/EC of the European Parliament and of the Council of 25 May 1999 on certain aspects of the sale of consumer goods and associated guarantees [1999] OJ L 171/12. Art 7 Directive prohibits explicitly the exclusion of the consumer rights conferred by the Directive in a consumer contract. See with regard to European private law also Art 6 (2) Rome I Regulation (n 3): Mandatory consumer protection laws existing at the place of the habitual residence of the consumer shall prevail over the laws chosen by the parties in the consumer contract.

[388] The CISG is pursuant to Art 2 lit a not applicable in case the goods are intended for personal, family or household use as far as the seller knew or should have known this intention.

[389] See, eg, Art 1 (2) lit a Directive 1999/44/EC (n 387): Pursuant to the Directive, a contract concluded between a natural person for a purpose which can be regarded as being outside his trade or profession with another person acting in the exercise of his trade or profession (eg, a commercial seller) is deemed to be a consumer contract – regardless whether the commercial seller has known or ought to have known about this intention.

[390] F Ferrari in Schlechtriem and Schwenzer (n 34) Art 90 CISG para 4. Contra with regard to European directives R Herber, "Mangelfolgeschäden nach dem CISG und nationales Deliktsrecht" [2001] IHR 187, 191.

[391] See, eg, with regard to European private international law Art 25 (1) Rome I Regulation (n 3).

II. Payment Terms

1. The suggested clause

§ 2 TERMS OF PAYMENT

(1) The stipulated contract price is exclusive of value added tax. The Purchaser shall at Seller's request provide the Seller with the necessary documentation required by the competent tax authorities as evidence of an export tax exemption. The Purchaser shall reimburse the Seller for any value added taxes levied on the seller in the country of dispatch or the country of destination due to either the agreed terms of delivery, any failure to duly provide the requested documentation referred to above or any other circumstances attributable to the Purchaser. Any taxes, fees, duties and other charges which are levied on the Seller in connection with the performance of the Contract in the country of destination of the Products (if any) shall be solely borne by the Purchaser and the Purchaser agrees to pay or reimburse the Seller for any such taxes which the Seller is required to pay.

(2) If the Parties have not agreed on other terms of payments, all payments shall be made to the bank account notified by the Seller without any reservation or deduction. All bank charges and fees shall be borne by the Purchaser.

(3) If the Contract provides for payment by means of a letter of credit, the Purchaser shall within two (2) weeks after the conclusion of the Contract open an irrevocable and transferable letter of credit in accordance with and subject to the Uniform Customs and Practice for Documentary Credits published by the International Chamber of Commerce (UCP 600) in favor of the Seller in the amount of the Contract Price, confirmed by a first class European bank with a branch at Seller's place of business and available at sight payment against the presentation of the documents further described in the Contract. The letter of credit shall have an expiry date of at least four (4) months from the contractual delivery date respectively the end of the contractual delivery period. All bank charges and fees shall be at the Purchaser's expense.

(4) If the Seller does not receive payment from the Purchaser when such payment has become due, the Seller is entitled to charge interest at an annual rate of eight (8) percentage points above the rate for main refinancing operations of the European Central Bank (ECB) (http://www.ecb.int/home/html/index.-en.html) as applicable throughout the period of delay. This provision shall apply mutatis mutandis if a letter of credit is not opened in time. Any further rights and remedies of the Seller provided by the Contract or under the applicable governing law shall remain unaffected.

(5) The Purchaser may only set off claims against the Seller in accordance with the governing law of the Contract that are owed in the same currency as the corresponding claim of the Seller arising out of the Contract and that are either undisputed between the Parties or have been finally adjudicated. The aforementioned rule shall apply mutatis mutandis to any right of retention of the Purchaser.

C. The International Sales Terms

2. Annotations

209 Payment terms in a more narrow sense (eg, the determination of the contract price, due dates and methods of payment) are generally individually tailored for each sales transaction and for this reason better addressed in the main contract document (see above). However, **payment terms** in a broader sense cover also legal issues that may equally apply in a multitude of sales transactions. That holds true in particular with regard to the allocation of the tax burden (if any) amongst the parties, general requirements for specific methods of payments (for instance payment by means of a letter of credit), applicable interest rates in case of default in payment as well as restrictions of set-off rights against monetary claims of the seller.

Subparagraph 1

210 Duties and taxes can have a major impact on the overall cost calculation. The terms of a sales contract must therefore explicitly deal with the allocation of these costs between the parties. The most important tax with regard to a sales transaction is indirect taxation by means of **value added tax** (VAT). Within the EU, indirect taxation has been largely harmonized by the European Directive 2006/112/EC on the common system of value added tax (the "VAT Directive")[392] and its preceding instruments. Similar principles are acknowledged by jurisdictions outside the EU as well.

211 Deliveries of goods under a commercial sales contract[393] are generally exempted under EU law from VAT in the country of dispatch but taxable in the country of destination (the "**country of destination principle**").[394] This principle is stipulated in Art 138 (1) VAT Directive[395] in relation to trade within the Union whereas Art 146 (1) lit a VAT Directive requires the Member States to exempt the supply of goods dispatched or transported to a destination outside the EU from VAT as well.[396] Accordingly, VAT is generally levied only on the purchaser by the taxation authorities in the country of destination (either by means of import VAT or (in case of a transaction within the Union) acquisition VAT).[397]

212 The seller may, however, face **tax liability** with respect to payment of VAT in the country of dispatch if he cannot provide the tax authorities with satisfactory evidence that the requirements for an export tax exemption were fulfilled in the given case.[398] Furthermore, VAT may also be imposed on the seller in the country

---

[392] Council Directive 2006/112/EC of 28 November 2006 on the common system of value added tax [2006] OJ L347/1.

[393] A taxable person is a person who independently carries out in any place any economic activity, see Art 9 (1) VAT-Directive.

[394] See 2 (1) lit b VAT Directive. The acquirer can however deduct the VAT due on the acquisition provided the goods are used for activities for which a right of deduction exists, see P Terra and P Wattel, *European Tax Law* (5th (abridged student) edn Wolter Kluwer, Alpena an den Rijn 2008) 144.

[395] Art 138 (1) VAT Directive: Member States shall exempt the supply of goods dispatched or transported to a destination outside their respective territory but within the Union, by or on behalf of the vendor or the person acquiring the goods, for another taxable person, or for a non-taxable legal person acting as such in a Member State other than that in which dispatch or transport of the goods began.

[396] In this case (delivery outside the EU), the tax exemption in the country of dispatch applies regardless whether the deliveries are taxable in the country of destination, see Art 146 (1) lit a VAT-Directive.

[397] K Tipke and J Lang (eds), *Steuerrecht* (21th edn Dr. Otto Schmidt, Köln 2013) § 14 paras 96, 111.

[398] Art 131 VAT-Directive permits the EU member states to lay down further conditions with regard to tax exemptions in order to prevent "evasion, avoidance or abuse" of the VAT exemptions

of destination if he is responsible according to the agreed delivery terms for the importation of the goods. For this reason, § 2 (1) expressly stipulates the purchaser's **obligation to reimburse** the seller for any VAT paid to either domestic or foreign tax authorities due to either the purchaser's failure to submit the requested documentation (inter alia) evidencing export of the goods, the peculiarities of the delivery terms or other circumstances attributable to the purchaser. All other taxes levied on the seller in relation to the sales transaction outside his own jurisdiction are also for the account of the purchaser.[399]

Subparagraph 3

§ 2 (3) lays down further requirements with regard to payment by letter of credit in case the parties have agreed on this payment method. In particular, the purchaser is obliged pursuant to § 2 (3) to arrange for a **letter of credit** that is confirmed by a reputable bank located at the seller's place of business and will not expire any earlier than four months from the scheduled delivery date.[400]

Subparagraph 4

Already under the CISG, the Seller is entitled to claim **interest** in case of default in payment whereas default does not (contrary to some domestic laws) require a prior reminder to be sent to the purchaser, Art 78 (1) CISG.[401] Given that Art 78 CISG does not stipulate the applicable interest rate, recourse must be had to the supplementary domestic law.[402]

Swiss domestic law (Art 104 (1) CO) provides for an **interest rate** of 5 % p.a. in case of default in payment whereas merchants can alternatively claim a (higher) interest rate amounting to the bank discount rate[403] applicable at the place of payment. However, according to Art 104 (2) CO, the parties remain free to agree on a deviating interest rate.[404] § 2 (4) stipulates an alternative interest rate that is in accordance with

---

stipulated in the VAT-Directive. Domestic VAT laws of EU member states may accordingly demand satisfactory evidence that an export has taken place as well as (with regard to intra-community transactions) information on the identity of the purchaser of the goods. In particular if the purchaser is in charge for the arrangement of export shipment, the seller may obtain the necessary evidence only with the assistance of the purchaser.

[399] A similar allocation of the tax burden with regard to all duties, taxes and other charges payable upon import of the goods is provided by almost all Incoterms (to the exception of the DDP term), see ch B.IV above.

[400] See for further details on letter of credits and recommendable contract clauses from the perspective of the seller in this regard ch. B.III.2 above.

[401] Art 78 CISG applies also in relation to other monetary claims such as a claim of damages by either party, J Gotanda in Kröll/Mistelis/Perales Viscasillas (n 34) Art. 78 CISG para 7. However, the payment of the contract price is without doubt the most important claim falling within the ambit of this Article.

[402] Pursuant to other views, the question of the applicable interest rate constitutes an "internal gap" of the CISG and must accordingly be determined on the basis of its general principles. Some arbitral tribunals have taken recourse to Art 7.4.9 (2) UPICC 2010 as an expression of the CISG's general principles in that regard, see n 155 above for further reference.

[403] The meaning of the term "bank discount rate" contained in Art 104 CO (*Bankdiskonto*) is however controversial, see Schwenzer (n 181) para 66.09 with further references.

[404] Though the wording of Art 104 (2) CO suggests that the parties can only agree on higher interest rates, the Swiss Federal Supreme Court has held that the parties may agree on lower interest rates as well, see BG (12 Dec 1991) BGE 117 V 349.

the minimum level set forth in the European Late Payment Directive, amounting to eight percentage points over the interest rate set by the European Central Bank (ECB) for its most recent main refinancing operations.[405] The ECB publishes the applicable bid rate for main refinancing operations (either as a fixed or a minimum bid rate) on its website.[406]

Subparagraph 5

216 The CISG does not contain rules in relation to the parties' **set-off rights**. This matter therefore falls within the ambit of the supplementary domestic law.[407] The relevant provisions with regard to set-off in the Swiss Code of Obligations are not of a mandatory character. It follows that the purchaser's set-off rights can in principle be excluded in their entirety, as Swiss jurisprudence has so far not established any specific restrictions.[408]

217 All the same, § 2 (5) does permit a set-off by the purchaser if the counterclaim has either been mutually acknowledged by the parties or finally adjudicated by a court or an arbitration tribunal, provided that the counterclaim is in each case owed in the same currency as the main claim. In these circumstances, an exclusion of set-off rights to the detriment of the purchaser seems unreasonable.

III. Delivery Terms

1. The suggested clause

§ 3 TERMS OF DELIVERY

(1) The Seller may withhold delivery until due payments have been made (or, as the case may be, a letter of credit has been opened) by the Purchaser in accordance

---

[405] See in particular the European Directive 2011/35/EU of 16 February 2011 on combating late payment in commercial transactions (recast) [2011] OJ L 48/1: Pursuant to Art 3 (1) in connection with Art. 2 No 5–7 Directive, all EU member states have to set the statutory level of interest for late payment which the debtor is obliged to pay at a rate of at least (!) eight percentage points plus a "reference rate" defined as the interest rate applied by the European Central Bank to its most recent main refinancing operations, alternatively the marginal rate resulting from variable-rate tender procedures; in case of a member state whose currency is not the Euro, the equivalent rate set by its national bank will apply.

[406] See <http://www.ecb.eu/stats/monetary/rates/html/index.en.html>. The rate for main refinancing operations (fixed rate) amounts currently to 0.5 % (from 8 May 2013 onwards).

[407] Art 126 (1) CO. See further ch A.IV.5 above.

[408] See Schwenzer (n 181) para 77.23. Other legal systems are more restrictive: Pursuant to German law, set off rights cannot be excluded in standard form contracts if the counter-claim has either been finally adjudicated or acknowledged by the other party, see § 309 No 3 German Civil Code. The German Federal Supreme Court has applied this restriction also to commercial contracts, see BGH (16 Oct 1984) [1985] NJW 319, 320. Furthermore, pursuant to BGH (7 Apr 2011) [2011] NJW 1729 ff. an exclusion of set off rights (in this case contained in an architecture agreement) in standard form contracts may also be invalid if the exclusion covers reciprocal claims of the other party, in particular (pursuant to German domestic law) warranty claims. Under English law, "no set off" clauses are generally enforceable though they may under specific circumstances fall foul of the reasonableness requirement imposed by the Unfair Contract Terms Act 1977, see McMeel (n 206) para 23.45 with reference to *Stewart Gill Ltd v Horatio Myer & Co Ltd* [1992] EWCA Civ. More recently (upholding a no set off clause) *FG Wilson (Engineering) Ltd v. John Holt & Co (Liverpool) Ltd18* [2012] EWHC 2477 (Comm).

with the Contract and all other obligations owed by the Purchaser under the Contract that are necessary for the performance of the delivery of the Products have been discharged.

(2) Partial deliveries of the Products shall be permitted throughout the delivery period.

(3) In case of a delay in delivery or any other performance owed by the Seller under the Contract, the Seller shall only be liable for damages if the delay was caused negligently or intentionally. Seller's liability for any damages shall in this case be limited to an amount of 0.5 % of the Contract Price for the Products (net) for each full week of delay up to a maximum amount of 5 % of the Contract Price (net) in the aggregate. Any claim for damages shall also be capped at this maximum amount if the Purchaser declares the avoidance of the Contract due to the delay. This limitation of liability shall not apply in any of the events stipulated in § 6 (5)[409] of the present International Sales Terms.

(4) The time of delivery agreed upon between the Parties shall not be of the essence. Accordingly and subject to any further prerequisites of the applicable governing law of this Contract, the Purchaser is only entitled to declare the Contract avoided by reason of any delay if the delay is attributable to the Seller, the Purchaser has threatened the Seller with avoidance in writing after the date of delivery and an additional period of time of reasonable length, at least however […] weeks, has not resulted in the delivery of the Products. § 10 (Force Majeure) shall remain unaffected.

(5) If delivery is delayed at the Purchaser's request or otherwise for reasons attributable to the Purchaser by more than fourteen (14) days after notice was given of the readiness for dispatch by the Seller, the Seller may charge the Purchaser liquidated storage costs for each commenced month thereafter amounting to 0.5 % of the Contract Price of the Products up to a maximum of 5 % of the Contract Price. The Seller remains entitled to claim further proven general damages in excess of the liquidated amount. Other rights and remedies provided by this Contract and/or applicable governing law, in particular the right to declare the Contract avoided, shall remain unaffected.

(6) Unless otherwise explicitly agreed in writing by the Seller, the Purchaser shall be solely responsible for the installation and erection of the Products.

[alternatively]

§ 3 TERMS OF DELIVERY

(1) The Seller may withhold delivery until due payments have been made by the Purchaser (or, as the case may be, a letter of credit has been opened) in accordance with the Contract and all other obligations owed by the Purchaser under the Contract that are necessary for the performance of delivery have been discharged.

(2) Partial deliveries of the Products shall be permitted throughout the delivery period.

(3) In case of a delay in delivery or any other performance owed under the Contract that was caused intentionally or negligently by the Seller, the Seller shall

---

[409] This reference must be replaced with a reference to § 6 (2) International Sales Terms if the second alternative of § 6 is used (see below).

C. The International Sales Terms

pay liquidated damages amounting to 0.5 % of the Contract Price for the Products (net) for each full week of delay up to an overall maximum of 5 % of the Contract Price (net) in the aggregate for any event of delay provided the Purchaser can prove that he has suffered any loss at all. The liquidated damages payable under this clause shall subject to § 3 (4) below constitute the sole and exclusive remedy of the Purchaser for delay. This limitation of liability shall not apply in any of the events stipulated in § 6 (5) of these International Sales Terms below.

(4) The time of delivery agreed upon between the Parties shall not be of the essence. Accordingly and subject to any further prerequisites of the applicable governing law of this Contract, the Purchaser is only entitled to declare the Contract avoided by reason of any delay if the delay is attributable to the Seller, the Purchaser has threatened the Seller with avoidance in writing after the date of delivery and an additional period of time of reasonable length, at least however [...] weeks, has not resulted in the delivery of the Products. In case of an avoidance of the contract pursuant to this § 3 (4), the Purchaser is entitled to claim further proven general damages in excess of the liquidated damages payable up to a maximum amount of 5 % of the Contract Price. For the avoidance of doubt, all damage claims (liquidated plus general damage claims) shall in the aggregate be capped at an amount of 10 % of the Contract Price. § 10 (Force Majeure) shall remain unaffected.

(5) If delivery is delayed at the Purchaser's request or otherwise for reasons attributable to the Purchaser by more than fourteen (14) days after notice was given of the readiness for dispatch by the Seller, the Seller may charge the Purchaser liquidated storage costs for each commenced month thereafter amounting to 0.5 % of the Contract Price of the respective Products up to a maximum of 5 % of the Contract Price. The Seller remains entitled to claim further proven general damages in excess of the liquidated amount. Other rights and remedies provided by this Contract and/ or applicable governing law, in particular the right to declare the Contract avoided, shall remain unaffected.

(6) Unless otherwise explicitly agreed in writing by the Seller, the Purchaser shall be solely responsible for the installation and erection of the Products.

2. Annotations

a) The first alternative:

Subparagraph 1

218 Retention rights based on Art 58 (1) 2, (2) CISG for the benefit of the seller are not sufficient to protect the seller against default in payment.[410] This problem is greatly minimized if the parties agree on a letter of credit as the applicable payment method, as the seller thereby secures payment (by means of a binding payment commitment of the issuing bank) already before the contractual goods are delivered. The existence of an appropriate **retention right** (beyond the scope of Art 58 CISG) may, however, even in this case, remain important on two counts: On the one hand, the seller may want to withhold delivery if the purchaser does not open the letter of credit before the delivery date.[411] On the other hand, the retention right contained

---

[410] See ch B.III above.
[411] It would appear that § 3 (1) confirms a right that may already exist under Art 71 (1) CISG in this event, see OGH (6 Feb 1996) CISG-online 224.

III. Delivery Terms

in § 3 (1) may become relevant if the seller cannot enforce his payment claims against the bank under the letter of credit.

Subparagraph 2

In the absence of a contractual right to make partial delivery or of corresponding trade usages, **partial delivery** is not permitted under the CISG.[412] This is evident in cases where the parties agree on a specific delivery date: The seller is in delay with delivery if he has only made partial deliveries up to that date. By the same token, a (partial) delivery ahead of the agreed delivery schedule amounts to an infringement of the contract by the seller as well.[413] Even if the parties have agreed on a delivery period instead of a specific delivery date, partial deliveries are generally permitted only on the basis of a corresponding contractual agreement.[414] Accordingly, § 3 (2) allows partial deliveries explicitly at least within the delivery period stipulated in the main contract document.

Subparagraph 3

Delays in delivery are commonplace in international trade. At the same time, under the applicable CISG rules, liability for delays in delivery does not require fault on part of the seller and is in principle unlimited (subject to the foreseeability doctrine and the purchaser's duty to mitigate his losses pursuant to Art 77 CISG). A reasonable contractual **limitation of liability** is for this reason from the seller's perspective clearly desirable. § 3 (3) aims to achieve this goal on two counts: On the one hand, according to § 3 (3), the seller's liability for damages incurred by delay in delivery presupposes fault (hence at least negligence) on his part. Secondly, § 3 (3) caps the maximum amount of liability for damages due to the delay at 5 % of the contract value, which appears to reflect the industrial standard in international sales contracts to a certain extent.[415] The cap includes also explicitly damages incurred by the purchaser *after* a termination of the contract triggered by the delay: This clarification is from the seller's perspective of major importance as the clause may otherwise (*contra proferentem*) be construed as applying solely to damages incurred *until* the contract has been terminated.[416] Finally, as a consequence of the statutory restrictions laid down in Art 20 CO as well as Art 100, 101 CO, this

219

220

---

[412] B Piltz in Kröll/Mistelis/Perales Viscasillas (n 34) Art 33 CISG paras 32 f.; U Magnus in Staudinger (n 29) Art. 51 CISG para 10; for a different view see C Widmer in Schlechtriem and Schwenzer (n 34) Art 31 CISG para 44. The purchaser is however pursuant to Art 51 CISG (in the absence of a fundamental breach of the seller) not entitled to reject partial deliveries, see OGH (21 Jun 2005) CISG-online 1047.
[413] B Piltz (n 34) para 4–70 f.
[414] B Piltz (n 34) para 4–72.
[415] See for instance § 10.1 of the ICC Model International Sales Contract (n 11) that provides for the payment of liquidated damages in lieu of general damages capped at 5 % of the contract price plus a further cap amounting to 10 % of the contract price if the purchaser terminates the contract due to the delay. Pursuant to the FIDIC-conditions (n 9), the separate cap on liability in case of delay will in principle no longer apply if the employer terminates the contract, see § 8.7 (2) General Conditions.
[416] See, eg, the English case *Bovis Construction Ltd v Whatlings Construction* [1994] B.L.R. 25, 45: A liquidated damages clause for delay did according to the court not prevent claims for general damages occurred after termination of the contract.

C. The International Sales Terms

limitation of liability will not apply in case of intentional misconduct, gross negligence or culpably caused bodily injury attributable to the seller.[417]

Subparagraph 4

221   **Avoidance of the contract** is the second remedy available to the purchaser under the CISG in case of delay. Though standard terms in sales contracts (particularly those drafted by lawyers with a common law background) often stipulate that (capped) liquidated (respectively general) damages constitute the purchaser's "sole and exclusive remedy" in case of delay[418], it is from the author's point of view rather questionable whether such a clause would be enforceable if it were literally construed. Without a right to declare the contract avoided at some point, the purchaser would be bound by the contract even in case of a substantial delay for an unlimited period of time – a result that would already on its face appear to be grossly unfair. Accordingly, § 3 (4) does not do away with the right to declare the avoidance of the contract but rather clarifies and restricts its scope of application.

222   Contrary to some domestic sales laws,[419] a sales contract governed by the CISG can in the absence of a fundamental breach or a contractual agreement stipulating otherwise only be declared avoided by the purchaser on the ground of the (physical) non-delivery of the goods if an **additional respite** set by the purchaser has lapsed to no avail, Art 49 (1) CISG. Against this background, § 3 (4) provides in the first place more legal certainty for the benefit of both parties by expressly defining the length of the respite[420] in lieu of the rather vague "time of reasonable length" stipulated in Art 49 (1) lit b in connection with Art 47 CISG. Secondly, by adhering to the *Nachfrist* doctrine, § 3 (4) intends to clarify again that time is not of the essence of the contract. This seems especially appropriate whenever Incoterms are used given that some domestic courts have (in the author's opinion, quite wrongly) interpreted the mere incorporation of specific Incoterms (in particular the terms CIF and FOB) in a sales contract as (rebuttable) evidence that timely delivery is of the essence of the contract.[421]

---

[417] It is however difficult to imagine that a delay with delivery may cause bodily injury in a legal sense. See on this issue U Magnus in HM Flechtner, RA Brand and MS Walter (eds), *Drafting Contracts under the CISG* (OUP, New York 2008) 472, who considers this scenario as unlikely though not impossible. Magnus draws the example of a delayed delivery of spare parts that leads to the collapse of a machine, resulting in bodily injuries of its operators. From the author's perspective, however, it is doubtful whether a causal link between delay and bodily injury would exist in this case: If a purchaser is or ought to have been aware that the operation of the machine would be unsafe without the replacement of the spare part but goes ahead with its operation nevertheless, it would appear that his own behavior rather than a delay with delivery of the spare part in question has legally caused the accident.

[418] See for instance the model clause suggested by Klotz (n 339) 239: "Liquidated damages paid in accordance with the foregoing provision shall be the Purchaser's sole remedy for any delay in delivery for which the Seller is responsible under the Agreement."

[419] See in particular English law that treats stipulations as to time in a contract generally as "conditions" of the contract whereas a breach of a condition entitles the innocent party regularly to terminate the contract with immediate effect, see McMeel (n 206) para 20.17.

[420] The duration of the respite (in weeks) must be specified by the user of the International Sales Terms pursuant to the particularities of the respective contractual goods (eg, regular delivery periods).

[421] OLG Hamburg (28 Feb 1997) CISG-online 261. See n 69 above for further reference.

III. Delivery Terms

Subparagraph 5

The purchaser's **failure to take delivery** pursuant to Art 60 CISG in a timely fashion entitles the seller to damages pursuant to Art 61 (1) lit b CISG. Given that these damages will in all likelihood predominantly contain expenditures incurred by the seller for the further storage of the goods, § 3 (5) aims to relieve the seller from the burden to prove the exact amount of these expenses by way of a liquidated damages clause. At the same time, § 3 (5) permits the seller to claim further (proven) general damages for this breach that are in excess of the stipulated liquidated damages. 223

b) The second alternative

The second alternative of the clause offers a more favorable solution from the purchaser's perspective with regard to the cap on liability for delay in case the first alternative is not acceptable for the purchaser. The alternative version of § 3 is potentially also more in line with the equivalent clauses contained in the standard model sales contracts that are regularly used in international commerce.[422] At the same time, the suggested alternative should still be acceptable for the seller given that his liability for delay is also reasonably limited. 224

Instead of a mere limitation of his right to recover general damages, the purchaser is pursuant to the amended § 3 (3) entitled to claim **liquidated damages** up to 5 % of the contract price. But, contrary to the common law understanding of "liquidated damages", § 3 (3) does require (as a prerequisite for a claim for liquidated damages) evidence that the purchaser has at least suffered some damages.[423] This approach is from the author's point of view more balanced than the traditional construction of liquidated damages clauses under English or US law: According to § 3 (3), the purchaser is still relieved from the burden to prove corresponding losses. On the other hand, liquidated damages will not become due if no damages have been suffered at all. This scenario is of some relevance in commercial reality: One may for instance imagine the case of a seller who has agreed to supply certain machinery and equipment for a manufacturing plant that is still under construction. If it were also assumed that the seller is in delay in delivering the contractual goods, however the whole project (eg, the construction of the plant) has in the meantime be postponed for a substantial period of time anyway, the delay will apparently not cause any damage at all. In this case, the purchaser would under common law in principle still be entitled to claim liquidated damages as agreed upfront (prior to the postponement of the project).[424] 225

The second enhancement of the amended § 3 from the purchaser's perspective comprises a higher cap on liability if the purchaser declares the **avoidance** of the contract pursuant to Art 49 (1) lit b CISG: In this event, the purchaser may 226

---

[422] See for similar though not identical solutions in particular § 10 of the ICC Model International Sales Contract (n 11) as well as §§ 14, 15 ORGALIME S 2012 (n 10).

[423] This is in line with the Swiss and (apparently also) the German legal concept of "pauschalierter Schadensersatz", see ch A.IV.7 above.

[424] See B Eggleston, *Liquidated Damages and Extension of Time* (3rd edn Wiley Blackwell, Oxford 2009) 78, with reference to the English case *BFI Group of Companies Ltd v. DCB Integration Systems Ltd* (1987).

pursuant to § 3 (4) and contrary to the original clause claim additional general damages up to another 5 % of the contract value.

IV. Retention of Title

1. The suggested clause

§ 4 TRANSFER OF TITLE

(1) Title to the Products shall not pass to the Purchaser until the Seller has unconditionally received the full amount of the contract price due under this Contract. The transfer of risk shall remain unaffected by this retention of title.

(2) Until title to the Products has passed to the Purchaser pursuant to the foregoing, the Purchaser shall insure the Products with a reputable insurance company for their full replacement value against all risks and shall keep the Products in good repair and condition. Until transfer of title, the Purchaser is not entitled to pledge, transfer ownership as security, lease or otherwise dispose of the Products without Seller's prior written approval. The Purchaser may however resell the Products in the ordinary course of business provided he receives payment from his customer or retains title so that the property is transferred to Purchaser's customer only after fulfillment of the customer's obligation to pay.

(3) If the relevant domestic property laws do not recognize a retention of title or provide for additional requirements such as but not limited to registration requirements etc., the Purchaser undertakes to support the Seller at Seller's request in order to either fulfill any of these requirements or to establish a comparable security interest for the Seller in relation to the Products. Costs reasonably incurred by the Seller in this regard shall be borne by the Purchaser.

2. Annotations

227 A **reservation of title** clause becomes important in particular if the contractual goods have already been delivered, the purchaser is in default of payment and the seller for this reason declares the avoidance of the contract.[425] Though the seller can claim restitution of the goods in this case also if title to the goods has already been unconditionally transferred,[426] only a reservation of title offers sufficient protection in the event of the purchaser's insolvency: According to the applicable national insolvency laws, an enforceable reservation of title will in all likelihood permit a privileged claim for separation and recovery of the contractual goods from the bankrupt estate, whereas the seller would without a reservation merely rank as an unsecured creditor entitled only to a dividend proportionate to the value of his claim.[427]

---

[425] If the parties agree on payment by means of a letter of credit as suggested in the main sales document above, a retention of title clause should usually not become relevant at all given that the payment is in this case regularly rendered at the time of delivery of the goods respectively shortly thereafter.

[426] See Art 81 (2) CISG. Pursuant to some domestic laws, ownership in the goods is in this case (termination of the contract) automatically and retroactively revested in the seller, see EM Kieninger (ed), *Security Rights in Movable Property in European Private Law* (CUP, Cambridge 2004) 227 f.

[427] See, eg, Federal Court of Australia, South Australian District (28 Apr 1995) CISG-online 218.

IV. Retention of Title

It has already been discussed above[428] that a "retention of title" clause can never- 228
theless often not provide the seller with appropriate security for payment of the
contract price in an international sales transaction, as the property and insolvency
law in many jurisdictions – in particular outside the EU[429] – does not acknowledge
any retention of title. Furthermore, even if the retention of title is enforceable in the
relevant jurisdiction, it will still be up to the seller to enforce a claim for restitution of
his (retained) property. For this reason, § 4 should only serve as a **"fall back scenario"**
in case that more appropriate means to secure payment (eg, an advance payment of
the contract price, payment via letter of credit or the provision of suitable payment
guarantees by reliable third parties such as banks or insurance companies on behalf of
the purchaser) of the contract price are not obtainable or have failed in an individual
case. For instance, in case of payment by letter of credit, the retention of title clause
may become important if the bank refuses payment under the credit due to mere
technicalities and the seller must accordingly enforce his claim for payment directly
against the purchaser.

Subparagraph 1

§ 4 (1) contains only a "simple" and not a "prolonged" respectively a **"current** 229
account" retention of title clause.[430] Accordingly, ownership in the contractual
goods will contrary to the "current account" retention of title clause pass to the
purchaser once the contract price for these goods has been paid in full, regardless
whether the seller has other due and open claims arising from an ongoing business
relationship with the purchaser. Though this limitation primarily serves the purchaser's interests, it also provides greater legal certainty in an ongoing business
relationship as the time of the passage of title to the goods would otherwise hardly
be foreseeable. Apart from that, many jurisdictions do not acknowledge "current
account" retention of title clauses in the first place.[431]

For the same reasons, § 4 (1) also does not extend the reservation of title to the 230
proceeds that the purchaser receives in the event of a subsequent resale of the reserved
goods by means of an anticipatory assignment of such (future) claims to the seller.[432]

---

[428] See ch A.V.2 above.

[429] In accordance with Art 9 (1) of the European Late Payment Directive (n 405), all domestic laws of the EU member states must acknowledge an expressly agreed retention of title clause. The member states remain however free to stipulate further prerequisites for a valid retention of title.

[430] See for this terminology H v Houtte, *The Law of International Trade* (2nd edn Sweet & Maxwell, London 2002) para 4.62.

[431] See Kieninger (n 426) 435 (using the term "all sums clause") and 417ff for detailed country reports. The enforceability of a "current account" retention of title clause is however inter alia acknowledged by German law, see BGH [1994] NJW 1154 and English law, see *Aluminium Industrial Vaasen B.V. v Romalpa Aluminium Ltd* [1976] 1 WLR 676 (CA).

[432] A "prolonged" retention of title clause (respectively a "proceeds clause") is industrial standard in general sales terms used for domestic transactions in Germany and its enforceability is principally acknowledged by German law, see RM Beckmann in J v Staudinger (ed), *Kommentar zum Bürgerlichen Gesetzbuch* (Sellier de Gruyter, München 2004) § 449 BGB paras 99 ff. A number of other jurisdictions do however either not acknowledge a proceeds clause or require certain formalities and publicity that render the assignment of claims or the taking of a charge over the proceeds largely nugatory in reality, see Kieninger (n 426) 364. The same restrictions apply with regard to a retention of title clause that aims (in case of delivery of raw materials and their subsequent transformation into new products by the purchaser) to extend to newly produced goods as well given that this clause is also not given effect in the vast majority of jurisdictions, see Kieninger (n 426) 396.

C. The International Sales Terms

231   The last sentence of § 4 (1) simply clarifies for the avoidance of any doubt that the delayed passage of title should not influence the transfer of risk as the passing of title is (unless otherwise agreed) pursuant to some domestic laws linked to the transfer of risk.[433]

Subparagraph 2

232   The purchaser's duties in relation to the contractual goods before transfer of title stipulated in § 4 (2) with regard to insurance, maintenance and repair represent the industrial standard. They are intended to protect the seller's **proprietary interests** until the property rights have been vested in the purchaser. The clause does, however, explicitly permit the purchaser to resell the contractual goods in the "ordinary course of business" as a purchaser (in particular a purchaser who resells the products on a regular basis as a "middle man") would otherwise be unduly restricted. The limitation of this permission to reselling in the "ordinary course of business" means that the purchaser must resell the goods in accordance with usual and customary practices that would exclude any underselling of the goods and – as further clarified in § 4 (2) – the resale of the goods without first obtaining the contract price or the reservation of title towards the end customer. But these restrictions cannot prevent a third party from acquiring title to the goods by way of a "bona fide transaction".

Subparagraph 3

233   § 4 (3) deals with cases where the contractual goods have been transferred into a jurisdiction that does either not acknowledge any reservation of title or demands compliance with certain formal requirements as a condition precedent for an operative retention of title. According to the suggested clause the purchaser is in this case obliged to assist the seller to fulfill any **further legal requirements** existing in the relevant jurisdiction (such as but not limited to a registration requirement) or to furnish alternative security.

V. Product Defects

1. The suggested clause

§ 5 QUALITY DEFECTS AND DEFECTS OF TITLE

(1) In case the Products do not conform with the contractual obligations as to quantity, quality or description ("Quality Defects") or are not free from enforceable rights of third parties, including but not limited to enforceable rights based on intellectual property ("Defects of Title") already at the time of transfer of risk, the Purchaser shall have the remedies provided by the UN Convention on Contracts for the International Sales of Goods (CISG) subject to the following provisions. These remedies (as amended hereafter) constitute Purchaser's sole and exclusive remedies for any Quality Defect or Defect of Title. The Purchaser is in particular not entitled to rescind the contract based on any mistake as to the actual condition of the Products.

---

[433] See, eg, Sec 20 (1) SGA 1979: Risk is presumptively transferred at the time of the transfer of property.

V. Product Defects

Quality Defects

(2) The Products shall only be deemed to be non-conforming if they do not comply already at the time of transfer of risk with the specifications laid down in this Contract, which shall conclusively describe the applicable conformity standard of the Products. In the absence of agreed specifications, the Products shall only be deemed defective if they are at the time of transfer of risk not fit for the purpose for which products of the same description would ordinarily be used. The application of any further conformity standards implied by law or otherwise is explicitly excluded. The Seller shall in particular not be responsible for the fitness of the Products for any particular purpose or for compliance of the Products with any legal requirements existing outside of Seller's country of residence.

(3) Accordingly, the Seller shall not be responsible for any non-conformity arising after the transfer of risk such as but not limited to any defect due to faulty use, maintenance or modifications of the Products, use of unsuitable spare parts, defective installation or erection by the Purchaser or any third party not acting on behalf of the Seller, natural wear and tear or damage or any other external influences not attributable to the Seller.

(4) In case of delivery of non-conforming Products, the Seller shall at his option and subject to any further preconditions pursuant to the applicable governing law either repair any defect or replace any Products or any portion thereof that are non-conforming. The Seller shall be given adequate time and opportunity to remedy the defect. For this purpose, the Purchaser shall grant the Seller access to the Products. Additional costs incurred by the Seller due to the relocation of the Products to a place other than the original place of destination shall be borne by the Purchaser. A right of the Purchaser to claim delivery of substitute Products is explicitly excluded.

(5) The Purchaser is entitled to a reduction of the contract price pursuant to the applicable governing law once either two attempts of the Seller to make good the defect have failed or the Seller has not undertaken such remedial measures within a reasonable time after receipt of a notice indicating a Quality Defect and lapse of an additional final respite set by the Purchaser. Subject to any further limitations set forth in § 6 below and by the applicable governing law, the same prerequisites shall apply for any claim for damages in lieu of performance. If the Quality Defect amounts to a fundamental breach of contract, the Purchaser is in this event alternatively entitled to declare the contract avoided subject to any further preconditions and restrictions set forth by the applicable governing law.

(6) Any and all remedies of the Purchaser for any Quality Defect are conditional upon prompt notice to be given by the Purchaser no later than seven (7) calendar days after the Purchaser has discovered or ought to have discovered the defect in accordance with his duty to examine the Products. The Purchaser shall examine the Products after handover within as short a period as is practicable in the circumstances whereas the period of time for the examination of the Products shall in any event not exceed a period of fourteen (14) days commencing upon handover of the Products. The Purchaser is not entitled to rely on any excuse for its failure to give the required notice. The Seller is not entitled to rely on this § 5 (6) if the lack of conformity relates to facts that he has or ought to have been aware of at the time of handover of the goods and which he did not disclose to the Purchaser.

C. The International Sales Terms

Defects of Title

(7) The Products shall only have a deficiency in title if they are not free from enforceable rights of third parties that exist already at the time of transfer of risk. Third parties' enforceable rights founded on intellectual property shall only be deemed to constitute Defects of Title to the extent that a) the intellectual property right is registered in the country of use specified in the Contract and such right is based on the identical invention disclosed and claimed in a property right registered and made public in Seller's country of residence and b) the ordinary use of the Products as foreseen in the Contract by the Purchaser is thereby impeded.

(8) If the Purchaser will be refrained from the regular use of the Products due to industrial or intellectual property rights in the Products of any third party, Seller shall upon Purchaser's request subject to the conditions and limitations stated in § 5 (7) at Seller's discretion and cost either:

(a) procure for the Purchaser the right to use the Product, or
(b) provide the Purchaser with a non-infringing replacement product or modify the Product so that it becomes non-infringing, provided that the replacement product/modified Product meets substantially the same functional specifications as the Product.
(c) refund the purchase price to the Purchaser upon return of the Products less a reasonable amount of depreciation for any period of use of the Products.
If Seller has not undertaken such remedial measures within a reasonable time after receipt of notice of default by the Purchaser, the Purchaser may subject to any preconditions under governing law declare the avoidance of the Contract and (subject to the limitations set forth in § 6 below) claim damages.

(9) The Seller shall only be liable for any Defect of Title if the Purchaser gives Seller prompt written notice pursuant to the applicable governing law, neither consents to any judgment or decree nor undertakes any other act in compromise of any claim without first obtaining Sellers' written consent. The Purchaser is not entitled to rely on any excuse for his failure to give the required notice. The Seller is not entitled to rely on a delayed notice of the Purchaser if he knew of the right or claim of the third party and the nature of it at the time of handover of the Products.

(10) The Purchaser loses the right to rely on a Quality Defect of the Products or on a Defect of Title if he does not give the Seller notice thereof at the latest within a period of one (1) year from the date of handover of the Products to the Purchaser, regardless of whether the defect has been or ought to have been detected by that time. This provision shall not apply if the defect relates to facts that the Seller has been or ought to have been aware of at the time of handover of the goods and which he did not disclose to the Purchaser.

2. Annotations

234   A reasonable **limitation** of the seller's overall risk exposure in the event of any defects of the contractual products can be achieved on two levels: First, a careful description of the required quality standards of the contract goods and the purpose for which they can (or cannot) be used reduces the number of situations in which the seller will be in breach of the contract. A limitation of applicable remedies on

V. Product Defects

the other hand restricts the seller's liability as a "tool of last resort" once a breach has been established.[434] Sales terms should ideally address both tiers.

Subparagraph 1

§ 5 (1) clarifies upfront that the International Sales Terms do not intend to create new remedies but must be interpreted instead as a mere modification respectively limitation of the existing remedies provided by the CISG in the event of any defect. § 5 (1) addresses also the problem that Swiss domestic law permits a rescission of the contract pursuant to Art 24 (1) 4 CO based on a fundamental mistake with regard to the quality of the contractual goods in addition to the regular sales law remedies and even after the transfer of risk.[435] Though Art 24 (1) 4 CO may only rarely apply (if at all) in case of defective generic goods[436] and the prevailing view assumes – rightly so from the author's point of view – that this provision is ruled out by the remedies of the CISG anyway[437], Swiss jurisprudence has apparently not yet explicitly acceded to this view. Accordingly, § 5 (1) expressly excludes any right to rescind the contract by reason of a fundamental **error as to the quality** of the goods.[438]

235

Subparagraph 2

Art 35 (1) CISG enables the parties from the outset to autonomously define the required **quality level** of the contract goods. It is also well accepted that conformity standards implied by the CISG pursuant to Art. 35 (2) CISG will be displaced by express agreements as to the required conformity standards pursuant to Art. 35 (1) CISG if express and implied standards are inconsistent with one another.[439] As a

236

---

[434] For an illuminating description of this distinction that applies also in other legal systems see the decision of the Wisconsin Supreme Court, *Murray v. Holiday Rambler Inc.* 83 Wis. 2 d 406, 414 (cited by ME Klinger, "The Concept of Warranty Duration: A Tangled Web" (1984–1985) 89 Dick L Rev 935, 947) that distinguishes between a "disclaimer of warranties" on the one hand and a "limitation of remedies" on the other hand as follows: "A disclaimer of warranties limits the seller's liability by reducing the number of circumstances in which the seller will be in breach of the contract; it precludes the existence of a cause of action. A limitation of remedies, on the other hand, restricts the remedies available to the purchaser once a breach is established."

[435] BG (7 Jun 1988) BGE 114 II 131, 139. Pursuant to Art 31 CO, a purchaser may rescind the contract in this event within one year after he has become aware of the defect whereas the Swiss Code of Obligations does not provide for a long stop period in case of hidden defects. For a critical appraisal with regard to the concurring application of Art 24 (1) 4 CO and the regular remedies under domestic Swiss sales law see H Honsell, "Die Konkurrenz von Sachmängelhaftung und Irrtumsanfechtung – Irrungen und Wirrungen" [2007] SJZ 137 ff. For a similar problem under English law (in particular due to the common law instruments of mistake and misrepresentation) see M Jewell, *An Introduction into English Contract Law* (2nd edn Nomos, Baden-Baden 1999) 115 ff. Pursuant to German sales law, a right to rescind the contract based on a mistake as to the fundamental properties of the goods in accordance with § 119 (2) German Civil Code is displaced by the regular sales law remedies, see D Reinicke and K Tiedtke, *Kaufrecht* (8th edn Carl Heymanns, Köln 2008) para 792.

[436] See C Brunner and M Vischer, "Die Rechtsprechung des Bundesgerichts zum Kaufvertragsrecht im Jahr 2007" jusletter (13. Oktober 2008) 7.

[437] This view is in particular convincing as the system of rights and remedies provided by the CISG would otherwise be substantially undermined; see for this problem in general Ferrari (n 65) 68.

[438] Art 24 (1) 4 CO is of a non-mandatory character, see I Schwenzer in Honsell et al (n 164) Art 24 CO para 33.

[439] S Kröll in Kröll/Mistelis/Perales Viscasillas (n 34) Art. 35 CISG para 64.

consequence, the parties are in principle free to define a quality standard that falls even short of the supplementary conformity standards contained in Art 35 (2) CISG.[440]

237 It remains questionable, however, whether an express contractual agreement on the required conformity standard of the goods would already rule out the **implied standards** set forth in Art 35 (2) CISG based on the view that Art. 35 (2) CISG constitutes merely a default rule.[441] In particular US-American courts have taken the apparently opposite view according to which Art. 35 (1) and (2) CISG will (subject to inconsistent requirements contained in agreed quality obligations on the one hand and quality standards implied by law on the other) apply cumulatively[442] if Art. 35 (2) CISG has not been excluded by way of an express disclaimer.[443] Also, even if Art. 35 (2) CISG is viewed as a supplementary provision, it should be taken into consideration that both courts of law and arbitral tribunals have in the past often assumed that conformity standards implied by law were (either implicitly) agreed on by the parties as the applicable conformity standard pursuant to Art 35 (1) CISG or the express agreement as to the conformity standard of the goods cannot (in particular due to a lack of comprehensive specifications) reasonably interpreted as a conclusive determination on the required quality. A good example is a finding by an arbitral tribunal of the Arbitration Institute of the Stockholm Chamber of Commerce, according to which an inclusion of "express warranties" into a sales contract that dealt in positive terms with general aspects of quality did not eliminate the implied quality standards set forth in Art 35 (2) CISG.[444]

---

[440] P Huber and A Mullis, *The CISG. A new textbook for students and practitioners* (Sellier, München 2007) 134.

[441] See in general H Flechtner, "Excluding CISG Article 35 (2) Quality Obligations: The "Default Rule" View vs the "Cumulation View", in *International Arbitration and International Commercial Law: Synergy, Convergence and Evolution. Liber Amicorum in Honor of Professor Eric Bergsten* (Kluwer Law International, 2011) 571 ff. providing an excellent discussion on different approaches of international case law.

[442] A general hesitance to accept the priority of express agreements of the parties towards implied warranties is also well established in common law systems: For instance, pursuant to § 2–317 UCC, express and implied warranties apply in principle cumulatively. Express warranties prevail only over inconsistent implied warranties if the cumulative application would be unreasonable whereas the implied "fitness for purpose" warranty remains untouched even by this exemption. In relation to English law see Sec 55 (2) SGA 1979 pursuant to which an express condition or warranty does not negate a condition or warranty implied by law unless inconsistent with it. Though German sales law seems to contain an even clearer order of priority as the CISG (see § 434 (1) German Civil Code that refers foremost to the "agreed quality" of the contract goods as the relevant standard whereas both suitability of the goods with either their intended or their customary use respectively compliance with the average quality of goods of the same kind (§ 434 (1) No 1, 2 German Civil Code) will only become relevant to the extent that the quality has not been (comprehensively) agreed expressly between the parties), the construction of this provision in light of the EC Directive 1999/44/EC (n 387) on consumer sales has robbed this order of priority some of its force.

[443] H Flechtner (n 441) 571, 578,

[444] Award of the Arbitration Institute of the Stockholm Chamber of Commerce (5 Jun 1998) CISG-online 379 (cited and reviewed by J Lookofsky, "Tooling Up for Warranties with the CISG Case Digest" in HM Flechtner, RA Brand and MS Walter (eds), *Drafting Contracts under the CISG* (OUP, New York 2008) 343, 356. In a similar direction Schlechtriem and Butler (n 34) para 138: "But, if the parties expressly or impliedly agreed upon a particular purpose, that purpose has become part of the characteristics of the goods in accordance with Art 35 I CISG." Overly broad however T Newmann, "Features of Article 35 CISG: Equivalence, Burden of Proof and Awareness" [2007] VJ 81, 83 ff, who is (based on Art 8 CISG) of the view that both express and implied

V. Product Defects

It would accordingly appear at a closer analysis that both the "default rule view" as well as the "cumulation view" are less divergent as one may think at first glance. In particular, the outcome may (at least in theory) often be quite similar given that the "cumulation view" still accepts the supremacy of Art. 35 (1) CISG in case of inconsistencies between both agreed quality standards and those implied by law, whereas the "default rule view" does not necessarily rule out Art. 35 (2) CISG whenever the agreed quality obligations cannot be construed as a conclusive statement. It follows that Art. 35 (1) CISG should in any event solely apply if the express quality obligations must be deemed to constitute a conclusive statement given that additional implied obligations set forth by Art. 35 (2) CISG may in this event always be considered as "inconsistent" – at least if this term is not too narrowly interpreted.[445] If this should, however, not be the case, Art. 35 (2) CISG may apply pursuant to both theories. The problem boils accordingly down to the essential question whether the parties have intended to create a truly comprehensive and exclusive set of quality obligations in relation to the contractual goods or not. 237a

§ 5 (2) hence aims to address the remaining risks of a cumulative application by clarifying that the technical specifications (if any) agreed between the parties rule out any supplementary conformity standards implied by law. Implied standards set forth in Art 35 (2) CISG will, according to the wording of the suggested clause, only become relevant if the parties have not agreed on any specifications. But they are limited in this case to the fitness of the goods for the ordinary purpose for which goods of a similar nature would be used and explicitly exclude the potentially dangerous conformity standard of **fitness for a particular purpose** that has been made known to the seller. 238

The seller should, however, be aware that the intended goal of this clause cannot (depending on the specific factual background in the individual case) always be accomplished. In particular, courts and arbitral tribunals may assume implied agreements of the parties with regard to conformity standards that prevail over the wording in general terms and conditions. Though this risk may be further reduced by means of an **entire agreement clause** (see below) that attempts to exclude supplementary oral agreements with binding contractual force, the effect of such a clause in general terms and conditions is in itself limited.[446] Secondly, a certain risk remains that a "warranty disclaimer may be struck down by a court or tribunal on the basis that a disclaimer will be considered as a "hidden limitation of liability".[447] Interestingly enough, contrary to the treatment of limitation of remedies/liability clauses, neither the CISG nor the majority of civil law systems contain (outside the area of consumer contracts) explicit restrictions with regard to disclaimer of warranties.[448] 239

---

statements of the purchaser as to specific purposes of the goods do already fall within the ambit of Art 35 (1) CISG if the seller could not have been unaware of such purpose.

[445] Contra Flechtner (n 441) 571, 581, who takes the view that the parties may very well agree on an exclusive regime (and will by that means effectively exclude Art. 35 (2) CISG) though the supplementary requirements set forth by Art. 35 (2) CISG would even in this event not necessarily be inconsistent with the exclusive regime set forth by the parties in the individual case.

[446] See ch C.XII below for further details.

[447] See for instance LG Karlsruhe (12 Jan 2007) [2008] MMR 136. For the position under Swiss law see Weber (n 169) Art 100 CO para 74.

[448] US law on the other hand lays down specific requirements with regard to the exclusion of implied warranties, see § 2–316 (2) UCC. Similarly, Art. 13 (1) of the English Unfair Contract Terms 1977 puts also disclaimers of implied warranties under scrutiny.

C. The International Sales Terms

240 As a consequence, a seller should always be careful when submitting product related statements to the purchaser, whether made orally or in writing. Risks can be substantially reduced if technical specifications of the products forming part of the contract are carefully and conclusively drafted.

Subparagraph 3

241 § 5 (1) already confirms that the contractual products are not subject to a "warranty of durability" and can accordingly be considered to be non-conforming only if they were already defective at the time of transfer of risk, see also Art 36 (1) CISG. Against this background, § 5 (3) is strictly speaking of a merely declaratory character. Nevertheless, the clause further illustrates the general idea that the seller cannot be made responsible for any detriments of the goods occurring after the **transfer of risk** – provided the roots of such detriments were not already inherent in the goods at that point of time.

Subparagraphs 4 and 5

242 § 5 (4) and § 5 (5) essentially effect some restrictions in relation to the **statutory remedies** available under the CISG in case of a quality defect.

243 According to the CISG, the purchaser is first and foremost entitled to demand **performance** of the contract, Art 46 (1) CISG. This general remedy is in the event of the delivery of non-conforming goods restricted to a right either to claim repair (subject to the "reasonableness" of this remedy, Art 46 (3) CISG) or to demand delivery of substitute goods (subject to the existence of a fundamental breach, Art 46 (2) CSIG. § 5 (4) states upfront that it is generally up to the seller to choose between repair or the delivery of substitute goods as the appropriate means in order to make good any defect. This provision is a clarification rather than an amendment of the CISG: Although the CISG in principle gives the purchaser the choice between a repair or substitute performance, this choice is substantially reduced both by the seller's right to remedy any failure even after delivery (either by repair or replacement) in accordance with Art 48 (1) CISG and by the high thresholds that apply in particular in relation to any demand of substitute performance.[449]

244 In deviation from the CISG, however, § 5 (4) excludes any right of the purchaser to claim the **delivery of substitute goods** even if the indicated prerequisites for such a claim under the CISG have been fulfilled. Such an exclusion has been considered as enforceable by the courts even under domestic laws that put general terms and conditions under stricter scrutiny than it appears to be the case under Swiss law – provided that the purchaser is still be entitled to other satisfactory remedies in lieu of performance.[450]

245 § 5 (5) leaves the remedies of price reduction (Art 50 CISG) and avoidance of the contract (Art 49 CISG) largely untouched. The former seems reasonable in particular if the seller opts for the exclusion (rather than a mere limitation) of damage claims:[451] In this event, a price reduction will constitute the purchaser's only remaining remedy if the thresholds for avoidance or for specific performance are

---

[449] See Schlechtriem and Butler (n 34) para 186.
[450] OGH (7 Sep 2000) CISG-online 642 (applying the CISG as well as German law as the "supplementary" domestic governing law of the contract).
[451] See ch C.VI below.

not fulfilled.⁴⁵² Accordingly, both courts of law as well as arbitral tribunals may be particularly tempted to reject an overly broad limitation of remedies that would essentially exclude almost all otherwise available remedies in lieu of performance – a view that is even accepted by legal systems (such as English law) that stick to the principle of contractual freedom with particular force.⁴⁵³

Both remedies are, however, made subject to **further qualifications**: The purchaser is allowed under § 5 (5) in any event only to either demand a price reduction or declare the contract avoided⁴⁵⁴ if and when two attempts of the seller to rectify the defect have failed or the seller has not made good the defect within a reasonable time after receipt of the respective notice and the lapse of an additional respite to no avail. The same requirements will also apply in relation to a claim for damages "in lieu of performance" pursuant to Art 74 CISG provided that this claim is not already excluded pursuant to § 6 of the suggested International Sales Terms. 246

Subparagraph 6

Art 38 and 39 CISG require the purchaser to examine the contractual goods within as short a period as is practicable in the circumstances and to notify the seller of a defect within a reasonable time after the defect has been or ought to have been discovered. Accordingly, Articles 38 and 39 CISG distinguish between a time period for the examination of the goods and a separate notification period that commences once the defect has or ought to have been discovered through the required **examination**.⁴⁵⁵ As regards the examination period, § 5 (6) merely reiterates upfront the wording of Art 38 CISG that requires the purchaser to examine the goods within as short a period as is practicable in the circumstances. Though there is no doubt that this wording is rather vague and may cause uncertainties,⁴⁵⁶ it 247

---

⁴⁵² See M Müller-Chen in Schlechtriem and Schwenzer (n 34) Art 50 CISG para 19, who takes the view that a cumulative exclusion of claims for damages and the price reduction remedy would be unenforceable.

⁴⁵³ An interesting recent English case illustrates that the existence of some remedy in lieu of performance may become crucial with regard to the enforceability of a limitation of remedies/liability clause contained in general terms and conditions (at least if the contract falls within the scope of the Unfair Contract Terms Act 1977), see *Regus (UK) Ltd v Epcot Solutions Ltd* [2008] EWCA Civ 361 para 30: In this case, a limitation of liability clause contained in standard rental terms of a provider of serviced office accommodation was finally upheld (contrary to the view of the court of first instance) and did hence pass the "reasonableness test" under the UCTA because the tenants were still entitled to claim the diminution in value of the services promised as damages. On the other hand, a limitation of liability in relation to "direct damages suffered in paying others to remedy the defects" that applied even in case of the failure of a limited obligation by the seller to repair defective goods was struck down as unreasonable, *Lobster Group Ltd v Heidelberg Graphic Equipment Ltd & Another* [2011] EWHC 1919 (TCC) para 128 f. However, the UCTA 1977 is not applicable in case of international supply contracts, s. sec 26 UCTA 1977.

⁴⁵⁴ These additional requirements will not do away with the further requirements that exist in case of an avoidance of the contract (i. e. a fundamental breach).

⁴⁵⁵ The prevailing opinion in the literature seems to assume some interdependence between the two periods: According to this opinion, a purchaser may catch up with a delayed examination by expediting its notice towards the seller, see Flechtner (n 97), criticizing a contrary judgment of the State Court Frankfurt in the notorious "Uganda used shoe case", see LG Frankfurt (11 Apr 2005), CISG-online 1014.

⁴⁵⁶ See V Behr, "Dealing with Non-Conformity – A Transaction Test Analysis of CISG Regulations on Examination and Notice Under Articles 38 Through 44" in HM Flechtner, RA Brand and MS Walter (eds), *Drafting Contracts under the CISG* (OUP, New York 2008) 429, 437.

C. The International Sales Terms

would in the author's opinion be inappropriate to replace the statutory wording with a fixed period for examination that may apply for a plethora of rather different contractual goods and circumstances. As an alternative, § 5 (6) stipulates a maximum (long stop) **period for examination**.

248 In relation to the notification period, § 5 (6) sets a fixed period of seven days instead of the more ambiguous "reasonable amount of time" pursuant to Art 39 CISG. From the author's point of view, the appropriate length of a **notification period** depends – compared to the examination period – much less on the particularities of an individual sales transaction and is accordingly better suited for a standardized determination in general terms and conditions.

249 Finally, § 5 (6) excludes the purchaser's right to rely on a **"reasonable excuse"** pursuant to Art 44 CISG for any failure to report a defect. A similar defense is also not available under the majority of domestic sales laws that provide for similar duties of the purchaser in relation to an examination of the goods and a corresponding notification of defects. Furthermore, given that the term "reasonable excuse" may trigger substantial legal uncertainties, it cannot be considered unduly harsh to exclude the application of Article 44 CISG in its entirety. From the author's point of view, the purchaser's legitimate interest in protecting his remedies in case of a defect is still preserved: In particular, under the suggested clause, the purchaser can expressly rely on Art 40 CISG in case the seller was aware or ought to have been aware of the defect.[457]

Subparagraphs 7–9

250 The seller's statutory responsibilities under the CISG with regard to **defects in title** are contained in Articles 41 and 42 CISG: Whereas Art 41 CISG deals with general defects in title, infringements of intellectual property rights, in particular caused by a resale or use of the contractual goods in the country of destination, are dealt with in Art 42 CISG.

251 The suggested terms leave both the seller's scope of responsibility under Art 41 CISG and the available remedies in case of general defects in title largely untouched. General defects in title (such as property or other security rights in the contractual goods claimed by third parties) that already existed at the time of delivery are foreseeable and manageable by the seller and a transfer of the goods into another jurisdiction should, contrary to an infringement of intellectual property rights, generally not cause any additional risk exposure. The only modification with regard to the scope of Art 41 CISG that is contained in § 5 (7) relates to the exclusion of the seller's responsibility for unjustified third-party claims. Accordingly, § 5 (7) does not oblige the seller to reimburse the purchaser for costs and expenses incurred as a result of a defense against unjustified or even frivolous claims. This restriction is in line with the vast majority of domestic sales laws[458] and should from the author's point of view be acceptable for the purchaser.

---

[457] It is also doubtful whether the application of Art 40 CISG can be excluded in case of a sales contract governed by (supplementary) Swiss law given that an exclusion may be considered as a hidden limitation of liability with the consequence that Art 100 CO applies, see I Schwenzer in Schlechtriem and Schwenzer (n 34) Art 40 CISG para 11.

[458] See, eg, USA: § 2–312 (3) UCC; Switzerland: Art 192, 197 CO; England: Sec 12 SGA 1979; Germany: § 435 German Civil Code.

V. Product Defects

§ 5 (7) follows a different approach with regard to the seller's responsibility for infringements of **intellectual property rights**. The transfer of the contractual goods into another jurisdiction may infringe existing intellectual property rights acknowledged in this jurisdiction even if (based on the generally accepted principle of territoriality)[459] both the use and resale of the products in the seller's country do not give rise to any concern. According to the prevailing view, a seller is under an indirect duty according to Art 42 CISG to investigate the existence of (registered) intellectual property rights in the relevant foreign jurisdiction (either the contemplated country of use or resale or – in the absence of any such contemplation of the parties – the country of the purchaser's residence).[460] However, a thorough research (even) of registered IP rights, such as trademarks, patents and utility models[461] in foreign jurisdictions may be difficult for the seller for a variety of reasons. According to § 5 (7), the seller will for that reason in deviation of Art 42 CISG be responsible for an infringement of an IP right in the foreign jurisdiction only if a similar property right has been registered in the seller's country of residence.[462] 252

It goes without saying that an exclusion of the seller's responsibility with regard to infringements of IP rights that are registered in the country of use but not in the jurisdiction of the seller may be difficult to swallow for the purchaser in individual cases. From the author's perspective, however, this result reflects last but not least the allocation of responsibilities that applies in the prevailing opinion also in the event of quality defects, as Art 35 CISG demands only compliance of the goods with public regulations acknowledged in the **country of dispatch** and not the country of use. 253

§ 5 (8) provides additionally for a limitation of available remedies once an infringement of IP rights (which the seller is responsible for) has been established. Given that a request for specific performance may meet with substantial obstacles (in particular if the third party whose IP right is at stake is unwilling to license the right at reasonable cost), the seller is entitled under § 5 (8) to refund the contract price instead. § 5 (9) clarifies finally that remedies based on defects of title are subject to a **timely notification** pursuant to Art 43 CISG whereas the purchaser cannot (similarly as in the case of quality defects) rely on an excuse pursuant to Art 44 CISG to submit this notice.[463] 254

---

[459] See Straus and Klunker (n 96).

[460] The prevailing opinion takes the view that a registration of the IP right in question in the relevant jurisdiction would justify the assumption that the seller could not have been unaware of that right, see Janal (n 98) 203, 212, with further references and a critical appraisal of this view.

[461] A number of countries offer utility model protection in addition to regular patent protection. A utility model (sometimes also referred to as a "petty patent") is similar to a patent though less stringent requirements (both procedurally and substantive-wise) have to be fulfilled for its acquisition and the term of protection is considerably shorter; for an overview of the countries that provide for utility model protection see the website of the World Intellectual Property Organization <http://www.wipo.int/sme/en/ip_business/utility_models/where.htm>.

[462] The suggested clause is influenced by the proposal of a patent indemnity clause by AJ Kasper in Kritzer et al (n 295) § 13–14. The wording of § 5 (7) seems also more reasonable from the perspective of the purchaser compared to a term that would solely accept an infringement of an intellectual property right registered in the seller's jurisdiction as a relevant contract breach: Such a clause would – based on the territorial restriction of IP rights – leave the purchaser almost completely unprotected given that the use or resale in the country of use does not infringe an IP right acknowledged in seller's jurisdiction on a stand-alone basis.

[463] § 5 (9) reiterates also § 43 (2) CISG: Accordingly, the seller is not entitled to rely on the omission of a notice if he knew of the right or claim on or before handover of the goods.

Subparagraph 10

255 Art 39 (2) CISG provides for a **long stop date** for the notification of (hidden) quality defects: Once a period of two years from the handover of the goods has lapsed and the purchaser has not submitted a notice indicating a defect of the goods to the seller, all remedies are lost – regardless of whether defects have or could have been detected during that time period.[464]

256 Though this "cut-off" period must be strictly distinguished from a limitation period,[465] Art 39 (2) CISG has nevertheless influenced the duration of the relevant **limitation period** set forth in Swiss domestic sales law: In order to avoid an (alleged) infringement of Art 39 (2) CISG by means of a literal application of Art 210 (1) CO Swiss courts have in the past regularly tried to align the limitation period in Art 210 (1) CO (that was only one year until changes in legislation in 2012) with the cut-off period stipulated in Art 39 (2) CISG.[466] Given that the present International Sales Terms have shortened the statutory limitation period provided by Art 210 CO for the benefit of the seller from two to one year (see the suggested § 7 on limitation of actions below), § 5 (10) accordingly shortens the "cut off" period to one year as well in order to align the two periods. At the same time, § 5 (10) extends the application of the "cut-off" period also to defects in title. By that means, the seller can limit the duration of his risk exposure as the applicable ten-year limitation period for claims based on a defect in title is – according to the Arts 127, 129 CO – at least arguably not subject to any contractual modification.

VI. Exclusion/Limitation of Damages Claims

1. The suggested clause

§ 6 LIMITATION OF DAMAGE CLAIMS

(1) Without prejudice to further limitations set forth below in this § 6 or elsewhere, damage claims of the Purchaser shall in any event only exist in case of negligence or intentional misconduct attributable to the Seller.

(2) Without prejudice to § 3 (Delay in Delivery) but notwithstanding anything to the contrary elsewhere, the Seller shall in no event and irrespective of the legal basis (contract, tort, indemnity or any other area of law) be liable to the Purchaser for loss of profit or revenue, wasted overhead, loss of production, loss of use, loss of data, cost of capital, cost of substitute goods, property damage external to the Products and any damage, expenditure or loss arising from such damage, any incidental, indirect or consequential damage or any of the foregoing suffered by any third party.

---

[464] OGH (19 Dec 2007) CISG-online 1628.

[465] A limitation period is the period during which the purchaser must perform a formal act such as bringing an action in front of a court respectively an arbitral tribunal in order to prevent that the claims will become time barred. The "cut-off period" contained in Art 39 (2) CISG on the other hand merely requires a notification of the purchaser whereas a warranty claim is (subject to a timely notification beforehand) still enforceable after the lapse of this period. Contrary to a limitation period, however, the "cut off period" is neither subject to discontinuation and/or suspension; see for further particulars ch C.VII below.

[466] That has been achieved either by way of an extension of the overall duration of the limitation period or by means of postponing its commencement, see ch A.IV.4 above.

VI. Exclusion/Limitation of Damages Claims

(3) Without prejudice to any further limitation of liability stipulated in this § 6 or elsewhere, Seller's overall liability arising from or connected to this Contract shall irrespective of the legal basis (contract, tort, indemnity or any other area of law) in the aggregate be limited to the Contract Price.

(4) The limitation of liability stipulated in the preceding subparagraphs of this § 6 shall apply regardless of whether any such damage or loss has been directly caused by the Seller or any of his subcontractors, agents, advisors or employees acting on his behalf.

(5) The aforementioned limitations of liability shall not apply in the following events for whose occurrence the burden of proof shall rest with the Purchaser:
a) gross negligence or willful misconduct attributable to the Seller. They do however apply in case of gross negligence of any other party acting for the Seller, including without limitation Seller's subcontractors, agents, advisors and employees but excluding Seller's legal representatives and executive staff.
b) in case of bodily injury culpably caused by an act or omission attributable to the Seller or
c) insofar as mandatory law provides otherwise.

(6) All limitations of liability stipulated in this § 6 shall also apply for the benefit of the Seller's subcontractors, agents, advisors, directors and employees.

[alternatively]

§ 6 EXCLUSION OF DAMAGE CLAIMS

(1) Without prejudice to § 3 (Delay in Delivery) but notwithstanding anything to the contrary elsewhere, the Seller shall in no event and irrespective of the legal basis (contract, tort, indemnity or any other area of law) be liable to the Purchaser for any damages, losses or expenditures, caused by defective products or otherwise, arising from or related to this Contract. This exclusion of liability applies regardless of whether any such damages, losses or expenditures have been directly caused by the Seller or by any of his subcontractors, agents, advisors or employees acting on his behalf.

(2) § 6 (1) shall not apply in the following events for whose occurrence the burden of proof shall rest with the Purchaser:
a) *gross negligence or willful misconduct attributable to the Seller. § 6 (1) does however apply in case of gross negligence of any other party acting on behalf of the Seller, including without limitation Seller's subcontractors, agents, advisors and employees but excluding Seller's legal representatives and executive staff.*
b) *in case of bodily injury culpably caused by an act or omission attributable to the Seller or*
c) *in so far as mandatory laws provide otherwise.*

(3) § 6 (1) shall to the same extent apply for the benefit of the Seller's subcontractors, agents, advisors, directors and employees.

2. General background

A contract clause limiting the seller's overall **liability for damages** is potentially the most important and often the most disputed provision in a sales contract. A reasonable limitation of liability is from the seller's perspective essential in order to control his overall risk exposure, particularly in case of defective contract goods or any delay in delivery. The seller must be especially aware of the fact that even an extended products liability insurance or third party liability insurance generally does not cover pure economic loss suffered as a result of defective goods, a delay in delivery or otherwise – even though the seller remains in principle fully responsible to compensate the purchaser for any such loss.

258   It has already been discussed above that the CISG – like many domestic legal systems[467] – allows the injured party to claim compensation for all (foreseeable) damages incurred due to a breach regardless of whether such damages are "direct" or "consequential" in nature.[468] Neither Art 79 (1) CISG nor the doctrine of **"foreseeability"** contained in Art 74 (1) CISG are able to render much comfort to the seller in that respect given that pure economic loss such as, among other heads of damages, lost profits and loss of production is generally foreseeable whenever the contract products were intended for production purposes.[469] This result has also been assumed in legal systems that apply similar restrictions on liability as does Art 74 CISG. The English case *Deepak Fertilizers Ltd v ICI Chemicals and Polymers Ltd* may serve as a good example in that regard: Both lost profits as well as wasted overheads caused by the destruction of a methanol plant (due to faulty construction plans provided under a know-how license agreement) were regarded by the English Court of Appeal as being "no more remote" than costs incurred for the reconstruction of the destroyed plant itself.[470]

259   By the same token, the **purchaser's risk exposure** arising from a sales contract is from the outset substantially lower:[471] Whereas the seller may face obstacles in relation to supplies of necessary raw materials and components or other flaws within the production process, transportation problems as well as a multitude of other impediments that may endanger timely and proper performance, the purchaser's contractual obligations that may trigger liability are basically limited to the timely payment of the contract price and taking over of the goods as provided by the contract. For that reason, the contract price generally serves as a cap on the purchaser's liability: If the seller claims lost profits or a loss of volumes, his claim cannot exceed the contract price minus saved expenses. It therefore seems justified that a limitation of liability clause in a sales contract is specifically tailored for the benefit of the seller.

260   Drafting an exemption clause requires special consideration. Many domestic jurisdictions apply a strict "contra proferentem" approach in particular with regard to the interpretation of limitation clauses contained in standard form contracts.[472] According

---

[467] Islamic law (that forms part of the civil laws in some Arabic States) does in principle not allow a recovery of lost profits as well as damages for any delay with delivery in the event of a contract breach and is therefore a notable exception, see FE Vogel and SL Hayes, *Islamic Law and Finance* (Kluwer Law International, New York 1998) 51 and N Saleh, "Remedies for Breach of Contract Under Islamic and Arab Laws" (1989) 269 Arab Law Quarterly 269, 280. For a general survey of national laws with regard to the recovery of damages in case of a contract breach JY Gotanda, "Damages in Lieu of Performance because of Breach of Contract" (Villanova University School of Law Working Paper Series 2006, P. 53) <http://law.bepress.com/villanovalwps/papers/art53/>.
[468] OGH (15 Jan 2013) CISG-online No 2398.
[469] See n 135 and 136 above.
[470] [1999] 1 Lloyd's Rep 387 para 90. But see also the latest relevant judgment of the House of Lords in the "Achilleas" case (n 134 above).
[471] See also J Hellner, "Consequential Loss and Exemption Clauses" (1981) 1 OJLS 13, 19.
[472] See with regard to general terms for instance Germany: § 305 c BGB; Switzerland: Uncertainty rule (*Unklarheitsregel*) that has been developed by case law, BG (17 Jul 1989) BGE 115 II 264; China: Art 41 Contract Law 1999. English law applies the "contra proferentem rule" with regard to

to the **"contra proferentem" rule**, the party that has proffered the disputed clause to the other party bears the risk of any potential ambiguities.[473] Although the CISG takes precedence over domestic law with regard to the interpretation and construction of contract terms, it is widely accepted that the "contra proferentem rule" has also found its way into the CISG via Art 8 (2) CISG.[474] Therefore, an exemption clause should to the utmost extent possible be transparent, unambiguous and comprehensive in order to accomplish its intended goal. The latter entails for instance a clarification of the scope of the intended limitation clause as well as a precise definition of the heads of losses falling within its ambit.

Another general drafting rule that needs to be taken into consideration is linked to the so-called **"blue pencil test"** that is strictly applied in some jurisdictions:[475] According to this test, the invalid part of the contractual clause in question is deleted and only a severable and grammatically meaningful remainder of the clause will survive. Therefore, a limitation clause should (as a rule of thumb) be drafted as severally as possible in order to ensure that a partial invalidity of the clause leaves the remainder of the provision intact. The Swiss Federal Supreme Court has so far – at least with regard to B2B-contracts – not applied a strict blue pencil test and even inseparable and overly broad clauses were accordingly upheld to the maximum legally permissible extent.[476] But this approach is not undisputed and some scholars have taken the view that a stricter course of action is required – in particular in relation to general terms and conditions.[477] 261

Finally, a limitation clause should explicitly stipulate that it **prevails** over any other contract terms. In commercial reality, many international contracts contain clauses that expressly impose liability upon one of the parties for particular breaches of contract while a limitation clause seeks at the same time to restrict or exclude exactly that kind of liability. Accordingly the contract may become inconsistent if neither clause contains an order of priority, and the enforceability of the limitation clause will be put at jeopardy. In order to clarify that a limitation clause will override any other inconsistent rule imposing liability on a contracting party, the term *notwithstanding* [anything to the contrary in this contract or elsewhere] should be used at the beginning of the clause. Non-native speakers often confuse this term with the expression "without prejudice", which means exactly the opposite.[478] 262

---

contractual clauses in general (even with regard to clauses individually drafted for one single transaction), see McMeel (n 206) para 8.4 ff; see also Art 4.6 UPICC: If contract terms supplied by one party are unclear, an interpretation against that party is preferred.

[473] M Schmidt-Kessel in Schlechtriem and Schwenzer (n 34) Art 8 CISG para 47.

[474] Brunner (n 114) Art 8 CISG para 45.

[475] In particular German case law applies a strict "blue pencil test" with regard to general terms and conditions (*Verbot der geltungserhaltenden Reduktion*), BGH (17 Feb 2004) [2004] NJW 1588, 1589.

[476] See Schwenzer (n 181) para 32.44 with further references. However, BG (18 December 2008) File No 4A_404/2008 has applied a strict blue pencil test in relation to a consumer contract. According to Ehle and Brunschweiler (n 175) 269, this judgment may also be of relevance in commercial contracts.

[477] See in particular Schwenzer (n 181) para 24.08; R Wey in Amstutz et al (n 168) Art 100 CO para 18.

[478] See Daigneault (n 238) 75.

3. Annotations

a) The second alternative:

Subparagraph 1

263 The second suggested alternative of the clause makes it rather plain and simple: Any damage claims are excluded **in their entirety** with the sole exception of claims based on delay in delivery that are already dealt with (and separately capped) in § 3 of the present International Sales Terms. § 6 (1) applies not only in relation to the seller's contractual liability but also explicitly covers the purchaser's concurring tort-based claims. The latter is especially important[479] given that a purchaser is generally believed[480] to be entitled to claim damages under tort in case of property damage (external to the goods) caused by defective goods in addition to the contractual claims for damages based on Art 74 CISG.[481]

264 Due to the fact that § 6 (1) excludes rather than limits the Seller's liability to pay damages, further stipulations as to specific heads of damages or losses are not necessary. On the contrary, the enumeration of specific heads could trigger ambiguities about the intended scope of the exemption.[482]

265 The seller should keep in mind that even such a broad exclusion of liability cannot provide protection against **damage claims by third parties** (who are not bound by the contract, including any limitation of liability clause stated in it) under tort. Claims by third parties under tort in case of defective goods are according to the tort laws of most legal systems generally limited to property damage (external to the contract goods) or bodily injury (as well as consequential loss resulting from either such property damage or bodily injury) and do not cover pure economic loss. In some jurisdictions, however, a manufacturer's product liability towards third parties extends also to pure economic losses in general.[483] The problem of a seller's continuing liability under tort law towards third parties could in principle be addressed by way of an indemnity clause providing for an obligation of the purchaser to indemnify the seller against any third-party claims to the same extent that the seller has disclaimed his liability to the purchaser.[484] However, from the

---

[479] Though the Swiss Federal Supreme Court has taken the view that a limitation of liability clause covers in principle also concurring claims under tort even in the absence of an explicit term to that effect (see inter alia BG (13 Jan 1994) BGE 120 II 58, 61), stricter standards may apply with regard to limitation of liability clauses contained in general terms and conditions, see Brunner (n 114) Art 5 CISG para 3.

[480] Huber and Mullis (n 440) 27.

[481] In case of bodily injury caused by defective products, domestic tort laws will in any event apply, Art 5 CISG. Swiss law does in principle acknowledge concurring claims under contract and tort, see Honsell (n 87) 111.

[482] In international commercial contracts, limitation of liability clauses are frequently used that stipulate the exclusion of all "direct, consequential, incidental" damages etc. That wording may leave room for doubts whether some categories of damages were not intended to be covered by the exclusion.

[483] For instance, Dutch Law permits in principle the recovery of pure economic loss under tort; see I Giesen and M Loos, "Liability for Defective Products and Services: The Netherlands" (2002) 6.4 EJCL para 2.5 (<http://www.ejcl.org/64/art64-6.html>).

[484] See for example the suggested (limited) indemnity clause in relation to property damages external to the goods contained in § 40 Orgalime S 2012 (n 10): "The Supplier shall not be liable for any damage to property caused by the Product [...] whilst it is in the possession of the Purchaser. [...] If the Supplier incurs liability towards any third party for such damage to property as

VI. Exclusion/Limitation of Damages Claims

author's point of view, it is questionable[485] whether such a clause is enforceable: An **indemnity** covering also claims of third parties under tort against the seller not only shifts liability for negligent acts of the seller to the purchaser. At the same time, the purchaser is in this event often not in a position to either take sufficient contractual precautions against potential risks resulting from such an indemnity (given that third parties, in particular "innocent bystanders", may be harmed by defective products but have no contractual relationship with the purchaser) or to procure adequate insurance coverage for these risks. As a result, § 6 does not contain an additional indemnity provision. Besides the discussed doubts as to its enforceability, this also reflects the commercial experience that usually neither contractual party is willing to provide indemnities to the other party even against third-party claims that are due to the negligent act or omission of the indemnified party.

As has already been discussed in detail, it remains unclear for the time being whether Swiss law may restrain limitation of liability clauses in general terms and conditions to a greater extent than it has been reflected in § 6. Some risks will therefore remain. They can be minimized if the first alternative of the clause is used. In the author's opinion, however, this second alternative of § 6 should be valid and enforceable as well. Though an **exclusion of liability** may undoubtedly entail stricter scrutiny than a mere limitation of certain heads of losses, it should be kept in mind that the purchaser remains not only entitled to demand the repair of defective goods but may also declare the avoidance of the contract (plus restitution of the contract price) in case of a fundamental breach. Finally, given that the purchaser may still demand a reduction of the contract price in case of a defect, he can also recover so-called "market-measured damages", representing a reduced market value of the defective goods in the absence of a fundamental breach. 266

Subparagraph 2

According to Art 100 (1) CO[486], liability cannot be excluded or restricted in case of gross negligence or intent. Further restrictions apply with regard to bodily injury 267

---

described in the preceding paragraph, the Purchaser shall indemnify, defend and hold the Supplier harmless." For a similar clause in the context of a model distributorship agreement W Döser, *Vertragsgestaltung im internationalen Wirtschaftsrecht* (C.H. Beck, München 2001) 72: "To the extent that Principal disclaims responsibility for warranties and liability for damages hereunder, Distributor shall indemnify Principal from, and hold it harmless against, all claims by third parties based upon Products supplied by the Principal to Distributor [...]."

[485] Under Swiss law, an indemnity clause in the indicated scope contained in general terms and conditions may fall within the ambit of the "unusual terms rule" (*Ungewöhnlichkeitsregel*) though an infringement of Art 19, 20 CO and Art 27 (2) CC may also be possible. For the admissibility of "risk-shifting clauses" (*Risikoüberwälzungsklauseln*) in general (subject to Art 27 CC) however Weber (n 169) Art 100 CO para 75. English law acknowledges "reverse indemnities" even in case of negligence of the indemnitee if the indemnity provision explicitly stipulates the same; see for example the decision of the House of Lords in *EE Caledonia Ltd v Orbit Valve Ltd* [1994] 1 WLR 1515, 1522.

[486] It has been submitted by some scholars that a limitation of liability clause covering also intentional misconduct or gross negligence would already be unenforceable under the CISG by reason of a violation of the good faith principle derived from Art 7 (1) CISG; see in particular U Magnus in Staudinger (n 29) Art 45 CISG para 46; in the same direction I Schwenzer and P Hachem, "The CISG – Successes and Pitfalls" (2009) 57 Am J Comp L 457, 473 f. It is respectfully submitted that this view is not entirely convincing: On the one hand, Art 7 (1) CISG deals only with the interpretation of the Convention in the light of inter alia the "observance of good faith in international trade" and does (in particular in accordance with Art 6 CISG) not stipulate manda-

C. The International Sales Terms

(Art 20 CO) and mandatory product liability laws. § 6 (2) reflects these outer limits. However, in the author's view, liability incurred by means of gross negligent acts of employees, subcontractors or other parties acting on behalf of the seller (excluding managing directors and executive employees) can in principle also be excluded if a sales contract is primarily governed by the CISG and supplemented by Swiss domestic law. Art 101 (2) CO permits an exclusion of liability even in case of intentional misconduct of auxiliary personnel of the seller whereas the CISG (in the absence of any provisions restricting the parties in their freedom to deviate from its provisions) does not take precedence over this article.[487] Accordingly, the counter-exemption stipulated in 6 (2) lit a does not cover grossly negligent (though intentional) acts by auxiliary personnel of the seller.

268 Finally, § 6 (2) places the **burden of proof** for the occurrence of any of the events stipulated in the counter-exemption on the purchaser. This appears to be a clarification rather than an amendment of the legal position under Swiss law: According to the Swiss Federal Supreme Court, it is generally up to the innocent party to prove that an exemption clause does not apply due to intentional or grossly negligent misconduct attributable to the breaching party.[488]

b) The first alternative

269 The first alternative provides for a **limitation** rather than the exclusion of the purchaser's damage claims. In order to reduce the seller's liability to a reasonable extent, this wording of § 6 introduces the principle of fault instead of strict liability, excludes certain heads of damages and provides for an overall cap on liability for damages.

---

tory rules and restrictions with regard to any limitation of liability. It is also rather doubtful whether mandatory liability in case of gross negligence reflects a generally accepted universal principle of contract law. For instance, restrictions set forth both in the UCC as well as in the English Unfair Contract Terms Act 1977 are apparently less concerned with the *degree* of fault but rather with the type of damages the parties intend to exclude. Sec. 2-719 (3) UCC does permit an exclusion of consequential damages unless such an exclusion is unconscionable: Limitation of consequential damages for injury to the person in the case of consumer goods is prima facie unconscionable but limitation of damages where the loss is commercial is not. According to the English UCTA 1977, a contractual limitation of liability inter alia in case of negligence is subject to a "reasonableness" test. Schedule 2 of the UCTA provides certain criteria for these tests but does not make reference to different degrees of fault. German law does allow an exclusion of liability in individually negotiated contracts save for intentional misconduct, see § 276 (3) German Civil Code; similarly Art 401 (4) of the Russian Civil Code. It should also be taken into consideration that the definition of the legal term "gross negligence" in common law jurisdictions may deviate from its meaning in civil law jurisdictions: For instance, pursuant to public policy considerations of the laws of New York, limitations of liability will not apply to exemption of willful or grossly negligent acts. However, the courts of New York have interpreted gross negligence as "conduct that evinces a reckless disregard for the rights of others or "smacks" of intentional wrongdoing", thereby applying a substantially higher threshold compared to German or Swiss law. On the other hand, according at least to the traditional view of English courts, a substantial difference between the legal concept of "negligence" and "gross negligence" has in principle not been accepted, see G Odry, "Exclusion of Consequential Damages: Write What You Mean" [2012] ICL Rev 142, 154 ff. with further references to English and New York case law.

[487] Contra Brunner (n 114) Art 4 CISG para 15, who takes the view that Art 101 (2) CO is not applicable in a contract predominantly governed by the CISG given that the CISG does not distinguish between liability directly incurred by the seller and liability imposed on the seller by reason of negligent acts of any auxiliary person acting on his behalf.

[488] See BG (2 Jun 1981) BGE 107 II 161, 167.

VI. Exclusion/Limitation of Damages Claims

Subparagraph 1

A damage claim under the CISG does not require **fault** on the part of the party in breach. It has already been submitted that the distinction between strict liability as foreseen by the CISG on the one hand and the principle of fault liability anchored in civil law jurisdictions is potentially less important than one might assume at first glance.[489] However, the distinction between fault and **strict liability** may from a commercial point of view remain especially relevant in case of distributors who simply resell goods to end customers and are not involved in either the construction, manufacture or even the packaging of the contractual goods. Although the mere resale of defective products generally does not constitute fault, the distributor would nevertheless face liability for any damage incurred through the defect because of the principle of strict liability maintained by the CISG.

Against this background, § 6 (1) replaces the seller's strict liability with the fault liability principle. This approach has so far not raised any substantial concerns among courts and can therefore be introduced even in general terms and conditions.[490]

Subparagraph 2

As an alternative to the exclusion of liability for damages (that is usually only accepted by a purchaser if the seller has substantial bargaining power), commercial contracts often exclude either party's liability for "**consequential**" and "indirect" damages.

However, it is dangerous from the seller's point of view to rely on such a clause that does not specify the intended limitation of liability more precisely. The majority of domestic legal systems as well as the CISG hold a breaching party liable for "direct" as well as for "consequential" damage caused by a contract breach, subject only to the doctrine of remoteness in common law countries and (with some modifications) under the CISG, respectively the existence of an adequate causal connection between breach and damage in civil law systems.[491] For that very reason, neither the CISG nor the majority of domestic laws provide a definition of either "direct" or "consequential" respectively "indirect" damage.

It follows that most legal systems are not adequately equipped to provide the necessary dogmatic foundation for the construction of "consequential" or "indirect" damages waiver clauses used in a commercial contract. Even legal systems that use these terms in their sales law statutes have generally not accomplished a satisfactory delineation between direct and consequential loss.[492] For instance, although the

---

[489] For a detailed analysis and the limited relevance of the distinction between fault and strict liability K Riesenhuber, "Damages for Non-Performance and the Fault Principle" [2008] ERCL 119 ff.

[490] See also n 29 above for further reference.

[491] Zweigert and Kötz (n 316) 601.

[492] See for this problem in general P Ostendorf and P Kluth, "Die Auslegung von Folgeschadenausschlussklauseln im internationalen Vertragsrecht" [2009] RIW 428 ff. For a notable exception see Sec 67 (1) of the Finnish Sale of Goods Act 355/1987 that defines the meaning of indirect damages in a comprehensive, clear and rather broad (!) manner, see the unofficial translation of the Finnish Ministry of Justice, <http://www.finlex.fi/en/laki/kaannokset/1987/en19870355>: Damages for breach of contract consist of compensation for expenses, price difference, lost profit and other direct or indirect loss due to the breach. (2) Indirect loss consists of the following: (1) loss due to reduction or interruption in production or turnover; (2) other loss arising because the goods cannot be used as intended; (3) loss of profit arising because a contract with a third party has been lost or

Uniform Commercial Code is one of the few domestic sales laws that elaborate on the term "consequential" damages, the statutory definition has not contributed much assistance for the construction of consequential damages waiver clauses.[493] At first glance, § 2–715 (2) UCC seems to interpret **consequential damage** as almost any loss that is not linked to the value of the goods (the latter being the so-called "market-measured" loss).[494] In particular, the wording of § 2–715 UCC indicates that "consequential damages" cover inter alia loss of profit[495], loss of production as well as any damage to property external to the goods. However, although some US courts have indeed applied such a broad understanding,[496] this interpretation is far from being undisputed: The official commentary on the UCC states the intention to incorporate the old common law doctrine of Hadley v Baxendale[497] which, in line with the majority view having evolved in England (see below), considers consequential damage as being only the damage that would not have occurred in the absence *of some special circumstances* applicable to the non-breaching party. Lost profits and loss of use may accordingly also under US law constitute direct damages in individual cases.[498]

275   **English courts** have interpreted the term "consequential damages" in exemption clauses in a particularly narrow manner. This is, for example, well illustrated by the decision of the English Court of Appeal in Hotel Services v Hilton Hotels.[499] In this case, the Hilton Hotel Group claimed damages from a lessor of innovative hotel minibars (so-called "Robobars") that enabled the hotel to bill each guest automatically in case of a removal of a drink from the bar in the hotel room. Hilton had rented Robobars for its hotels in London with the intention to prevent hotel guests

---

breached; (4) loss due to damage to property other than the goods sold; and (5) other similar loss that is difficult to foresee.

[493] Pursuant to § 2–715 (2) UCC, consequential damages include (from the perspective of an injured purchaser) any losses resulting from general or particular requirements and needs of the purchaser of which the seller at the time of contracting had reason to know and which could not reasonably be prevented by resale or otherwise as well as injury to person or property proximately resulting from any breach of warranty. Incidental damages (a separate category of damages acknowledged by US law) on the other hand include any commercially reasonable charges, expenses or commissions incurred in stopping delivery, in the transportation, care and custody of the goods after the purchaser's breach, in connection with return or resale of the goods or otherwise, see § 2–710 (2) UCC. Though there is no statutory definition of "indirect" damages in the UCC, the prevailing opinion interprets both "consequential" and "incidental" damages as subgroups of "incidental" resp. "special" damages whereas "direct" and "general" damages are used interchangeably as well, PS Turner, "Consequential Damages: Hadley v. Baxendale Under the Uniform Commercial Code" (2001) 54 SMUL Rev 655, 662 f.

[494] Damages based on the value of the goods (e.g. diminution of their value, costs related to a cover purchase etc.) are direct, respectively "general" or "ordinary" damages, see RR Anderson, "Incidental and Consequential Damages" (1987) 7 J L & Com 327, 328.

[495] Profits necessarily inherent in the contract will however always constitute direct loss even if a broad interpretation of "consequential" loss is applied, see GD West and SG Duran, "Reassessing the 'Consequences' of Consequential Damages Waivers in Acquisition Agreements" [2008] Bus Lawyer 777, 792.

[496] For a similar view apparently Gabriel (n 113) 207; Anderson (n 494) 335.

[497] T Diamond and H Foss, "Consequential damages for commercial loss: An alternative to Hadley v Baxendale" (1994) Fordham Law Review 665, 670, citing further relevant case law confirming that view.

[498] See in particular West and Duran (n 495) 790 f.

[499] *Hotel Services Ltd v Hilton International Hotels (UK) Ltd* [2000] EWCA Civ 74.

VI. Exclusion/Limitation of Damages Claims

from cheating and to increase profitability. After it turned out that the chillers of the Robobars were defective, Hilton did not only claim damages with regard to the costs of removal and storage of the bars but also lost profits. The Court of Appeal upheld the claim and rejected reliance of the lessor on an exemption clause in the lease contract that excluded any liability of the lessor for "consequential and indirect damages". In reaching this result, the court relied on the view that the line between direct damages and consequential losses had to be drawn "along the boundary between the first and second limbs of Hadley v Baxendale". As the claimed damages arose naturally, in the opinion of the court, according to the usual course of things from the breach of contract, they fell within the ambit of the first limb of Hadley v Baxendale and therefore constituted direct rather than consequential loss.[500]

It remains unclear whether a court or an arbitral tribunal in charge of interpreting a waiver for a consequential loss clause governed by the **CISG** would take recourse to the developments under common law or aim for an autonomous "international" interpretation of that term. In the author's view, however, there is a good likelihood that the basic understanding of "consequential damages" as developed by the courts in common law countries may have a certain impact on the interpretation – last but not least because Art 74 CISG shares some essential features with the "remoteness" doctrine anchored in common law. 276

Additionally, it should be taken into account that the picture is similarly blurred in **civil law jurisdictions**: For instance, indirect damages have been defined under Swiss domestic law as those damages which arise due to a new cause that would not have occurred without the first harmful event.[501] It is generally agreed that the definition of "consequential damages" is apparently based on identical considera- 277

---

[500] This position has inter alia been confirmed by *Regus (UK) Ltd v Epcot Solutions Ltd* [2008] EWCA Civ 361 para 28: "Loss of profits are often thought of as consequential losses, but may well be direct"; see also more recently *Markerstudy Insurance Company Ltd & Ors v Endsleigh Insurance Services Ltd* [2010] EWHC 281 (Comm) and *McCain Foods Gb Ltd v Eco-Tec (Europe) Ltd* [2011] EWHC 66 (TCC). See also the decision of the Court of Appeal in *British Sugar Plc v NEI Power Projects Ltd & Anor* [1997] EWCA Civ 2438, where the court held that increased production costs and loss of profit as the result of faulty power station equipment did not constitute consequential but direct loss. See further the decision in *Deepak Fertilizers and Petrochemicals Corp v ICI Chemicals & Polymers Ltd.* [1999] 1 Lloyd's Rep 387: Wasted overheads incurred during reconstruction of a plant following destruction, for which the defendant was contractually liable were considered as direct loss that did not fall within the ambit of a contractual clause excluding liability for consequential loss. The House of Lords has however so far not confirmed the legal position of the Court of Appeal, see *Caledonian North Sea Ltd. v British Telecommunications plc* [2002] 1 Lloyd's Rep 553 (Lord Hoffmann); see also McMeel (n 206) para 21.56 ff. The jurisprudence of the English Court of Appeal with regard to the construction of "consequential damages" has also recently been expressly rejected by Australian courts: The Supreme Court of Victoria turned down claims for costs of labor incurred in an attempt to cure defects of the contractual goods by the purchaser (in this case an afterburner used to incinerate gaseous emissions of a production plant) as well as extra costs of gas incurred due to the forced use of the old afterburner: The court based its decision on the view that all claimed damages fell within the ambit of a consequential loss waiver clause, see *Environmental Systems Pty Ltd v Peerless Holdings Pty Ltd* [2008] VSCA 26. For a general overview see also J Sidnell, "Consequential Damages: Are Exclusions of Consequential Damages Inconsequential?" [2010] CCCL Journal 2010, 106 ff.

[501] T Siegenthaler and J Griffiths, "Indirect and Consequential Loss Clauses under Swiss Law" [2003] ICL Rev 446, 451.

tions of causation.⁵⁰² The "parrot case"⁵⁰³ illustrates also that the scope of "direct losses" in a sales transaction may be much wider than expected, least from the point of view of the Swiss Federal Supreme Court: Although lost profits are generally (and contrary to English law) regarded as "consequential" or, as the case may be, "indirect losses", property damage external to the goods caused by defective contract goods has been explicitly identified as (potential) direct damage.⁵⁰⁴

278 The prevailing view under **German law** seems to favor a broader understanding of "consequential loss" that contains in particular damage to property external to the contractual goods respectively bodily injury.⁵⁰⁵ It is nevertheless rather doubtful whether German courts would adhere to that view with regard to the construction of this term in a limitation of liability clause. Besides the ongoing controversy in both jurisdictions, Swiss and German courts have regularly applied a "contra proferentem rule" in order to narrow down the scope of exemption clauses excluding or restricting the liability for "consequential losses". In the case of a shipyard relying on a contractual exemption clause that excluded the liability for both indirect and consequential loss (*indirekte und Folgeschäden*), the German Federal Supreme Court held that only "atypical and not foreseeable" damages fell within the ambit of the clause. As a result, the claimant, a customer of the shipyard whose ship was destroyed due to negligent acts of the shipyard's personnel during repair works, was in addition to compensation for the destruction of its property entitled to damages incurred by loss of use as well as costs of an expert report.⁵⁰⁶ The Swiss Federal Supreme Court has on the other hand interpreted an exemption clause limiting the contractual liability of an architect to "direct losses" in a standard form contract as a mere restatement that any liability would presuppose an adequate causal link.⁵⁰⁷ As a result, the clause was completely ineffective given that its impact was reduced to the mere confirmation of general statutory requirements for contractual liability under Swiss law.

279 To cut a long story short: The terms indirect and consequential damages used in a limitation of liability clause remain a "black box" in international contract law

---

⁵⁰² The Swiss Code of Obligations distinguishes explicitly between direct and consequential loss in the articles on sales law; see in particular Art 208 (2) and 208 (3) CO. Lost profit has predominantly been considered as a "consequential" loss, see Honsell (n 87) 107. On the other hand, damages of the goods itself can be claimed under Art 208 (2) CO as direct damages, see H Giger in Honsell et al (n 164) Art 208 CO para 36 ff.

⁵⁰³ See n 504 below.

⁵⁰⁴ See in particular the decision of the Swiss Federal Supreme Court, BG (28 Nov 2006) BGE 133 III 257: In this case, the seller had supplied the purchaser, a professional parrot breeder, with six infected parrots. The sold parrots infected also the existing stock of parrots and caused additional losses amounting to roughly 2 Mio Swiss Francs. Contrary to the view of the courts of the lower instances, the Federal Supreme Court considered the entire loss related to the infection of the existing stock of parrots as a "direct loss" giving that the infection of the existing stock were held to constitute a direct consequence of the supply of infected parrots. For a critical assessment of this decision and the recourse to considerations of causation as means to delineate direct and consequential loss in general H Honsell, "Der Mangelfolgeschaden beim Kauf – der Papageienfall des Bundesgerichts" [2007] recht 154, 155; further P Pichonnaz, "Defective Goods and Consequential Loss – A Swiss Case and Some Reflections on Limitation of Damages" (2012) 76 RabelsZ 819, 821 ff.

⁵⁰⁵ The qualification of "pure economic loss" (eg, lost profits/loss of use directly incurred due to defective goods) as either direct or consequential loss is however controversial, see P Ostendorf and P Kluth (n 492) 430.

⁵⁰⁶ BGH (29 Nov 1988) [1989] NJW-RR 953, 956. See also BGH (8 June 1994) [1994] DB 2073.

⁵⁰⁷ BG (18 Jul 2000) BGE 126 III 388.

and only few legal systems have been able to provide satisfactory solutions for their construction. That also holds true with regard to the CISG, as an autonomous "international" definition of consequential losses has so far not evolved. As a consequence, it is from the seller's perspective essential to explicitly exclude **specific heads of losses** such as loss of profits and revenue, loss of production and the like instead of relying on the mere exclusion of "consequential" and "indirect" damages. These specific heads of losses should also be excluded on a stand-alone basis rather than as sub-sets of "consequential damages": Otherwise, the seller may remain liable for all those losses of production and loss of profits etc. that were objectively foreseeable and would therefore constitute a "direct" rather than a "consequential" loss. Though this view is a peculiarity of English case law[508], it may also have a certain impact on the interpretation of limitation clauses governed by the CISG.

280 If these basic drafting rules are observed, it will not do any harm from the seller's perspective to also exclude the seller's liability for "consequential" damages separately and in addition to the exclusion of the more specific heads of damages.

Subparagraph 3

281 § 6 (3) provides for an additional overall **cap on liability** for those damage claims that have not already been excluded pursuant to § 6 (2). Accordingly, § 6 (3) will become relevant in particular with respect to damages and expenditures incurred as a result of repair work undertaken by the purchaser himself as well as costs of a cover transaction performed by the purchaser or other market measured damages. It should be noted that the cap set forth in § 6 (3) does not apply to any expenses incurred by the seller himself with regard to repair or replacement of defective goods or any restitution claim (i. e. refund of the contract price) in case of an avoidance of the contract.[509]

VII. Limitation of Actions

1. The suggested clause

§ 7 LIMITATION OF ACTIONS

(1) It is expressly agreed that the Purchaser cannot bring an action based on a quality defect before the arbitral tribunal or any court of law nor plead the existence of any such defect as a defense against any action of the Seller based on the non-performance by the Purchaser after one (1) year from the handover of the Products to the Purchaser and regardless of whether the defect has been or ought to have been detected by that time.

---

[508] *Markerstudy Insurance Company Ltd & Ors v Endsleigh Insurance Services Ltd* [2010] EWHC 281 (Comm) para 17: "The use of the phrase "including but not limited to" is a strong pointer that the specified heads of loss are but examples of the excluded indirect loss."

[509] The latter may in principle be achieved by the following addendum to the third subparagraph: *"The amount of this overall cap on liability shall be reduced by any costs incurred by the Seller to make good any defect or any refund of the contract price in case of an avoidance of the contract."* Such an addendum would however essentially restrain the purchaser from recovering any damages in case of an avoidance of the contract.

C. The International Sales Terms

(2) § 7 (1) shall also apply in relation to any claims of the Purchaser based on concurring claims under tort arising from defective Products.

(3) The statute of limitations of one year cannot be invoked by the Seller if it can be proven that he willfully deceived the Purchaser.

(4) Remedial measures of the Seller in case of any defect, including but not limited to either repair or replacement of the Products or any parts thereof shall not trigger the commencement of a new limitation period. Any such remedial measure by the Seller or any third party acting on his behalf shall not be deemed to constitute a tacit acknowledgement of debt or liability on the part of the Seller.

2. General background

282   The evaluation of the seller's scope of liability arising from a sales contract must also consider time aspects. The applicable limitation periods of the governing law[510] set the **time period** during which the parties may enforce claims based on a breach of contract or under tort. Once all applicable limitation periods have expired, no such claims can be brought any longer and the seller can liquidate any reserves that may have been set up, in particular to cover potential warranty claims.

283   Besides the significant impact of **limitation periods**, the parties to a commercial transaction often fail to pay adequate attention to this issue and to the impact of the governing law on the time limits of liability.[511] The whole matter is further complicated by the fact that the meaning of the terms in (international) commercial contracts stipulating time periods with regard to the conformity of the goods is often ambiguous and frequently gives rise to substantial misunderstandings.[512] In particular, if the parties agree on a specified "warranty period", "defects liability period" or "defects notification period" in a sales contract, the period may in each case be interpreted (either by the parties or by a court or an arbitral tribunal called upon to resolve a contractual dispute) in one (or, in the alternate, even as a combination of some) of the following manners:

---

[510] The applicable limitation period falls pursuant to the majority of conflict of laws statutes within the ambit of the governing law of the contract respectively the law governing the relevant non-contractual obligations; see, eg, with regard to the EU member states: Art 12 (1) lit d Rome I Regulation (n 3); Art 15 lit h Rome II Regulation (n 318); Switzerland: Art 148 PILA. Anglo-American law has traditionally considered limitation periods as forming part of the procedural law (therefore belonging to the lex fori) though this view has been more and more undermined in recent years, see I Schwenzer and S Manner, "The Claim is Time-Barred: The Proper Limitation Regime for International Sales Contracts in International Commercial Arbitration" [2007] Arb Int 2007, 293, 296 f. The applicable limitation periods of domestic sales laws for warranty claims based on non-conforming (moveable) goods deviate substantially: Spain: Six months (Art. 1490 Codigo Civil); Germany, Switzerland and France: 2 years (§ 438 (2) German Civil Code; Art. 210 (1) CO, Art 1648 Code Civil); Russia: 3 years (Art 196 Civil Code); USA, China and the United Nations Convention on the Limitation Period in the International Sales of Goods 1974: 4 years (§ 2–725 UCC; Art 129 Contract Law 1999; Art 8 UN-Convention), England: 6 years (Sec 5 Limitation Act 1980) whereas the limitation period will amount to 12 years in case the parties have entered into a "Deed" instead of a simple contract (Sec 8 Limitation Act 1980). The respective limitation periods in the various domestic legal systems commence regularly upon handover of the goods though some jurisdictions apply the "discovery rule" also for contractual claims (see for instance Art 129 of the Chinese Contract Law 1999 and Art 1648 of the French Civil Code).

[511] See Schwenzer and Manner (n 510) 294.

[512] See, eg, the existing controversy with regard to the "Defects Notification Period" provided by the FIDIC-conditions, see ch A.I above.

VII. Limitation of Actions

- An extension or, as the case may be, a shortening of the applicable statutory **limitation period**; i.e. the period during which the purchaser must perform a formal act such as bringing an action before a court or an arbitral tribunal.[513] 284
- An amendment of the **"cut-off provision"**[514] contained in Art 39 (2) CISG[515] that requires the purchaser to give notice of a defect during the stipulated period of time, all remedies being lost if (even latent) defects[516] have not been reported by the end of the period (though an action can be brought thereafter, subject to the applicable limitation period, provided that notice has been given in time beforehand). Unlike a limitation period, a cut-off period is not subject to any suspension or discontinuation.[517] 285
- The definition of the time frame (respectively the **life cycle**) during which the contract goods are to remain in good working condition, the stipulated period constituting neither a waiver of shorter cut-off or limitation periods nor a "guarantee of durability".[518] 286
- A **"guarantee of durability"** (respectively promissory warranty or "warranty extending to future performance") that may extend the seller's obligations regarding the quality of the goods both substantively and in terms of time.[519] Under a guarantee of durability, the seller is in principle liable for any defects that may occur throughout the indicated time period – regardless of whether or not (the roots for) these defects already existed at the time of the handover of the goods to the purchaser.[520] In addition, a guarantee of durability may (depending on the (supplementary) governing law) trigger an extension of the applicable limitation periods: Pursuant to some domestic laws, the applicable limitation periods for claims based on the breach of a guarantee of durability commence (similar to claims under tort in accordance with the "discovery rule") only once the defect has been (or ought to have been) detected. Although the CISG contains 287

---

[513] D Girsberger, "The Time Limits of Article 39 CISG (2005–2006) 25 J L & Commerce 241, 248.

[514] See for this terminology JO Honnold, *Uniform Law for International Sales under the 1980 United Nations Convention* (3rd edn Kluwer Law International, The Hague 1999) § 258.

[515] See Schwenzer and Manner (n 510) 300.

[516] OGH (19 Dec 2007) CISG-online 1628.

[517] See D Akikol, *Die Voraussetzungen der Sachmängelhaftung beim Warenkauf* (Schulthess, Zürich 2008) 352.

[518] That was apparently the interpretation chosen by a Swedish arbitral tribunal with regard to a contract clause pursuant to which the contract goods would last at least for a period of 30 years, see Arbitration Institute of the Stockholm Chamber of Commerce (5 Jun 1998) CISG-online 379: "It may well be that the representatives of [seller] have indicated or even 'promised' that the Press would last for at least thirty years. It may certainly be assumed that [purchaser] expected the Press to last for a considerable number of years even in the absence of such a promise, and that [seller] realized this. This obviously has a bearing on the issue of non-conformity as such, but the statements by [seller], if any, or [purchaser's] expectations cannot be construed to set aside or derogate from the limitation periods for examination and notices either under the Contract or under the CISG."

[519] See for instance the arbitral award of a CIETAC tribunal (21 Oct 2002) CISG-online 1557: A contractual clause providing the following wording was apparently interpreted as a guarantee of durability pursuant to Art 36 (2) CISG by the arbitrators: "The warranty period is one year from the date on which the acceptance testing is completed."

[520] However, the seller is also pursuant to a guarantee of durability regularly not liable for defects caused by faulty operation or maintenance by the purchaser or any third party as well as other external influences not attributable to him, see U Magnus in Staudinger (n 29) Art 36 CISG para 16. Furthermore, a guarantee of durability will regularly not do away with the notice period pursuant to Art 39 (1) CISG.

an explicit provision on "guarantees of durability" (i. e. Art 36 (2) CISG), their interaction with applicable limitation periods is not dealt with by the CISG and also falls within the ambit of the respective supplementary domestic law.

288　The stipulation of **"warranty periods"** etc. in sales contracts without further explanation as to their exact meaning may thus cause substantial ambiguities – in particular with regard to the critical question whether the stipulation of such a period in the contract amounts to a warranty of durability to the potential detriment of a seller.[521] Potential problems resulting from an ambiguous clause are well illustrated in a decision rendered by the English Court of Appeal:[522] In the case underlying that decision, the seller had delivered certain equipment and machinery for an industrial plant to the purchaser under an express warranty providing for a warranty period of "no longer than 24 months" from delivery. Though the goods were delivered already in 1995, the purchaser brought an action against the seller due to a defect of the contractual goods only in February 2002 and therefore after the expiry of the regular limitation period of six years under English law.[523] Accordingly, the court had to determine the parties' true intention in relation to the meaning of the **"warranty period"**. In this regard, the court had to resolve whether the indicated warranty period was intended to limit the duration of the seller's liability or – precisely on the contrary – postpone the commencement of the statutory limitation period until the end of the warranty period. One of the judges maintained the latter interpretation of the "warranty period" as a continuing warranty that would accordingly postpone the commencement of the limitation period until the lapse of the continuing warranty.[524] The majority of the judges, however, took a different view and rejected the interpretation of the contractual warranty period as a promissory warranty (i. e. a warranty of durability) – however, without offering an alternative interpretation of this clause.

289　Other jurisdictions are struggling with similar difficulties of construction. Although contractual clauses providing for **"guarantee periods"** have often been interpreted as "guarantees of durability" (*Haltbarkeitsgarantie*) under German law, it is controversial which statutory limitation period should apply in relation to claims under the guarantee and when the applicable limitation period starts to run in this event.[525] Swiss courts have on the other hand regularly interpreted "guaran-

---

[521] See for instance the clause on "warranty duration" suggested by S Cook, "Sample Agreement and Clauses" in HM Flechtner, RA Brand and MS Walter (eds), *Drafting Contracts under the CISG* (OUP, New York 2008) 3, 13, in order to "avoid the rather open-ended language of Art 36 II CISG": The wording of the suggested clause ("Goods [...] shall comply with the applicable written Specifications for a period of time of [one year] (however not to extend under any circumstances beyond such period") does from the author's perspective constitute a (limited) warranty of durability respectively a warranty extending to future performance of the goods; inter alia with the potential consequence of extended limitation periods. The suggested clause may also be interpreted as a combination of a warranty of durability with the determination of the life cycle of the products.
[522] *VAI Industries (UK) Ltd. v Bostock & Bramley & Ors* [2003] EWCA Civ 1069.
[523] See Sec 5 Limitation Act 1980.
[524] See inter alia para 35 of the judgment (Lord Justice Ward): "[...] If the warranty continues for two years it seems to me inevitable that it is a promise that for each day of the two year period the equipment will be free from defect."
[525] Pursuant to the prevailing opinion, the legal consequences of a guarantee of durability (*Haltbarkeitsgarantie*) in a sales contract governed by German (domestic) sales law are twofold: On the one hand, the guarantee relieves the purchaser from the burden to proof that a defect of the

tee periods" contained in contractual agreements as an amendment of statutory limitation periods, provided that the "guarantee periods" were longer than the statutory periods.[526] If, on the other hand, the guarantee periods fall short of the statutory limitation periods, Swiss courts will most likely assume an intention of the parties to extend the statutory notice periods (i. e. "cut off periods") without an amendment of the applicable statute of limitations.[527]

Even under US sales law, that has specifically addressed this issue in § 2–725 UCC, the delineation between a **"warranty of durability"** and a mere limitation period has proven to be difficult.[528] § 2–275 (2) UCC stipulates that the limitation period does not begin to run, contrary to the usual manner, upon tender of delivery but on discovery of a breach in the event that a "warranty explicitly extends to future performance". Traditionally, US courts have been reluctant to assume that the parties have agreed on a warranty extending to future performance.[529] However, in individual cases, even standard warranty period clauses were interpreted as warranties of durability.[530]

290

3. Annotations

Subparagraph 1

Given the existing uncertainties described above, the parties are best advised to stipulate the intended effect of time periods in relation to the conformity of the goods as precisely as possible. From the seller's perspective, the use of the terms

291

---

contractual goods did already exist at the time of transfer of risk. On the other hand, rights and remedies arising out of a breach of the guarantee are pursuant to the prevailing opinion not subject to the regular limitation period applicable in case of defective goods amounting to two years from handover of the contract goods, (§§ 438 (1) No 3, 218 German Civil Code) but to the general limitation period amounting to three years in accordance with §§ 195, 199 German Civil Code). Furthermore, the general limitation period will in this event only start to run once the purchaser has become (or ought to have become aware) of the defect, see T Grützner and M Schmidl, "Verjährungsbeginn bei Garantieansprüchen" [2007] NJW 3610, 3614.

[526] Cf. BG (13 Jul 1937) BGE 63 II 180.

[527] See, eg, BG (26 Oct 2004) File No 4 C. 246/2003. The contractual clause in dispute in this case (concerning a construction contract) provided for a guarantee period of two years. Pursuant to the Swiss Federal Supreme Court, this period (considerably shorter than the applicable limitation period amounting to five years) was neither a limitation period nor a warranty of durability but merely an extension of the (statutory) time period in which defects must be notified. Contrary to German law, warranties of durability have in the past been interpreted as setting also the applicable limitation period, see BG (5 Sep 2002) BGE 128 III 416 ff: In this case concerning a construction contract, the parties had agreed on a warranty of durability amounting to a period of 10 years. Pursuant to the view of the court, this period did also constitute the applicable limitation period (and the guarantee of durability did accordingly not trigger a new limitation period commencing with the detection of the (latent) defect).

[528] See J White and RS Summers, *Uniform Commercial Code* (5th edn West Group, St. Paul 2000) 415. For an excellent in-depth analysis of the duration of warranties under US sales law Klinger (n 434).

[529] JJ Corey, "Contract Warranties and Remedies" (1991–1992) 14 Campbell L Rev 323, 339.

[530] See, eg, US Court of Appeals for the Sixth Circuit, *Standard Alliance Industries, Inc. v The Black Clawson Company* (20 Oct 1978) 587 F.2 d 813 para 36: The relevant clause in this case read as follows: "Seller warrants the equipment manufactured by it will be free from defects in workmanship and material. [...] If any part be found within one year from date of delivery to have been defective when delivered [...] and provided immediate notification in writing is given to the Seller, the Seller will replace or repair such part."

"warranty period" or "guarantee period" should from the outset be replaced with a clear reference to "**limitation periods**". By that means, the seller can ensure that he will neither agree on a "warranty of durability" nor provide for a mere amendment of applicable "cut-off periods". Based on this reasoning, § 7 (1) refers explicitly to the legal consequences of a limitation period.

292 The limitation period for contractual claims based on quality defects stated in § 7 (1) shortens the applicable statutory limitation period pursuant to Swiss domestic sales law, which provides (since the legislative amendment undertaken in 2012) for a regular two year limitation period, **Art 210 (1) CO**. The present International Sales Terms also provide for the shortening of the "cut-off" period contained in Art. 39 (2) CISG to one year (see § 5 (10)) in order to avoid a discrepancy between the two time periods.[531]

293 § 7 (1) extends its application also to **defenses** of the purchaser based on (statute barred) warranty claims against potential claims for payment by the seller. Otherwise, Art 210 (5) CO may still permit the use of time barred warranty claims as a defense against the seller's claims (for payment) provided that the purchaser has given notice of the defect in a timely manner.

Subparagraph 2

294 The Swiss Federal Supreme Court has not yet determined whether Art 210 (1) CO applies also in relation to concurring **claims under tort** by way of analogy.[532] But the prevailing opinion in the legal literature rejects an analogous application of Art 210 (1) CO and opts instead for the application of the general limitation period for tort claims (Art 60 (1) CO). As a result, in the absence of a contractual agreement stipulating otherwise, a seller may face claims of the purchaser under tort due to defective goods even after the lapse of the limitation period stipulated for contractual claims, as Art 60 (1) CO has absorbed the "discovery rule" and the limitation period for tort claims therefore does not begin to run before the purchaser has or ought to have discovered the damage caused by defective products.

295 **Art 60 (1) CO** is not of a mandatory character and therefore subject to amendment by contractual agreement. From the author's point of view, an alignment of the limitation period for contract claims with concurring claims under tort should also not trigger substantial concerns as to the potential infringement of the "unusual terms rule" though a certain risk remains that the clause may be considered by courts as unduly burden the legal assertion of concurring claims in tort. Accordingly, § 7 (2) extends the application of the (amended) limitation period for contractual claims of one year (commencing upon delivery of the goods) also to potential concurring tortious claims of the purchaser based on quality defects of the goods.

---

[531] See for the relationship between the two periods Schwenzer and Manner (n 510) 301, who takes the view that limitation periods agreed by the parties in relation to claims based on the non-conformity of the goods would have to respect Art 39 (2) CISG and can accordingly only be set between a minimum period of two years and a maximum period of six to eight years. It is not entirely clear whether this restriction will pursuant to Schwenzer and Manner also apply if the parties amend the "cut-off" provision in accordance with the limitation period. From the viewpoint of the author, such an amendment should clearly be considered as valid and enforceable given that Art 39 (2) CISG is not a mandatory piece of law.

[532] Honsell (n 87) 91 with further references.

VII. Limitation of Actions

Given that claims based on **defects in title** do not fall within the ambit of Art 210 (1) CO and are subject to the mandatory general limitation period of ten years (Arts 127 (1), 129 (1) CO), claims based on defects in title have been carved out of the scope of § 7.[533] But a similar result is accomplished by way of the extended application of the "cut-off period" to claims based on defects of title (see § 5 (10) International Sales Terms above).

296

Subparagraph 3

The seller cannot rely on the one-year limitation period if he willfully deceived the purchaser with regard to any defect at the time of the conclusion of the contract, **Art 210 (6) CO**. Art 210 (6) CO is a mandatory provision and must hence be sustained. Accordingly, claims based on defects that have already been known but not revealed to the purchaser by the seller at the time of the conclusion of the contract will become time barred only after ten years, see Art 127 CO.

297

Subparagraph 4

Remedial measures undertaken by the seller, either by way of repair or replacement of defective goods or parts thereof can (depending on the respective governing law and the particulars of the individual case) trigger a new limitation period even in the absence of a contractual agreement to that end and hence lead to an "evergreen warranty".[534]

298

Under Swiss law, remedial measures performed during the applicable limitation or warranty period may – similar as in other jurisdictions[535] – be interpreted as an **acknowledgement of liability** to the purchaser, thereby causing a re-run of the applicable limitation period pursuant to Art 135 No 1 CO for the repaired parts of the goods.[536] § 7 (4) aims to avoid this effect by clarifying that any remedial measure undertaken by the seller (either by way of replacement or repair) or any

299

---

[533] See however G Benedick and M Vischer, "Vertragliche Modifikation der Verjährungsregeln im Gewährleistungsrecht beim Unternehmenskauf", Jusletter 4. September 2006 para 29, who suggest that the duration of the limitation period for warranty claims based on defects of title is in principle subject to amendment by the parties despite Art 127, 129 CO.

[534] This term is coined by Kritzer et al (n 295) § 12:11. The German expression *Kettengarantie* means essentially the same.

[535] Germany: § 212 German Civil Code; Russia: Art 203 Russian Civil Code (see also Art 471 (4) with regard to guarantees of durability); USA: See for a discussion of the controversial question whether a remedial promise may postpone the commencement of the limitation period inter alia US Court of Appeals of the First Circuit (30 Apr 2008) *Trans-Spec Truck Service Inc. v. Caterpillar Inc* 524 F.3 d 315. Pursuant to § 2–725 (2) lit c UCC (2003), that has so far not been enacted by the states, a (new) right of action accrues when a remedial promise is not (respectively not properly) performed when performance is due. Under English law, a fresh accrual of action by way of acknowledgement prerequisites an acknowledgment act made in writing and signed by the person making it, see Sec. 29, 30 Limitation Act 1980. See however *VAI Industries (UK) Ltd. v Bostock & Bramley & Ors* (n 522) para 42 ff: Replacement of parts was deemed to constitute a new contract (and accordingly fresh limitation periods were commencing) whereas remedial measures were pursuant to the opinion of the Court of Appeal performed in consideration for a waiver to sue for defective design.

[536] See Appellationsgericht Basel-Stadt (26 Sep 2008) CISG-online 1732 para 10; upheld by the Swiss Federal Supreme Court, see BG (18 May 2009) CISG-online 1900.

third party acting on his behalf is not intended to constitute a (tacit) acceptance or an acknowledgement of any legal liability to do so. Even though Art 135 CO is of mandatory character[537], there is from the author's point of view a good likelihood that § 7 (4) will be upheld: In particular, a purchaser is not entitled to an acknowledgment of liability in case of any remedial measure carried out by the seller and the seller should accordingly have the option to clarify the legal meaning of his own unilateral actions in general terms upfront.[538]

300 However, the seller should keep in mind that the suggested clause offers in any event no protection in case of an express assumption of liability in an individual case. As a consequence, any remedial work carried out by the seller should always be accompanied by a statement that these measures are solely made as a gesture of goodwill and do not contain any acknowledgement of liability.

VIII. Export Control Regulations

1. The suggested clause

§ 8 EXPORT CONTROL REGULATIONS

(1) Delivery obligations of the Seller are subject to the condition that required export licenses are issued and that no other restrictions imposed by mandatory export control regulations of the European Union, the United States of America or any other relevant jurisdiction (regardless whether these restrictions were at the time of contract conclusion foreseeable or not) exist. In the event that the delivery of the Products is prevented by export control regulations or other legally mandated restrictions for more than three (3) months from the scheduled delivery date, both parties are entitled to declare the avoidance of the Contract.

(2) The Purchaser undertakes to comply with all export control regulations of the national export control authorities applicable to him, in particular the authorities in the European Union and in the United States of America. In particular, the Purchaser undertakes not to directly or indirectly export or re-export the Products to any country for which such export may be prohibited by the aforementioned regulations. Failure to comply strictly with all laws relating to embargoes, sanctions, export and re-export applicable to the Purchaser shall entitle the Seller to declare the avoidance of the Contract.

---

[537] RK Däppen in Honsell et al (n 164) Art 135 CO para 1.

[538] The validity of a similar clause under German law has been controversially discussed: According to one opinion, a corresponding clause (when used in general terms and conditions of a seller) infringes § 307 German Civil Code (and hence constitutes an unfair deviation from statutory law) respectively § 305 c BGB, see M Menges, "Vertraglicher Ausschluss der Kettengewährleistung zulässig" [2008] ZGS 457, 462; C Auktor and HJ Mönch, "Nacherfüllung – nur noch auf Kulanz?" [2005] NJW 1686, 1688. For the enforceability of such a clause in general terms and conditions governed by German law however M Schwab, *AGB-Recht* (2nd edn C.F. Müller, Heidelberg 2008) para 1058.

2. Annotations

Subparagraph 1

International sales contracts usually require the seller to obtain necessary **export licenses**. This general rule is also reflected by the Incoterms 2010: Only one out of the 11 Incoterms (the rarely used EXW clause) shifts this obligation to the purchaser.[539]

A temporary or permanent impediment to delivery of the goods caused by **export control regulations** (in particular those enacted after the conclusion of the contract) may cause substantial problems for the seller: Although Art 79 (5) CISG permits the purchaser to terminate the contract in this case at a certain point of time (once the delay in delivery amounts to a fundamental breach), a corresponding right of the seller does not exist in this event. The seller may under the CISG also be held liable for damages based on his failure to perform – subject to the limited exception in Art 79 (1) CISG that may only apply in exceptional circumstances.

Against this background, § 8 (1) turns the issuance of required export licenses (if any) into a condition precedent for the existence of any delivery obligation of the seller. Additionally, the clause permits both parties to declare the avoidance of the contract[540] if the delivery is prevented by export control regulations (in particular but not limited to applicable EU and US export regulations) or other legally mandated restrictions for a period of more than three months. As a result, the fact that the seller ought to have been aware of impeding **export control regulations** will on a stand-alone basis not trigger liability towards the purchaser. However, the clause does not do away with the seller's general obligation to take all reasonable action to obtain a required export license.[541]

Subparagraph 2

The seller may face **criminal liability** under domestic laws even if he is not responsible for the export of the goods[542] if he makes the goods available to a purchaser in spite of his awareness that the purchaser may subsequently infringe relevant export control regulations. Besides criminal sanctions, an illegal re-export of the goods by the purchaser may substantially harm the seller's reputation and business standing. Though it has been submitted that the CISG may already exempt the seller from his delivery obligations in this event,[543] an explicit contractual termination right provided by § 8 (2) may provide the seller with additional legal certainty.

301

302

303

304

---

[539] See ch B.IV.2 above.

[540] An outstanding export license may pursuant to some domestic laws already render the contract invalid, see in relation to German export control law for instance § 31 (1) AWG. See with regard to other jurisdictions E Geisinger et al, "The impact of international trade sanctions on contractual obligations and on international commercial arbitration" [2012] IBLJ 405 ff.

[541] See also Murray et al (n 352) 129.

[542] This situation may for instance occur if the parties agree on delivery of the goods on an "ex works" basis.

[543] I Schwenzer in Schlechtriem and Schwenzer (n 34) Art 79 CISG para 32, referring to "moral unacceptability" as grounds for a refusal to perform.

IX. Avoidance by the Seller

1. The suggested clause

§ 9 AVOIDANCE OF THE CONTRACT BY THE SELLER

Without prejudice to any such right or other remedies provided by the applicable governing law of this Contract, the Seller is entitled to declare the Contract avoided without any further preconditions if
a) the Purchaser fails to make payment of the Contract Price to the Seller under this Contract within thirty (30) days after it has become due and payable or fails to open a letter of credit pursuant to the Contract within such period after the due date, or
b) the Purchaser fails to perform his contractual obligations whose performance is necessary for the delivery of the Products or to take delivery pursuant to the Contract within fourteen (14) days after request of the Seller in that regard, or
c) a material deterioration of the Purchaser's creditworthiness has occurred or insolvency proceedings relating to the assets of the Purchaser are applied for or commenced.

2. Annotations

305 Art 64 CISG gives the seller a right to declare the contract avoided (i.e. to terminate the contract) if the purchaser's failure to perform any of his contractual obligations amounts to a **fundamental breach** or if the purchaser does not perform his primary obligation to pay the price and/or take delivery of the goods even after the lapse of an additional grace period of reasonable length set by the seller pursuant to Art 63 (1) CISG. § 9 International Sales Terms serves against this background essentially as a **clarification** of this remedy, which already exists under the CISG.

306 Having in mind that both the existence of a fundamental breach and (in the absence of the former) the appropriate length of a reasonable **grace period** may be difficult to ascertain in the individual case, § 9 lit a and b allows the seller to either (and without the need to first set a grace period) withdraw from the contract once the purchaser has failed to make payment (or failed to open a letter of credit, as the case may be) within 30 days after the due date or to perform upon request other obligations required for the delivery of the goods (including taking delivery) after the lapse of a specified period of time. Finally, sub-clause c) permits termination in the event of a material deterioration of the purchaser's creditworthiness.

307 Other termination rights available to the seller under the CISG or granted by other provisions of the International Sales Terms are not prejudiced by § 9 and therefore remain unaffected.

308 The seller should keep in mind that an opportunity to declare the avoidance of the contract due to a breach by the purchaser is restricted once payment has been made, see Art 64 (2) CISG.

X. Confidentiality Obligations

1. The suggested clause

§ 10 CONFIDENTIALITY

(1) The Parties shall keep all know-how, data and any other information (collectively hereinafter "Information") received from the respective other Party under this Contract confidential with respect to any third parties and shall use the Information solely for the purpose of this Contract.

(2) The confidentiality obligation shall not apply to Information which
a) is in the public domain at the time of disclosure or later becomes part of the public domain without any breach of this confidentiality obligation,
b) was known to the receiving Party prior to disclosure by the disclosing Party,
c) is disclosed to the receiving Party by a third party without any breach of a confidentiality obligation towards the disclosing Party,
d) has been independently developed by the receiving Party.

The receiving Party bears the burden of proof that any one of the foregoing requirements for an exemption is fulfilled.

(3) The confidentiality obligations stipulated in this § 10 shall remain in force after the Parties have discharged their performance obligations. They shall also survive an avoidance of this Contract.

2. Annotations

Confidentiality clauses (and non-disclosure agreements) are a common feature of international commercial contracts. Although many domestic laws protect confidential information to a certain extent under criminal and unfair competition laws[544] even in the absence of either a non-disclosure agreement or a corresponding intellectual property right,[545] both the scope and effect of this protection may be inadequate if confidential information is revealed to the other party on a **voluntary basis** without further explicit contractual restrictions. From the seller's perspective, a confidentiality clause may therefore become important in particular if detailed technical specifications and know how as well as other (unprotected) trade secrets related to the contractual goods are made known to the purchaser in the course of a sales transaction.

309

---

[544] The CISG does not contain any provisions with regard to the protection of trade secrets and other confidential information released in the course of a sales transaction.

[545] See with regard to Germany: §§ 17, 18 UWG; Switzerland: § 4, 6 UWG; England: See *De Maudsley v Palumbo and Others* [1996] FSR 447, confirming the "three point test" in relation to the protection of confidential information under common law (according to which the disclosed information i) must have the necessary quality of confidence about it ii) was disclosed or became known in circumstances that imported an obligation of confidence and iii) has been used or disclosed without authorization to do so); USA: Uniform Trade Secret Act (as adopted by some US-states) and the common law protection of trade secrets, see for a more detailed overview MA Woronoff in TL Stark (ed), *Negotiating and Drafting Contract Boilerplate* (ALM Publishing, New York 2003) 393 ff.

C. The International Sales Terms

Subparagraph 1

310   The remedies generally available under the applicable law (either the CISG or domestic laws) in the event of a breach of a confidentiality clause do not always adequately serve the interests of the harmed party. This holds true particularly with regard to a **damage claim**, as damage incurred through the breach of a confidentiality undertaking is notoriously difficult to prove and quantify. The parties can reduce this problem by means of a liquidated damages or penalty clause that relieves the injured party from the requirement to prove corresponding losses. Although this approach may be appropriate in individual contracts, § 10 does not provide for the payment of either a penalty or of liquidated damages, as a breach of confidentiality may take rather different forms and one single lump sum amount payable in case of an infringement of § 10 can hardly reflect an appropriate amount for all potential breaches.

Subparagraph 2

311   Non-disclosure obligations generally contain some exceptions regarding the protected information or the know-how submitted to the other party or the parties' duties with regard to the confidential information. These **limitations** are necessary in order to avoid overly broad (and as a potential result unenforceable) confidentiality obligations. In particular, information that is already in the public domain (or information that becomes part of the public domain without any breach of confidentiality by the receiving party) should be carved out, considering that a confidentiality clause would otherwise function in a manner similar to a non-compete obligation and may cause an inadmissible restraint of trade.[546]

Subparagraph 3

312   It is a different question whether a confidentiality clause should also contain a **time limit** or a geographical restriction in order to avoid overly broad restraints to the detriment of the receiving party. However, not only the time limits but also the geographical restrictions can generally not be considered as an appropriate means to reasonably limit the scope of a confidentiality clause: That is obvious with regard to geographical restrictions as a revelation of trade secrets by the receiving party outside a "protected" territorial area would harm the interests of the disclosing party almost to the same extent[547]. A time limit may also unduly harm the seller if the know how in question is not out-dated even after the lapse of the indicated time period.[548] EU competition laws also in principle permit the unlimited protection of know how if and to the extent that the information has not become part of the public domain.[549]

---

[546] See for instance the Australian case *Maggbury Pty Ltd v Hafele Australia Pty Ltd* [2001] HCA 70, in which the High Court of Australia held that a confidentiality undertaking that did neither carve out information being already in the public domain nor provided for a time limit constituted a restraint of trade and was accordingly unenforceable.

[547] LK Stevens, "When Should a Confidentiality Agreement Contain a Time Limit?" (1999–2000) 19 Franchise L J 3, 4.

[548] I Westermann, *Handbuch Know-how-Schutz* (C.H. Beck, München 2007) 91.

[549] See with regard to the block-exemption of post-contractual non-compete obligations in particular Art 5 (3) Regulation (EU) 330/2010 (n 278): "Paragraph 1(b) is without prejudice to the possibility of imposing a restriction which is unlimited in time on the use and disclosure of know-how which has not entered the public domain." See with regard to US law however Stevens (n 547).

XI. Force Majeure

1. The suggested clause

§ 11 FORCE MAJEURE

(1) Neither party shall be in breach of this Contract if and to the extent that the performance of the Contract is prevented or made excessively onerous by an Event of Force Majeure as defined below in § 11 (2). However, no ground for relief under this § 11 shall exist if the non-performing party could have reasonably expected both the impediment and its effects upon its ability to perform at the time of the conclusion of the Contract or reasonably avoided or overcome it or its effects.

(2) Any event that is beyond either party's reasonable control shall be deemed to constitute an "Event of Force Majeure" regardless of whether such event occurs before or after the conclusion of the Contract. An Event of Force Majeure shall include but shall not be limited to natural disasters or catastrophic events, nuclear accidents, fire, flood, typhoons or earthquakes, terrorism, acts or omissions by governmental authorities, allocations or restrictions upon the use of materials or manpower, war, riots, sabotage or revolutions, strikes or lockouts.

(3) If either Party claims that an Event of Force Majeure has occurred affecting its performance, it shall promptly notify the other Party. If the Event of Force Majeure continues for a period of ninety (90) calendar days or more upon notice, either Party may terminate the Contract in writing after to the lapse of that period.

(4) § 11 shall not prejudice any further exemption provisions provided either by these International Sales Terms or the applicable governing law.

2. General background

Force majeure clauses are undoubtedly among the most widely used "boilerplate" clauses in international commercial contracts. The **force majeure clause** is intended to excuse the failure of a party to fulfill its contractual duties due to an impediment beyond its reasonable control. However, it is up to the parties to define what kind of circumstances will constitute an event of force majeure and which legal consequences should ensue in that case. 313

The impact of an **event of force majeure** depends not only on the wording of the force majeure clause but also on the applicable governing law. Accordingly, the necessity and scope of a force majeure clause must be reviewed in the light of the governing law and other exemption provisions in the contract. Legal systems such as the CISG (and the common law) that apply the principle of strict liability with regard to breaches of contract also in relation to claims for damages and, as opposed to civil law systems, exempt the non-performing party from liability only under narrow circumstances,[550] justify the existence of a force majeure clause 314

---

[550] In particular, the doctrine of "frustration of contract" developed by English common law exempts the party only from liability if the obligation in question "has become incapable of being performed because the circumstances in which performance is called for would render it a thing radically different from that which was undertaken by contract", *Davis Contractors Ltd v Fareham U.D.C.* [1956] A.C. 696, 729. The impact of a force majeure clause against this background is clearly

potentially even to a greater extent than those jurisdictions that are based on the principle of fault liability. Although Art 79 CISG provides a statutory excuse in the event of non-performance, this exemption is limited both in scope and effect and has in reality only rarely relieved a non-performing party from liability.[551] Not only does the application of Art 79 (1) CISG require an unavoidable impediment to perform that is beyond the control of the respective non-performing party.[552] It is also a precondition that the impediment in question could not be foreseen by the non-performing party. Finally, Art 79 CISG limits the legal consequences of an event of force majeure even if the indicated strict prerequisites are fulfilled: According to Art 79 (5) CISG, the exemption provided under Art 79 (1) CISG does not do away with any remedy other than a damage claim.[553]

315   A force majeure clause must be distinguished from a **hardship clause** though both clauses overlap to a certain extent: Whereas a force majeure clause implies a disclaimer of liability in case of non-performance, the legal concept of "hardship" deals with a revision of the contract terms in cases where the performance of the contract becomes considerably more burdensome though not impossible.[554] The use of a separate hardship clause seems less important in a simple sales contract compared to long-term supply or construction contracts. If the seller is concerned about currency fluctuations or the increase of direct costs for raw material and individual components, it is advisable to address this issue by means of a **price adjustment clause** rather than a standardized "hardship provision".

---

illustrated by the decision of the Court of Appeal in *J Lauritzen AS v Wijsmuller BV, The Super Servant Two* [1990] 1 Lloyds Rep 1. A frustration of the contract brings the contract to an end, E McKendrick in HG Beale (ed), *Chitty on Contracts, General Principles* (31st edn Sweet & Maxwell, London 2013) para 23-071. US law has developed the concepts of frustration, impossibility as well as "commercial impracticability" (§ 2–615 UCC) as three separate subgroups of the general doctrine of excuse, see JM Bund, "Force Majeure Clauses: Drafting Advice for the CISG Practitioner" (1997–1998) 17 J L & Commerce 381, 395 ff.

[551] See CISG-AC Opinion No 7 (23 Apr 2007), Exemption of Liability for Damages Under Article 79 of the CISG (Rapporteur: AM Garro), para 2 ff.

[552] The term "impediment" refers pursuant to the prevailing view only to external circumstances that are not within the typical sphere of control of the affected party. Hence, personal impediments of a contractual party such as conduct of its own personnel, financial capability, procurement risk in relation to generic goods (on part of the seller) as well as the utility risk (on part of the purchaser) are generally excluded from the scope of Art 79 CISG, see I Schwenzer in Schlechtriem and Schwenzer (n 34) Art 79 CISG para 18 ff. See with regard to the procurement risk of the seller also BG (12 Jun 2006) CISG-online 1516; in relation to the utility risk inter alia BGH (27 Nov 2007) CISG-online 1611.

[553] However, though Art 79 (5) CISG applies without doubt also to any claim for specific performance pursuant to Art 46 CISG, there is widespread agreement that a performance claim does not exist in the event that performance is simply impossible.

[554] J Rimke, "Force majeure and hardship: Application in international trade practice with specific regard to the CISG and the Unidroit Principles of International Commercial Contracts" in *Pace Review of the Convention on Contracts for the International Sale of Goods* (Kluwer International 1999–2000) 197, 200 f. For the ongoing controversy whether the CISG precludes recourse to domestic laws respectively general principles derived from international "soft law" (eg the UPICC) that provide for specific provisions on "hardship" see I Schwenzer, "Force Majeure and Hardship in International Sales Contracts" (2008–2009) 39 Vict U Well L Rev 709, 724.

3. Annotations

Subparagraph 1 and 2

As § 6 (1) of the International Sales Terms replaces strict liability with a fault liability principle (or excludes the seller's liability for damages subject to intentional or grossly negligent misconduct in the entirety), a separate force majeure clause seems to be (at least from the seller's perspective) of only limited importance at first sight. But § 11 may well help to prevent the premature **termination** of the contract in case of a temporary impediment and also provides the non-performing party with a termination right in order to overcome the stalemate caused by a long-lasting impediment to performance (see below).

§ 11 applies for the benefit of both parties.[555] Although **reciprocity** is not a mandatory feature of a force majeure clause, it may help to promote the acceptability of the sales terms by the purchaser. As a consequence, however, the seller must be aware that the purchaser may have recourse to § 11 as well if the performance either of the payment obligations or of the obligation to take delivery is prevented by an unforeseeable impediment. It is not least of all for this reason that § 11 (1) does not significantly lower the general threshold for an excuse based on "force majeure" compared to Art 79 (1) CISG: Otherwise, the clause may backfire on the seller if the purchaser may too easily rely on its application. In line with the prevailing view on Art 79 CISG, however, an event of force majeure relieves the non-performing party pursuant to § 11 (1) even if the event renders performance excessively onerous though not impossible.[556]

§ 11 (2) defines the circumstances that constitute an event of force majeure. The indicated events reflect the typical enumeration that can be found in standard force majeure provisions.[557]

Subparagraph 3

A force majeure clause should last but not least state the **legal consequences** that emanate from an event of force majeure. At least from the perspective of the seller, who can rely on the suggested § 6 for an exclusion or limitation of liability for damages, § 11 (3) will not provide any additional shelter when it comes to liability for damages as an event of force majeure is by its usual definition not caused by culpable behavior of the non-performing party. But § 11 (3) essentially limits the right of the other party to terminate the contract pursuant to Art 49 (2) CISG or Art 64 (2) CISG given that only the lapse of the 90-day period permits a declaration of avoidance.

At the same time, § 11 (3) grants a termination right in case of an event of force majeure also to the non-performing party once the indicated period of 90 days has lapsed to no avail – a similar right is not available under the CISG, where the non-

---

[555] See for a similar arrangement inter alia § 13 of the ICC Model International Sales Contract (n 11) as well as Art 41 Orgalime S 2012 (n 10).

[556] See L Nottage, "Changing Contract Lenses: Unexpected Supervening Events in English, New Zealand, U.S., Japanese and International Sales Law and Practice" (2007) 14 Ind J Global Legal Stud 385, 404.

[557] See for instance the force majeure clause promoted by the ICC, *ICC Force Majeure Clause 2003* (ICC Publication No 650, Paris 2003).

performing party has no termination right pursuant to Art 49 and Art 64 CISG based on its own failure to perform.

Subparagraph 4

321 A force majeure clause should also clarify whether exemptions from liability provided by the governing law remain applicable or will be replaced by the clause.[558] Given that § 11 (4) serves as a **"catch all clause"** because other suggested terms and conditions of the International Sales Terms deal already with typical obstacles that may prevent the seller from the (timely) performance of the contract, § 11 (4) clarifies that both statutory as well as contractual exemptions will not be prejudiced.

XII. Entire Agreement, Written Form, Severability and Anti-Assignment Clause

1. The suggested clause

§ 12 MISCELLANEOUS

(1) This Contract contains the entire understanding between the Parties and fully replaces any other agreements or understandings between the Parties on its subject matter entered into before the conclusion of this Contract. Accordingly, this § 12 (1) shall prevail over Arts 8 (3) and 11 CISG.

(2) No amendment to this Contract shall be valid unless made in writing. The same shall apply with regard to any amendment to this written form requirement. For the avoidance of doubt, the written form requirement shall be deemed complied with in any case of exchange of communications via E-mail or facsimile.

(3) Should any of the provisions of this Contract be or become invalid or otherwise unenforceable, this shall not affect the validity and enforceability of the remaining contractual provisions. The invalid or unenforceable provision will be automatically replaced by a valid and/or operative provision which most effectively serves the economic purpose and effect intended by the original provision.

(4) The Purchaser is not entitled to assign any rights or claims arising from or related to this Contract to any third party without the prior written consent of the Seller.

2. Annotations

322 The suggested "miscellaneous" clause contains four typical "boilerplate" terms that are fairly standard in international commercial contracts: § 12 consists in particular of an entire agreement or "merger-clause" (§ 12 (1)), a written form requirement or no-oral modification ("NOM") clause (§ 12 (2)), a severability clause (§ 12 (3)) as well as an anti-assignment clause (§ 12 (4)).

---

[558] T Plate, "Die Gestaltung von 'force majeure' Klauseln in internationalen Wirtschaftsverträgen" [2007] RIW 42, 43.

Subparagraph 1 (merger clause)

A **merger clause** combined with a written form requirement can in principle substantially contribute to the fundamental aim of a seller to control his overall risk exposure under a sales contract. However, notwithstanding the importance of these two clauses, the parties to an international commercial contract are often not sufficiently aware of their precise effect and the role of the governing law of the contract with regard to both the interpretation and scope of application. The latter is especially important as the legal effect of the merger clause and of the written form requirement is subject to significant limitations imposed by domestic laws as well as international instruments. 323

The purpose of an entire agreement (merger) clause is, first of all, the provision of legal certainty: The merger clause is intended to ensure that the contractual terms and conditions stipulated in the written document(s) contain the **entire understanding** between the parties and prevail over any other (oral) agreement that may have been reached before the conclusion of the final contract. Accordingly, the merger clause takes a backward look: Its concern is to "merge" all relevant contractual agreements into one single contract document. Amendments or alterations of the contract *after* the conclusion of the contract on the other hand are dealt with by the written form requirement that is discussed below.[559] 324

Under domestic laws, merger clauses aim to reinforce the assumption already made by the majority of legal systems, namely that a written contractual document represents the understanding between the parties in an exhaustive manner. Anglo-American law has firmly established this principle by way of the **"parol evidence rule"** that excludes (subject, however, to rather far-reaching exceptions) any evidence as to prior agreements or contemporaneous oral agreements that contradict or supplement a written term in the contractual document.[560] Civil law jurisdictions apply a weaker assumption of completeness.[561] Not only are the parties generally entitled to rebut the assumption that the written text reflects the entire agreement.[562] It is also widely accepted that (oral) agreements take precedence over 325

---

[559] See for this distinction O Meyer, "Die privatautonome Abbedingung der vorvertraglichen Abreden – Integrationsklauseln im internationalen Wirtschaftsverkehr" (2007) 71 RabelsZ 562, 564.

[560] In case of a "partially integrated" document, however, evidence of prior agreements or negotiations is admissible in order to supplement the written document. Furthermore, such evidence is permitted to interpret ambiguous terms, see with regard to US law RB Risdon and WA Escobar, "Merger" in TL Stark, *Negotiating and Drafting Contract Boilerplate* (ALM Publishing, New York 2003) 563 ff. § 2–202 UCC contains further exemptions from the parol evidence rule in relation to sales contracts: Pursuant to this provision, a written contract may also be supplemented or explained (though not contradicted) by course of dealing, usage of trade or performance. The parol evidence rule is limited in a similar manner pursuant to English law given that the courts permit "extrinsic evidence" if it can be shown that the document was not intended by the parties to express their entire agreement. However, according to the "exclusionary rule", extrinsic evidence may not be used for the purpose of interpretation of the written contract given that the latter constitutes a question of law and not of fact, see AG Guest in Chitty on Contracts (n 550) para 12-097 and para 12-119. For a comparison between US and English law with regard to the "parol evidence rule" and merger clauses also Meyer (n 559) 565, 577 ff.

[561] AL Zuppi, "The Parol Evidence Rule: A Comparative Study of the Common Law, the Civil Law Tradition, and Lex Mercatoria" (2007) 35 Ga J Int'l & Comp L 233, 258.

[562] German law applies the (rebuttable) assumption that a written contract contains the entire agreement, see for instance BGH (5 Jul 2002) [2002] NJW 3164. French law takes a similar view: Though Art 1348 CC contains a "parol evidence rule", Arts 1341(2) CC and 110-3 French

C. The International Sales Terms

standard terms in case of conflict.[563] Though this order of priority does not do away with the assumption of completeness of a written instrument even in case of standard form contracts, it may have an effect on the validity or scope of merger clauses drafted in general terms and conditions.[564]

326 The CISG does not contain a parol evidence rule or any similar instrument. On the contrary, Arts 8 (3) and Art 11 CISG explicitly permit recourse to any other means (including negotiations, course of conduct and trade usage) to determine the content of a sales contract[565] whereas a written contract governed by the CISG may (in the absence of a merger clause) not even establish a firm (though rebuttable) **assumption of completeness**.[566] Furthermore, the prevailing opinion derives an implied order of priority from the CISG in which (oral) agreements prevail over contradicting standard terms.[567]

327 It is a different question whether the parties may by way of a merger clause deviate from Arts 8 (3) and 11 CISG. According to Art 6 CISG, this option undoubtedly exists in case of an individually negotiated clause that is drafted in a sufficiently clear manner. Merger clauses contained in **general terms and conditions** may face stricter scrutiny.[568] A general tendency of courts to interpret merger clauses contained in general terms and conditions governed by the CISG in a

---

Commercial Code stipulate explicitly that commercial contracts can be proven by any means, see S Vogenauer, *Interpretation of Contracts: Concluding Comparative Observations*, University of Oxford Faculty of Law Legal Studies Research Paper Series, Working Paper No 7/2007, <http://papers.ssrn.com/Abstract=984074> 12.

[563] See for instance Germany: § 305 b German Civil Code; Switzerland: Schwenzer (n 181) para 45.09; with regard to English law see the decision of the English High Court in *Indian Oil Corp v Vanol Inc* [1991] 2 Lloyd's Rep 634: At least a negotiated written (!) contract prevails over general terms and conditions.

[564] A merger clause in a standard form contract governed by German law is based on this reasoning of almost no legal effect: § 305 b German Civil Code stipulates explicitly the priority of individually negotiated clauses (whether oral or written) over standard terms and renders a merger clause largely ineffective; see P Ulmer in P Ulmer et al (eds), *AGB-Recht* (10th edn Dr. Otto Schmidt, Köln 2006) § 305 b BGB para 13. The merger clause will at best be interpreted as a mere clarification of the assumption of completeness that does already exist in the absence of such a clause. A merger clause that opts for an irrefutable assumption of completeness is invalid under German law, see J Dammann in Wolf et al (n 386) Anh. § 310 BGB para S 118. The approach chosen by the Principles of European Contract Law is similar, see Art 2:105 (2) PECL: "If the merger clause is not individually negotiated it will only establish a presumption that the parties intended that their prior statements, undertakings or agreements were not to form part of the contract. This rule may not be excluded or restricted." Less restrictive however Art 2.1.17 UPICC: "A contract in writing which contains a clause indicating that the writing completely embodies the terms on which the parties have agreed cannot be contradicted or supplemented by evidence of prior statements or agreements. However, such statements or agreements may be used to interpret the writing." Pursuant to English law, a standard entire agreement clause will not exclude liability in relation to pre-contractual misrepresentations, *Axa Sun Life Services Plc v Campbell Martin Ltd & Ors* [2011] EWCA Civ 133.

[565] See in particular CISG-AC Opinion No 3 (23 Oct 2004), Parol Evidence Rule, Plain Meaning Rule, Contractual Merger Clause and the CISG (Rapporteur: R Hyland) para 2.1 ff.

[566] M Schmidt-Kessel in Schlechtriem and Schwenzer (n 34) Art 8 CISG para 34. See however also CISG-AC Opinion No 3 (n 565) para 2.7, where it is acknowledged by the commentators that contractual writing will at least "receive special consideration under the CISG".

[567] M Schmidt-Kessel in Schlechtriem and Schwenzer (n 34) Art 8 CISG para 58.

[568] See with regard to sales contracts governed by the CISG also CISG-AC Opinion No 3 (n 565) para 4.6: "Under the CISG, a merger clause does not generally have the effect of excluding extrinsic evidence for purposes of contract interpretation. However, the merger clause may prevent recourse

restrictive manner is well illustrated by a decision of the US Federal District Court of the Southern District, New York: In this case, the court regarded a merger clause contained in general sales terms as inoperative (regardless of the question whether the general terms were validly incorporated into the contract in the first place) as the parties did not "share an intent to be bound by the merger clause".[569]

Although there is no specific **statutory control** of general terms under Swiss law, it seems nevertheless likely that a court would interpret a merger clause rather narrowly (also through a "contra proferentem" approach, but also simply based on an assumed priority of oral agreements over standard terms).[570] Accordingly, it seems questionable whether the legal impact of § 12 (1) goes beyond the mere establishment of a (rebuttable) assumption of completeness of the written document. In order to reinforce at least the latter, § 12 (1) explicitly excludes Arts 8 (3) and 11 CISG.[571] 328

Subparagraph 2 (written form requirement)

In a similar manner, written form requirements may serve the legitimate end to avoid disputes about existence and content of potential oral modifications to a contract subsequent to its conclusion.[572] According to the relevant provisions of the CISG, the parties can in the absence of any **written form requirement** and because of the general absence of any requirements as to form (as stipulated in Art 11 CISG) generally modify their contract at any time by mere oral agreement, Art 29 (1) CISG. Contrary to "merger clauses", however, written form requirements are explicitly (and contrary to many domestic jurisdictions[573]) acknowledged by the CISG. Art 29 (2) CISG states that a written form requirement contained in a sales contract is not prejudiced by a subsequent oral agreement and the parties can accordingly not implicitly eliminate the written form requirement.[574] The same result should in principle be accomplished if the written form requirement is contained in general 329

---

to extrinsic evidence for this purpose if specific wording, together with all other relevant factors, make clear the parties' intent to derogate from Article 8 for purposes of contract interpretation."

[569] US District Court, South District of New York (26 Aug 2006) CISG-online 1272.

[570] Art 29 (2) 2 CISG may impose additional restrictions: Though this provision covers – based on a literal construction – only amendments effected after the contract conclusion, it may be applied by way of analogy also in relation to the "initial" content of the contract, see Brunner (n 114) Art 8 CISG para 15.

[571] See also the recommendation by HM Flechtner, "Adressing Parol Evidence Issues in Contracts Governed by the CISG" in H Flechtner, RA Brand and MS Walter (eds), *Drafting Contracts under the CISG* (OUP, New York 2008) 329, 333.

[572] F Wagner-von Papp, "European Contract Law: Are No Oral Modification Clauses Not Worth the Paper They Are Written On?" [2010] CLP 511, 520.

[573] See for a comprehensive comparative analysis in this regard F Wagner von Papp (n 572) 511, 524 ff.

[574] For a contrary position see in particular (domestic) Swiss and German law: Pursuant to the case law of both the Swiss and the German Federal Supreme Court, the parties can by means of an oral amendment of the written contract also impliedly exclude the application of a (simple) written form requirement contained in the original agreement, see for instance BG (29 Apr 1998) BGE 125 III 263, 268; BGH (2 Jun 1976) BGHZ 66, 378, 371. It would appear that English law applies a similar approach though this matter has not yet been finally resolved by the courts, see, eg, *Spring Finance Ltd v HS Real Company LLC* [2011] EWHC 57 para 53 with reference to differing decisions of the Court of Appeal.

C. The International Sales Terms

terms and conditions that have been accepted by the other party.[575] It would also appear that a regular written form requirement will due to Art. 29 CISG be sufficient to prevent valid subsequent oral agreements. Accordingly, the "double barreled" written form requirement[576] is strictly speaking not mandatory though may serve as additional evidence against the assumption of an implicit derogation from the first sentence of Art. 29 (2) CISG by means of a subsequent oral agreement.

330 According to the second sentence of Art 29 (2) CISG, which appears to have been influenced by the common law concepts of "waiver" and "estoppel"[577], a party can however be precluded due to its **"conduct"** from asserting a written form requirement if the other party has relied on the same. It is still controversial what kind of conduct is required to trigger this provision. It would appear, however, that a simple (oral) agreement on a modification of or addendum to the written contract can on a stand-alone basis not constitute relevant "conduct", as the benefit of a written form requirement (as expressly acknowledged by Art 29 CISG) would otherwise become nugatory. In particular, if the parties were not aware of the written form requirement at the time of an amendment, only the unreserved performance or acceptance of performance of the other party in accordance with any amendments (orally) agreed upon should suffice to bring Art 29 (2) 2 CISG into play.

331 It is another question whether the parties may opt out of Art 29 (2) 2 CISG in their written sales contract. The prevailing view seems to reject that option based on an alleged mandatory character of this provision.[578] Although Art 6 CISG casts some doubt on this view, § 12 (2) does for that reason not attempt to exclude Art 29 (2) 2 CISG.[579] As a consequence, § 12 (2) can only offer limited protection against oral amendments of the International Sales Terms and the seller should continuously act in a careful manner whenever he communicates orally with the purchaser after the conclusion of the contract.

331a Problems may occur (similar as in many domestic laws) with regard to the question which means of communication actually fulfill the requirement of being made in writing. Art. 13 CISG (that can be applied in relation to contractual written form requirements as well) stipulates that "Writing" includes telegram and telex. Given that both telegram and telex have since long been replaced by telefax and email, the prevailing opinion amongst scholars wants to include these means of communication by way of an analogous application of Art. 13 CISG. However, the application by analogy remains disputed in particular in relation to electronic means such as emails.[580] As a consequence, the seller is best advised to define the

---

[575] EE Bergsten, "Amending the Contract: Art 29 CISG" in CB Andersen and UG Schroeter (eds), *Sharing International Commercial Law across National Boundaries: Festschrift for Albert H Kritzer on the Occasion of his Eightieth Birthday* (Wildy, Simmonds & Hill Publishing, London 2008) 48, 58.

[576] This term has been coined by Schwenzer, Hachem and Kee (n 26) para 14.13.

[577] P Schlechtriem and UG Schroeter in Schlechtriem and Schwenzer (n 34) Art 29 CISG para 23.

[578] For this view, R Hillmann, "Article 29(2) of the United Nations Convention on Contracts for the International Sale of Goods: A New Effort at Clarifying the Legal Effect of 'No Oral Modification' Clauses" (1988) 21 Cornell Int'l L J 449, 461; P Perales Viscasillas, "Modification and Termination of the Contract (Art 29 CISG)" (2005–2006) 25 J L & Commerce 167, 179; Brunner (n 114) Art 29 CISG para 3.

[579] But see Klotz (n 339) 321, who recommends the use of a "no modification by conduct clause" that excludes the application of Art 29 CISG in the entirety.

[580] See for a thorough treatment of this problem P Perales Viscasillas in Kröll/Mistelis/Perales Viscasillas (n 34) Art. 13 CISG para. 6 ff.

"writing" requirement in more detail in the contract. Accordingly, the suggested clause clarifies that both use of email and fax will meet the written form requirements. It would of course also be possible to achieve the opposite result by way of an explicit exclusion of this means of communication.

Subparagraph 3 (severability clause)

§ 12 (3) consists of two parts: The first part of the severability clause aims to preserve the remainder of the contract in the event that a contractual term is invalid or unenforceable. This first **"preservative" part** of the clause corresponds with general rules of Swiss contract law: Art 20 (2) CO assumes the (rebuttable) intention of the parties to uphold a contract that is only partially invalid.[581] Against this background, § 12 (3) reinforces a legal principle that is already acknowledged under statutory law although the preservation of the contract is pursuant to § 12 (3) (and contrary to Art 20 (2) CO[582]) not a mere (rebuttable) assumption but a binding undertaking. 332

The second part of § 12 (3) contains a **"reformation clause"** that purports to replace an invalid provision with a valid one coming as close as possible to the economic intent of the original clause. Swiss jurisprudence has generally applied a similar approach (regardless of the existence of a corresponding "reformation clause" in the contract) and enforced overly broad provisions up to the legally permitted extent.[583] This jurisprudence has, however, met with criticism and its applicability in the area of general terms and conditions is controversial.[584] 333

Subparagraph 4 (non-assignment clause)

The potential **transfer** of individual rights and claims arising from a sales contract to a third party may become important on two counts: On the one hand, the seller may want to ensure that the purchaser cannot freely assign both primary obligations (in particular claims of performance) and potential warranty claims to a third party. On the other hand, the assignment of the claim for payment by the seller may secure the financing of a sales transaction and minimize the need to collect debts. 334

It is a widely accepted though not entirely undisputed principle of private international law that the governing law of the assigned claim will, among other things, determine its **assignability**.[585] Hence, a court having to resolve a dispute 335

---

[581] This rule does not apply in all legal systems: For instance, pursuant to German law, a partial invalidity of a contract triggers (by means of a (rebuttable) assumption) in principle the invalidity of the contract as a whole, § 139 German Civil Code. Different rules apply however in the event of a (partial) invalidity of general sales terms, § 306 (1) German Civil Code.

[582] Art 20 (2) CO is not a mandatory provision, see P Gauch et al, *Schweizerisches Obligationenrecht: Allgemeiner Teil. Band I* (9th edn Schulthess, Zürich 2008) para 695.

[583] See n 476 above.

[584] See Schwenzer (n 181) para 24.08.

[585] See, eg, with regard to the EU member states: Art 14 (2) Rome I Regulation (that has however not solved the controversial discussion whether the governing law of the assigned claim should also control the proprietary aspects of an assignment and accordingly potential "erga omnes" effects of an anti-assignment clause; see A Flessner,"Die internationale Forderungsabtretung nach der Rom I-Verordnung" [2009] IPRax 35, 42 who argues that "erga omnes effects fall within the ambit of Art 14 (1) Rome I-Regulation and are accordingly not determined by the governing law of the assigned claim). Pursuant to Art 145 Swiss PILA, the contractual assignment

between the (alleged) assignee and the original debtor will most likely apply Swiss law with regard to the scope and impact of the present § 12 (4), as the CISG covers this subject neither explicitly nor by means of general principles.

336 Contrary to many other legal systems, an anti-assignment clause governed by Swiss law has **"erga omnes" effects** and therefore prevents (once applicable) the acquisition of the assigned claim by any third party.[586]

XIII. The governing law of the contract

1. The suggested clause

§ 13 GOVERNING LAW

(1) **This Contract is governed by Swiss material law to the inclusion of the United Nations Convention on Contracts for the International Sale of Goods (CISG).**

(2) **The material laws of Switzerland shall also apply with regard to any non-contractual obligations arising from or related to this contract, in particular any concurring claims under tort.** *This choice of law does however not extend to obligations arising out of an act of unfair competition, the restriction of competition or an infringement of intellectual property rights.*

2. Annotations

Subparagraph 1

337 The private international laws of many jurisdictions permit the parties of an (international) commercial contract in contrast to consumer and employment contracts[587] to freely choose the **governing law** of their contractual relationship (the "lex contractus") provided that the contract is not solely linked to one single jurisdiction and accordingly entails a genuine international element.[588] At least under European but also Swiss private international law, the parties can also choose

---

of a claim including potential "erga omnes" effects of an anti-assignment clause are however governed by the lex contractus of the assigned claim. A prevailing choice of law between assignor and assignee is invalid if this choice has not been permitted by the debtor of the claim in the individual case, Art 145 (1) 2 PILA.

[586] See Chapter A.IV.6 above.

[587] See for instance Art 6 (1), (2) and Art 8 (1), (2) Rome I Regulation (n 3). Though the parties may pursuant to these provisions choose the governing law even in case of consumer or employment contracts (as defined by the Rome I Regulation), this choice will be of a rather limited effect given that mandatory laws applicable in the jurisdiction of the consumer's habitual residence respectively the working place of the employee prevail over the chosen governing law.

[588] See with regard to member states of the EU Art 3 (1), (3) Rome I-Regulation (n 3); Switzerland: Art 116 (1) PILA. Though this is not explicitly stated, the choice of a foreign law requires pursuant to Swiss private international law an international link as well, see M Amstutz in Honsell et al (n 251) Art 116 PILA para 7. Other jurisdictions have more or less recently expressly enacted the principle of party autonomy as well, see, inter alia, China: Arts 3 and 41 of the Law on the Application of Laws to Foreign-related Civil Relationships of the People's Republic of China; Japan: Art. 7 of the Act on General Rules for Application of Laws (Law No 78); Russia: Art. 1210 (1) Civil Code; USA: § 187 Restatement (2nd), Conflict of Laws; see also G Rühl, "Regulatory Competition in Contract Law: Empirical Evidence and Normative Implications" [2013] ERCL 61, 64 f.

XIII. The governing law of the contract

a "neutral" law, i. e. the laws of a jurisdiction that has no objective links with either the place of business of the parties or the place of performance.[589]

The **freedom of choice** with regard to the governing law is even more far-reaching if an arbitral tribunal instead of a court of law is in charge of resolving a potential contractual dispute between the parties. Many domestic arbitration laws as well as international conventions explicitly stipulate in line with the arbitration rules of the major arbitration institutions[590] that the governing law of the contract is first and foremost to be determined by the parties themselves.[591] Even states that do not permit the choice of the governing law by the parties pursuant to their general conflict of laws provisions are on a regular basis more generous if the parties have opted for arbitration instead of litigation.[592] In the case of an arbitral tribunal having its seat in Switzerland (as suggested by the arbitration clause of the present International Sales Terms, see § 14 below), the then applicable Art 187 PILA leads to the same result. Against this background, § 13 (1) should generally be upheld both by the courts and by arbitral tribunals whenever the seller and the purchaser are based in different jurisdictions and the transaction is of a commercial character for both parties. 338

The rationale behind the choice of law contained in § 13 (1) has already been discussed above.[593] In the author's opinion, the choice of a "state law" is for the present purpose also clearly more recommendable than the choice of general principles of the lex mercatoria or of legal principles of international contract law developed by academic scholars and adopted by international organizations. Although (if so 339

---

[589] H Heiss, "Party Autonomy", in F Ferrari and S Leible (eds), *Rom I Regulation* (Sellier, München 2009) 1, 2. Conflict of laws rules of the US states are in principle still more restrictive: § 187 (2) Restatement (2nd), Conflict of Laws, requires either a substantial relationship between the parties respectively the transaction and the chosen law or another reasonable basis for the choice. § 1–301 UCC (2003) (not yet adopted by the US states) lowers the threshold for a valid choice of law provision at least in business to business contracts, see ML Moses, *The Principles and Practice of International Commercial Arbitration* (2nd edn CUP, Cambridge 2012) 72.

[590] See for instance Art 21 (1) ICC Arbitration Rules 2012; Art 33 (1) Swiss Rules of International Arbitration 2012.

[591] Germany: § 1051 (1) Code of Civil Procedure; Switzerland: Art 187 (1) PILA; France: Art 1496 NCPC; England: Sec 46 (1) Arbitration Act 1996; Art. VII (1) European Convention on International Commercial Arbitration. Arbitral tribunals seated in the EU are according to the prevailing opinion not bound by the Rome I Regulation, see inter alia D Martiny, in *Münchener Kommentar zum Bürgerlichen Gesetzbuch* (5th edn C.H. Beck, München 2010) Art. 1 Rom I-Regulation para 100; T Pfeiffer "Die Abwahl des deutschen AGB-Rechts in Inlandsfällen bei Vereinbarung eines Schiedsverfahrens" [2012] NJW 1169, 1170; J Kondring, "Flucht vor dem deutschen AGB-Recht bei Inlandsfällen" [2010] RIW 184, 187. However, this still prevailing view is (at least outside the scope of application of the European Convention on International Commercial Arbitration that prevails over the Rome I Regulation pursuant to Art. 25 Rome I-Regulation) more and more disputed, s. for instance P Mankowski, "ROM I-VO und Schiedsverfahren" [2011] RIW 30 ff. as well as B Yüksel, "The Relevance of the Rome I Regulation to International Commercial Arbitration in the European Union" [2011] JPIL 149, 164.

[592] For instance, the regular private international law of Brazil (to be applied by state courts) and other Latin American jurisdictions does not permit a choice of law by the parties. However, if the parties have entered into an arbitration agreement, they may choose the governing law of their contract even if the seat of the arbitration is located in these jurisdictions; s. M Albornoz, "Choice of Law in International Contracts in Latin American Legal Systems" [2010] JPIL 959, 23, 44 (inter alia) with reference to Art. 9 of the Brazilian Civil Code's Introductory Law (litigation) as well as Art. 2.1 Lei 9307 (arbitration).

[593] See ch A.II above.

requested by the parties and contrary to the courts of law[594]) arbitral tribunals are generally entitled to apply "soft law" such as the Unidroit Principles for International Commercial Contracts 2010, the Principles of European Contract law or the "lex mercatoria" in general[595], the CISG offers, contrary to at least some of these instruments, specific provisions for sales contracts and can provide greater legal certainty given that international case law has interpreted and applied the CISG for more than 30 years. Secondly, a variety of legal gaps is not addressed by "soft law" instruments and would in this case have to be solved on the basis of domestic (state) law in any case.[596]

340   It has also already been discussed above[597] that some legal issues are outside the scope of a governing law clause. According to generally acknowledged principles of private international law, the parties can on a regular basis not choose the applicable property laws that will govern the transfer of title of the contract goods. The same applies with regard to the question of the legal capacity of both natural persons and corporate entities that is subject to the domestic laws applicable at the place of domicile or the place of incorporation.[598] Finally, certain "overriding mandatory" rules of foreign jurisdictions such as export control regulations, antitrust laws and so forth as well as rules of "international public policy" can have a direct impact on a sales transaction. Though this holds in principle true regardless of whether the parties opt for arbitration or litigation as the appropriate means for dispute resolution, an arbitral tribunal does enjoy more independence also in that regard.[599] Nevertheless, in order to prevent an overbroad choice, § 13 (1) is explicitly limited to the governing law of the contract (in deviation of the suggested provision contained in the first edition of this book) and avoids a general reference to any and all legal matters that may arise out of or in relation to the contract. By that means, this clause may in principle be used in the vast majority of jurisdictions and regardless whether the parties have opted for arbitration or litigation.

---

[594] The vast majority of jurisdictions do not permit the choice of "non-state" (soft) law if courts of law are in charge of resolving a contractual dispute, see in particular Art 3 (1) Rome I Regulation (n 3). Therefore, the choice of "soft law" in a contract will necessarily fail whenever the parties have not concluded a valid arbitration agreement.

[595] Contrary to the "lex mercatoria" whose existence, scope and precise content remains a highly controversial matter, the Unidroit Principles of International Commercial Contracts 2010 (UPICC) as well as the various European instruments (eg, the Principles of European Contract law (PECL) as well as the Draft Common Frame of Reference (DCFR) prepared by the Study Group on a European Civil Code and the Research Group on EC Private Law) offer carefully drafted sets of rules that are specifically tailored for international commercial transactions. For the various existing instruments of soft law in general M Bonell "The CISG, European Contract Law and the Development of a World Contract Law" (2008) 56 Am J Comp L 1 ff.

[596] The combined choice of the CISG and the UPICC (respectively other "soft law" principles) on the other hand would create a complicated three-layer structure of governing laws (CISG, UPICC and domestic laws as supplementary law) and also lead to further ambiguities given that the CISG and the UPICC deviate in some areas, see in particular R Herber, "Lex Mercatoria and Principles – gefährliche Irrlichter im Internationalen Kaufrecht" [2003] IHR 1, 9.

[597] See ch A.V above.

[598] See for instance Art 7 EGBGB.

[599] Horn (n 254) 213. For applicable limitations in case of arbitration GC Moss, "International Arbitration and the Quest for the Applicable Law" [2008] Global Jurist 1 ff.

Subparagraph 2

In order to provide for a coherent legal framework, § 13 (2) chooses Swiss law 341 also as the governing law with respect to concurring **claims under tort** as these claims may substantially overlap with contractual claims.

At least under European private international law, the freedom of choice of law 342 extends nowadays (subject to certain prerequisites) to concurring claims under tort that may in the context of a sales transaction in particular arise if defective products have caused either property damage (in particular those external to the contract goods) or bodily injury. Art 14 (1) lit b Rome II Regulation[600] permits the choice of the applicable law with regard to (concurring) claims under tort even before the occurrence of a harmful event giving rise to such claims. For the time being, however, it is still unclear whether a valid choice of law (with respect to non-contractual claims) can be made in general terms and conditions given that Art 14 (1) lit b Rom II Regulation requires a "freely negotiated contract".[601] Furthermore, a choice is according to the explicit restrictions set forth in Art 6 (4) and Art 8 (2) Rome II Regulation not permitted with regard to non-contractual obligations arising out of an act of unfair competition, the restriction of competition or from an infringement of an intellectual property right. Given that the Rome II Regulation must be applied by state courts within the EU, but may also become relevant for arbitral tribunals with a legal seat in a member state of the European Union[602] (and may to that extent prevail over domestic arbitration laws), the optional sentence of the suggested choice of law provision[603] may be added whenever a domestic court of an EU member state respectively an arbitral tribunal with a seat within the EU has jurisdiction (in particular pursuant to a corresponding forum selection clause or arbitration agreement) in order to reduce risks that this choice of law provision is held to be inoperative.[604]

Swiss private international law seems to permit a corresponding choice at least in combination with an arbitration agreement without further preconditions: According to **Art 187 PILA**, an arbitral tribunal must resolve a dispute primarily on the basis of the law chosen by the parties.[605] Although Swiss jurisprudence has so far not determined whether concurring claims under tort fall within the ambit of Art 187 PILA as well, it is generally accepted that Art 187 PILA prevails over any other conflict of laws provision contained in the PILA. A literal interpretation of

---

[600] See n 318.

[601] See Heiss (n 589) 8 f. However, the choice of the governing law of the contract will on a regular basis indirectly also determine the applicable material laws in relation to concurring tort claims, see Art 4 (3) as well as Art 5 (2) Rom II Regulation.

[602] According to the wording of the Rome II Regulation it remains unclear whether only courts of law or also arbitral tribunals (with a legal seat in the EU) are bound by it. However, pursuant to Recital No 8, the Regulation "should apply irrespective of the nature of the court or **tribunal** seized" [emphasis added].

[603] Based on the clause suggested by M Walter in P Ostendorf and P Kluth, *Internationale Wirtschaftsverträge* (C.H. Beck, München 2013) § 13 para 76.

[604] P Ostendorf, "Die Wahl des auf internationale Wirtschaftsverträge anwendbaren Rechtsrahmens im Europäischen Kollisionsrecht: Rechtswahlklauseln 2.0" [2012] IHR 180, 182.

[605] Pursuant to the prevailing view, Art 187 PILA excludes the direct application of any other conflict of laws provisions of the PILA, see PA Karrer in Honsell et al (n 251) Art 187 PILA para 20.

Art 187 PILA, which refers to "disputes" in general without providing any further limitation in this respect, seems to further support the view that the parties may choose the applicable law also with regard to concurring claims under tort.[606]

XIV. Arbitration and Litigation

1. The suggested clause

§ 14 ARBITRATION

(1) All disputes arising from or related to the Contract, regardless of their legal basis (contract, tort or otherwise), shall be submitted to the International Court of Arbitration of the International Chamber of Commerce (ICC) and shall be finally settled under the ICC Arbitration Rules 2012 (hereinafter the "Rules") by one (1) arbitrator appointed in accordance with the Rules. The language to be used in the arbitration proceedings shall be English. The seat of arbitration shall be [...] Switzerland.

(2) *The parties remain, however, entitled to apply to any competent judicial authority for interim or conservatory measures in accordance with the Rules.*

[alternatively]

§ 14 EXCLUSIVE JURISDICTION

(1) *Without prejudice to § 14 (2) and § 14 (3) below, the Parties agree to submit any dispute arising from or related to the Contract, regardless of its legal basis (contract, tort or otherwise) to the exclusive jurisdiction of the courts of [...].*

(2) *The Seller remains entitled to bring an action also at the principal place of business of the Purchaser.*

(3) *Both parties remain entitled to apply to any competent judicial authority for interim or conservatory measures.*

[alternatively]

§ 14 NON-EXCLUSIVE JURISDICTION

The Parties agree to submit any dispute arising from or related to the Contract, regardless of its legal basis (contract, tort or otherwise) to the non-exclusive jurisdiction of the courts of [...].

---

[606] Swiss private international law is however more restrictive with regard to proceedings conducted by Swiss courts of law: In this case, the parties can only opt for the tort laws of the forum state (hence Swiss law) instead of the otherwise applicable law whereas even that limited choice is subject to a mutual agreement of the parties concluded *subsequent* to the harmful event, see Art 132 PILA. It is also controversial whether concurring tort claims are governed by the (chosen) governing law of the contract by means of an accessory application in the absence of a (valid) choice in that respect. Though Art 133 (3) PILA provides for a similar mechanism as the Rome II Regulation (see for the latter T de Boer, "Party Autonomy and its Limitations in the Rome II Regulation" [2007] YPIL 19, 27), the prevailing view assumes that Art 135 PILA (the specific conflict of laws provision of the PILA on product liability) ousts Art 133 (3) PILA, see RP Umbricht and N Zeller in Honsell et al (n 251) Art 135 PILA para 14.

2. General background

The contractual machinery for the **resolution of disputes** is generally more important for the purchaser than for the seller: The seller is rarely compelled to institute legal proceedings against the purchaser as he will usually receive the contract price (being the essence of what he can expect under the contract) at an early stage of the transaction. The purchaser on the other hand may have to enforce warranty claims based on defective goods even after the delivery of the goods and payment of the contract price. 343

This does not mean, however, that issues of dispute resolution can be neglected by a seller: The chosen **means of and the place for dispute resolution** may directly influence both the interpretation and the enforceability of individual contract clauses. Additionally, the seller may want to enforce claims for the contract price or for damages if the purchaser repudiates the contract notwithstanding the fact that the goods have not yet been delivered. 344

In a commercial contract, the parties can in principle freely decide whether disputes arising from or in connection with the contract are to be resolved by way of litigation conducted by domestic courts of law or by way of arbitration. It is not possible to stipulate a general preference for either means of dispute resolution that applies in all cases. Arbitration does provide the parties with greater leeway in relation to the choice of the governing law of the contract (and the acceptance of that decision by a tribunal) and is without doubt more appropriate in relation to international sales transactions with links outside the European Union. On the other hand, litigation can be substantially cheaper (in particular if the value of the matter in dispute is small) and is therefore also a viable option at least with regard to disputes that are solely linked to the European Union/the European Economic Area (to the exception of Liechtenstein that is not a member of the Lugano Convention). 345

a) Arbitration

Arbitration is a private system of dispute resolution that offers some advantages over litigation in particular with regard to an international commercial transaction. Due to the most prominent international convention in this field, the United Nations Convention on the Recognition and Enforcement of Foreign Arbitral Awards of 1958 (the "New York Convention")[607] that has been adopted by currently 149 countries in the world (status as of 31 July 2013), it is generally much easier to enforce an arbitral award than the judgment of a court of law[608], as the New York Convention obliges the contracting states to recognize and enforce international arbitral awards (Art III New York Convention) subject only to their compliance with fundamental proce- 346

---

[607] The Convention can be found at http://www.uncitral.org/pdf/english/texts/arbitration/NY-conv/XXII_1_e.pdf. The Convention applies whenever an arbitral award is made in a state other than the state where the recognition and enforcement of such award is sought, Art I (1) New York Convention.

[608] The judgment of a domestic court will only be recognized and enforced in an another state if bi- or multilateral treaties concluded by the affected states provide for the same or the domestic procedural laws of the enforcing state permit the enforcement of foreign judgments in the individual case. A number of domestic civil procedural laws still adhere to the principle of reciprocity: Foreign judgments are accordingly (at least pursuant to the applicable statutes) in this case only recognized if (inter alia) the courts of the foreign jurisdiction in question do also recognize judgments rendered by courts of the enforcing state, see, eg, § 328 (1) No 5 German Code of Civil Procedure.

dural and material legal principles.⁶⁰⁹ By the same token, the parties are in case of a valid arbitration agreement also able to stay out of the other party's domestic courts as any court of a contracting state of the **New York Convention** is obliged to decline its jurisdiction if seized upon in a matter that falls within the ambit of an arbitration agreement (Art II (3) New York Convention).

347 Two different kinds of arbitration exist: The parties can either opt for **institutional arbitration** where the proceedings will be administered by a permanent arbitration institution pursuant to the rules of that institution (for instance the Arbitration Rules of the International Chamber of Commerce (ICC), the Rules of the London Court of Arbitration (LCIA), the Swiss Rules of International Arbitration of the Swiss Chambers of Commerce, the Commercial Arbitration Rules of the American Arbitration Association or the Arbitration Rules of the German Institution of Arbitration). Alternatively, the parties can agree on ad-hoc arbitration that will be conducted in accordance with the rules set by the parties themselves.⁶¹⁰

348 Although both institutional and ad-hoc arbitration fall within the ambit of the New York Convention and therefore enjoy its benefits (Art 1(2) New York Convention), institutional arbitration provides the parties with greater legal security and reliability. The rules of the major arbitral institutions do not only lay down the general framework for the arbitral proceedings. They also explicitly resolve **default situations** such as the failure of both parties to agree on a sole arbitrator, respectively a refusal of either party to appoint an arbitrator in case the parties have agreed on three arbitrators.⁶¹¹ Additionally, not all domestic arbitration laws accept a contractual agreement providing for ad-hoc arbitration. Notably Chinese law considers corresponding arbitration clauses as invalid and unenforceable at least if the elected seat of arbitration is located in China.⁶¹²

349 The parties to an arbitration agreement are free to determine the **legal seat** of arbitration. The choice of the legal seat is decisive with regard to the applicable domestic arbitration laws that govern the arbitration proceedings as such (the "lex

---

⁶⁰⁹ Pursuant to Art V (1) of the New York Convention, recognition and enforcement of an arbitral award may be refused if either the arbitral agreement is invalid or fundamental principles of legal procedure have not been observed (see Art V (1) lit b-d New York Convention). Furthermore, recognition and enforcement may also be denied if the subject matter of the dispute in question is not capable of settlement by arbitration (pursuant to the laws of the state where enforcement is sought) or an enforcement would be contrary to public policy in accordance with the laws of the country in which recognition and enforcement is sought ("under the law of that country"), see Art V (2) lit a and lit b New York Convention.

⁶¹⁰ Instead of drafting their own procedural rules from scratch, the parties can pick established procedural rules such as the UNCITRAL Arbitration Rules if they want to go along with ad hoc instead of institutional arbitration, see for this option N Blackaby et al, *Redfern and Hunter on International Arbitration* (5th edn OUP, Oxford 2009) para 1.153. The latter is highly advisable whenever the parties opt for ad-hoc arbitration given that the UNCITRAL rules contain inter alia provisions dealing with default of either party to appoint an arbitrator.

⁶¹¹ See, for instance, Art 12 ICC Arbitration Rules 2012.

⁶¹² Art 16 of the Chinese Arbitration Law provides that an arbitration agreement must (with regard to arbitration proceedings conducted in China) expressly designate a competent arbitration commission (i. e., an arbitration institution), see J Tao and C v Wunschheim, "Articles 16 and 18 of the PRC Arbitration Law: The Great Wall of China for Foreign Arbitration Institutions" (2007) 23 Arb Int 309, 323. It is also still controversial whether a non-chinese arbitration institution will be regarded as a "competent arbitration commission" by Chinese arbitration laws, see M Barth and G Johnston, "Vereinbarung einer Schiedskommission als Wirksamkeitsvoraussetzung der Schiedsklausel – Zur Nichtanerkennung eines chinesischen ICC-Schiedsspruchs in Deutschland" [2007] SchiedsVZ 300, 303.

arbitri").⁶¹³ The lex arbitri usually contains basic rules for the arbitral proceedings such as the constitution of the tribunal, default proceedings and judicial review of an award, but also determines whether the dispute is arbitrable in the first place.⁶¹⁴ The majority of the provisions contained in the various domestic arbitration laws is usually not of a mandatory character⁶¹⁵ and may accordingly be set aside by the rules of the arbitration institution selected by the parties. Once the legal seat has been chosen, however, mandatory provisions of the seat country's lex arbitri must be observed by the tribunal.⁶¹⁶

b) Litigation

Arbitration is not always the preferred means for the resolution of an international contractual dispute. **Litigation** may be considerably cheaper in individual cases and also puts more emphasis on the strict application of legal principles than arbitration. As already stated, however, the "weak spot" of litigation in an international contract dispute materializes once a party aims to enforce the judgment of a domestic court in a foreign jurisdiction: States have so far shown considerably more reluctance to acknowledge and enforce judgments of foreign courts than arbitral awards. 350

These problems do not arise if either party seeks to enforce a judgment of a court located in the EU or the EEA (to the exclusion of Liechtenstein⁶¹⁷) in another EU/EEA member state. The courts of the member states of the EU/the EEA are under EC Regulation No 44/2001⁶¹⁸ (the called **"Brussels I Regulation"**), respectively its successor instrument, Regulation (EU) No 1215/1012⁶¹⁹ as well as the Lugano Convention⁶²⁰ obliged to acknowledge and enforce any court decision dealing with a commercial or civil law matter rendered by a court of another member state, subject only to compliance of the decision with fundamental procedural and substantive rules. According to Art 23 of both instruments⁶²¹, the parties can also agree on the 351

---

⁶¹³ The lex arbitri must be distinguished from the governing law of the contract (i.e. the substantive law applied by the tribunal to the merits of the dispute) but also from the law governing the arbitration agreement as such (i.e. the substantial validity of the arbitration clause) given that the majority of arbitration laws consider the arbitration agreement as a separate contract. Though there is a strong assumption that an arbitration agreement will be governed by the same law as the main contract (provided the parties have not explicitly stipulated otherwise), this view is not universally accepted: Another opinion favors the law of the seat of the arbitration (hence the lex arbitri) as the applicable law of an arbitration clause, see A Tweeddale and K Tweeddale, *Arbitration of Commercial Disputes. International and English Law and Practice* (OUP, Oxford 2007) para 7.20.

⁶¹⁴ JF Poudret and S Besson, *Comparative Law of International Arbitration* (2ⁿᵈ edn Sweet & Maxwell, London 2007) para 112.

⁶¹⁵ Moses (n 589) 65.

⁶¹⁶ Poudret and Besson (n 614) para 117.

⁶¹⁷ Liechtenstein has still not acceded to the Lugano Convention, see R Schütze, *Rechtsverfolgung im Ausland* (4ᵗʰ edn De Gruyter, Berlin 2009) para 615 ff.

⁶¹⁸ Council Regulation (EC) No 44/2001 of 22 December 2000 on jurisdiction and the recognition and enforcement of judgments in civil and commercial matters, [2001] OJ L12/1.

⁶¹⁹ Regulation (EU) No 1215/2012 of the European Parliament and of the Council of 12 December 2012 on jurisdiction and the recognition and enforcement of judgments in civil and commercial matters (recast), [2012] OJ L 351/1. This Regulation replaces the Brussels I Regulation (Art. 80) and will pursuant to its Art. 66 (1) apply to legal proceedings instituted on or after 10 January 2015.

⁶²⁰ The Lugano Convention has recently been revised and by that means further aligned with the current version of the Brussels I Regulation.

⁶²¹ Respectively Art. 25 Regulation (EU) No 1215/1012.

(exclusive) jurisdiction of any national court located inside the EU/EEA. A corresponding choice must be respected by all courts of EU/EEA member states provided that at least one of the parties[622] resides either in the EU or in the EEA.[623] An (exclusive) **agreement on jurisdiction** is therefore a viable alternative to arbitration whenever both parties are based in the EU/EEA and the likelihood that a judgment may have to be enforced abroad seems remote.

352 Litigation instead of arbitration is, however, much less recommendable in cases where a court judgment is to be enforced **outside the EU/EEA**. Although bilateral conventions may oblige domestic courts to enforce foreign judgments in individual cases and some national procedural rules do also provide for the general recognition of foreign judgments (sometimes, inter alia, subject to the principle of reciprocity) substantial legal uncertainties whether a judgment will eventually be enforced remain in this case.

353 This substantial advantage of arbitration over litigation with regard to enforceability may be reduced greatly once the **Hague Convention of 30 June 2005**[624] on Choice of Courts Agreements finally enters into force. The Hague Convention tries to establish a mechanism similar to the New York Convention with regard to judgments of domestic courts residing in member states of the Convention that have based their jurisdiction on an exclusive agreement on jurisdiction between the parties.[625] The Convention also applies in relation to concurring claims under tort with the exception of claims by natural persons based on bodily injury.[626] However, at this point in time, (still) only Mexico has acceded to the Convention whereas both the USA and the European Union have signed though (as of 2013) not yet ratified this instrument.

---

[622] According to Art. 25 Regulation (EU) No 1215/1012, a jurisdiction clause providing for the jurisdiction of a court of any EU member state falls within the ambit of this provision regardless of the domicile of the parties. Hence, from 10 January 2015 onwards, courts of EU member states must also accept the prorogation of their jurisdiction even if both parties are domiciled outside of the EU, s. J von Hein, "Die Neufassung der EuGVVO" [2013] RIW 97, 104.

[623] An agreement on jurisdiction pursuant to Art 23 Brussels I Regulation respectively the Lugano Convention may however not contradict the exclusive jurisdiction of a court stipulated in the instruments, see Arts 22 and 23 (5). An agreement is pursuant to Art 24 also disregarded if the defendant appears in front of a court to which he has been summoned, see A Briggs, *Agreements on Jurisdiction and Choice of Law* (OUP, Oxford 2008) 239. Domestic laws of the member states must not invalidate an agreement on jurisdiction falling within the ambit of Art 23 by taking recourse to stricter domestic laws dealing with unfair contractual provisions, see R Hausmann in Reithmann and Martiny (n 262) para 6391. In case of consumer contracts, however, courts must invalidate agreements on jurisdictions that infringe the European Directive 93/13/EEC (n 161) respectively domestic rules that have transformed the Directive into national laws, see recently ECJ, Case C-243/08 *Pannon GSM Zrt* (not yet published).

[624] <http://www.hcch.net/index_en.php?act=conventions.text&cid=98>.

[625] For the current status of the Convention see the website of the Hague Conference on Private International Law: <http://www.hcch.net/index_en.php?act=conventions.status&cid=98>. An obligation to recognize both foreign judgments as well as agreements on jurisdiction exist only in relation to judgments rendered by courts of member states of the Convention.

[626] See Art 2 Hague Convention: "This Convention shall not apply to the following matters: [...] j) claims for personal injury brought by or on behalf of natural persons; k) tort or delict claims for damage to tangible property that do not arise from a contractual relationship [...]".

XIV. Arbitration and Litigation

c) Alternative Dispute Resolution

In particular in the area of construction, standard form contracts such as the FIDIC conditions[627] often provide for so-called **"multistep dispute resolution"** mechanisms.[628] According to this machinery, the parties must first attempt to resolve their dispute amicably, either by negotiation at a certain business level and/or by mediation (collectively "alternative dispute resolution") before they can proceed with arbitration or, as the case may be, litigation.[629]   354

There is no doubt that this approach may be useful to resolve a complex dispute. In a standard sales transaction, however, **alternative dispute resolution** procedures seem less suitable as a precursor to arbitration/litigation. Besides the problem that mandatory ADR procedures may considerably extend the overall duration of legal proceedings, poorly drafted ADR clauses that do not unambiguously stipulate when the parties are permitted to move on to arbitration or litigation may cause substantial legal uncertainty and additional costs. Although arbitral tribunals and the courts have generally been reluctant to enforce ambiguous ADR clauses, the risk remains that an arbitral tribunal will deny its jurisdiction on the ground that neither negotiations nor mediation attempts were appropriately conducted first.[630]   355

Some domestic laws demand the prior performance of alternative dispute resolution as a condition precedent before the parties can proceed with either litigation or arbitration. For instance, according to Section 108 of the English Housing Grants, Construction and Regeneration Act 1996, the parties to a contract that involves construction operations[631] must first refer any dispute to an **adjudication** board[632] whenever construction works are being carried out in England, Scotland or Wales and regardless of whether English law is the governing law of the contract.[633] But in general, a standard sales transaction will not fall within the ambit of these statutory provisions.   356

3. Annotations

a) The Arbitration Clause:

Subparagraph 1

§ 14 (1) contains an arbitration agreement that opts for **institutional arbitration** in accordance with the Arbitration Rules of the International Chamber of Commerce (ICC). The ICC is probably the most prestigious arbitration institution and therefore widely accepted in the international commercial world. Apart from the general advantages of institutional arbitration, the ICC Arbitration Rules 2012 provide also for a specific system of quality control: Pursuant to Art 33 ICC Arbitration Rules 2012,   357

---

[627] See n 9 above.
[628] Moses (n 589) 47.
[629] S Leonhard and K Dharmananda, "Peace Talks before war: The Enforcement of Clauses for Dispute Resolution before Arbitration" (2006) 23 J Int Arbitrat 301 ff.
[630] Leonhard and Dharmananda (n 629) 302 with further reference to case law.
[631] Though the definition of "construction operations" under the Act is rather broad, relevant operations (such as construction, maintenance, repair, alteration) must be carried out in relation to buildings or structures that form part of the land, see Sec 105 (1) of the Act.
[632] Adjudication is an alternative dispute resolution mechanism that concludes (contrary to conciliation and mediation) with a binding, although not final decision, see N Gould and M Abel, "Adjudication in the UK – recent developments" [2005] SchiedsVZ 167, 190 f.
[633] See Gould and Abel (n 632) 190 f.

C. The International Sales Terms

the final award of the tribunal is subject to the approval of the ICC Court (a permanent body of the ICC composed of international renowned experts of international commercial arbitration) as to its form. The ICC Court may also recommend amendments as to points of substance though the tribunal is not bound by any such recommendations.

358 It goes without saying that other arbitration institutions are also recommendable and may even be considerably cheaper than the ICC. In any event however, it is clearly advisable to choose one of the renowned institutions and to use their model arbitration clauses[634] in order to avoid the danger of **"pathological arbitration clauses"** that may be inoperative. Pathological arbitration clauses[635] typically refer contractual disputes to arbitration institutions that do not or have ceased to exist[636] or cannot be unambiguously identified or cause confusion by combining an arbitration agreement with the choice of courts of law.[637] The international case law is full of examples where "pathological arbitration clauses" have not only caused major obstacles for the parties in successfully proceeding with the resolution of a dispute but also increased the overall costs of the legal proceedings.[638]

359 The choice of a renowned (in particular West European or North American) arbitration institution also offers another substantial benefit: The terms and conditions of many industrial **insurance policies** often accept neither the use of ad-hoc arbitration nor less renowned arbitration institutions as a means[639] of dispute resolution, and non-compliance with this requirement may put the seller's insurance cover at risk. In any event, the seller is best advised to carefully check the requirements of his third-party/product liability insurance with his insurance broker to make sure that the arbitration clause complies with the terms of the insurance policy.

360 Arbitration pursuant to the ICC Arbitration Rules is expensive.[640] **Costs** may, however, be greatly reduced if the parties appoint a sole arbitrator instead of a three person tribunal. § 14 (1) accordingly opts for a sole arbitrator, considering that the legal and factual complexity of a dispute related to a standard sales transaction is in all likelihood considerably lower than the complexity of a dispute that may for instance arise from a construction contract.[641]

361 § 14 (1) is drafted in accordance with the model arbitration clause proposed by the ICC. However, some changes were made: On the one hand, the clause makes explicit reference to concurring **claims under tort**. Even though the latter is in

---

[634] See for instance the model arbitration agreements promoted by the London Court of Arbitration (LCIA) (<http://www.lcia.org/Dispute_Resolution_Services/LCIA_Recommended_Clauses.aspx >), the Swiss Chambers' Arbitration Institution (<https://www.swissarbitration.org/sa/en/clause.php>), the American Arbitration Association (<http://www.clausebuilder.org>) and the German Institution of Arbitration (<http://www.dis-arb.de/en/17/clause/dis-arbitration-clause-id22 >).

[635] For the origin of this phrase see Tweeddale and Tweeddale (n 613) para 4.45.

[636] A Frignani, "Drafting Arbitration Agreements" (2008) 24 Arb Int 561, 565.

[637] See for this specific problem S Stebler, "The Problem of Conflicting Arbitration and Forum Selection Clauses" (2013) 31 ASA Bull 27 ff.

[638] See for examples S Breßler et al, "Pathologische Schiedsklauseln – Beispiele aus der Beratungspraxis" [2008] IHR 89 ff.

[639] See R Koch, "Schiedsgerichtsvereinbarungen und Haftpflichtversicherungsschutz" [2007] SchiedsVZ 281 ff.

[640] See Appendix III, ICC Arbitration Rules 2012.

[641] The parties must agree on and nominate the sole arbitrator within 30 days from the receipt of the claimant's request by the defendant. Failing an agreement, the sole arbitrator will be chosen and appointed by the ICC-court, see Art. 12 (3) ICC Arbitration Rules 2012.

principle covered by the phrase "arising from or related to the contract"[642], an explicit reference may enhance legal certainty even further, as national courts of different legal backgrounds may review both the validity and scope of an arbitration clause. Deviating from the standard clause recommended by the ICC, the suggested clause also contains an explicit reference to the "ICC Court" as the arbitration institution. This amendment is strictly speaking only necessary if the legal seat of the arbitration is in China.[643] However, this wording may also help to prevent the (remote) risk that a Chinese court may (wrongly) refuse the enforcement of an award in China. Explicit reference to the ICC court does no harm in all other cases where no links to China exist at all.

The choice of the (legal) seat of arbitration is not only a mere choice of convenience but also has substantial legal impacts as the tribunal must apply mandatory provisions of the lex arbitri and only the domestic courts residing in this state may (pursuant to an internationally accepted general principle) annul the award.[644] Against this background, the Swiss Code on Private International Law (PILA) as the applicable lex arbitri (in case of a seat in Switzerland) offers both a reliable legal framework and substantial leeway for the parties. In particular, Art 190 (1) PILA accepts the finality of an arbitral award as a matter of principle and allows an appeal[645] pursuant to Art 190 (2) PILA only in case of irregularities in relation to the constitution of the tribunal, errors of the tribunal with regard to the scope of its jurisdiction or infringements of either fundamental procedural rules (equality of the parties and/or the right to be heard) or the material "ordre public", which has been narrowly interpreted by the Swiss Federal Supreme Court.[646] In theory, and contrary to the vast majority of arbitration laws enacted elsewhere, the parties can even exclude this rather limited appeal provided that neither party has its place of business in Switzerland, see Art 192 PILA.[647] Besides the problem whether this

362

---

[642] See for instance the decision of the US District Court, Northern District of California (24 Oct 1996) *Twi Lite International, Inc v Anam Pacific Corp*, Yearbook of Commercial Arbitration XXIII (1998) 910 ff, dealing with an arbitration clause that covered only disputes "arising out of the contract" but omitted reference to disputes "relating to the contract". Pursuant to the court, the phrase "arising out of" did on a stand-alone basis not cover claims of misappropriation of trade secrets but only disputes relating to the interpretation and performance of the contract itself (to the exclusion of any collateral issues). For a review of this decision see also P Gillies, "Enforcement of International Arbitration Awards – The New York Convention" (2005) 9 Int'l Trade and Bus L Rev 19, 34.

[643] See the explicit recommendation by the ICC (<http://www.iccwbo.org/Products-and-Services/Arbitration-and-ADR/Arbitration/Standard-ICC-Arbitration-Clauses/>) with regard to arbitration conducted in China. However, it is still unclear whether Art 16 of the Chinese Arbitration Act acknowledges arbitration proceedings conducted in China but administered by a foreign arbitration institution at all, see Tao and Wunschheim (n 612) 323. Accordingly, the parties should at best avoid China as the seat of arbitration whenever they elect a non-Chinese arbitration institution.

[644] R Goode, "The Role of the Lex Loci Arbitri in International Arbitration" (2001) 19 Arb Int 19, 30. However, not all jurisdictions adhere strictly to that principle, see for instance with regard to India JK Schäfer, "Der lange Arm der indischen Justiz – Aufhebung von ausländischen Schiedssprüchen bei indischem Nexus" [2008] SchiedsVZ 299 ff.

[645] Pursuant to Art 191 PILA, an appeal may only be taken to the Swiss Federal Supreme Court.

[646] AK Schnyder and M Liatowitsch, *Internationales Privat- und Zivilverfahrensrecht* (2nd edn Schulthess, Zürich 2006) 183. In the essence, only fundamental and internationally accepted legal principles will qualify as forming part of the "ordre public" pursuant to Art 190 (2) lit e PILA, SVW Berti and AK Schnyder in Honsell et al (251) Art 190 PILA para 73.

[647] Pursuant to the Swiss Federal Supreme Court, an exclusion of any and all appeals pursuant to Art 192 PILA must be made in an explicit and unambiguous manner. Though express reference to

exclusion would be enforceable in general terms and conditions, it is from the author's point of view not recommendable to do so given that a (limited) **appeal** against a manifestly wrong award is in the interest of both parties.

363 According to Art II (1) of the New York Convention, an arbitration agreement must be recognized by the domestic courts of a contracting state (other than the seat state) if the agreement was made in writing. In accordance with Art II (2) of the New York Convention, this includes clauses contained in signed contracts or in an exchange of letters or telegrams. But an arbitration clause contained in general terms and conditions will not meet the **formal requirements** of the Convention if the other party has accepted those terms merely by way of conduct (eg, by means of performance of the contract).[648] At the same time, certain doubts remain whether the formal requirements of Art II (2) of the New York Convention are fulfilled if the parties sign a contract that incorporates general terms by way of reference but does not refer explicitly to an arbitration clause contained in these terms.[649]

364 Some domestic arbitration laws of the contracting states have established a **lower threshold** with regard to the requirements as to form.[650] But domestic arbitration laws (even those of the seat state) need not necessarily prevail over Art II New York Convention in the state where enforcement is sought. Though more lenient domestic laws may play a role under Art VII of the New York Convention,[651] enforcing states are not obliged (at least pursuant to the New York Convention) to enact or apply more generous legislation.

365 Considering that acceptance by way of conduct will not deemed to be sufficient for the purpose of creating a **valid agreement** to arbitrate, it is also for that reason of eminent importance that the purchaser countersigns a document that incorporates the arbitration clause.

Subparagraph 2

366 An arbitral tribunal (once established) is usually entitled both under its own procedural rules[652] in case of institutional arbitration and according to many national

---

Art 192 PILA in the contractual clause is not strictly necessary, a mere reference to the finality of the award will not be construed as an exclusion of Art 192 PILA, see BG (21 Oct 2008) (2009) 27 ASA Bull 290, 300.

[648] In this case, the formal requirements of Swiss law contained in Art 178 (1) PILA (that are relevant both for arbitral tribunals with a legal seat in Switzerland as well as for Swiss courts) are not fulfilled as well, see W Wenger and C Müller in Honsell et al (n 251) Art 178 PILA paras 5 and 15.

[649] In the affirmative however R Hausmann in Reithmann and Martiny (n 262) para 6687.

[650] Art 7 (6) of the UNCITRAL model law on arbitration stipulates that a reference in a contract to a document containing an arbitration clause constitutes a valid arbitration agreement provided that the contract is in writing and the reference is such as to make that clause part of the contract. Art 178 (1) PILA has been similarly interpreted, see BG (7 Feb 2001) (2001) 19 ASA Bull 529.

[651] See, eg, the decision of the German Federal Supreme Court, BGH (21 May 2005) [2005] SchiedsVZ 306 ff: In this case, the BGH held that Art VII of the New York Convention did not only justify the application of German arbitration laws tailored for national awards (though § 1061 German Code of Civil Procedure refers solely to the provisions of the New York Convention with regard to international awards) but also the even more lenient provisions of Dutch law as the relevant governing law of the arbitration agreement.

[652] Art 28 (1) ICC Arbitration Rules 2012; Art 34 Commercial Arbitration Rules of the American Arbitration Association; Art 25.1 LCIA Arbitration Rules; Art 26 Swiss Rules of International Arbitration; § 20 of the Arbitration Rules of the German Institution of Arbitration. See also for a

procedural laws[653] to issue **interim or conservatory measures** at the request of either party. The ICC Arbitration Rules 2012 have additionally established the alternative of an "**emergency arbitrator**"[654] that will be appointed by the President of the ICC Court even before the establishment of the arbitral tribunal (and until the file has been transmitted to an already established arbitral tribunal) within two days of receipt of a corresponding application of either party. The emergency arbitrator may grant interim measures in the form of an order (Art. 29 (2) ICC Arbitration Rules 2012) that is with respect to any question, issue or dispute determined in the order though not binding for the arbitral tribunal, Art. 29 (3) ICC Arbitration Rules 2012. Any of these **measures must, however, be recognized and enforced by the competent** courts of the state in which their enforcement is sought. This procedure can cost a considerable amount of time and hence deprive such interim measures of their essential advantage.[655] Furthermore, given that any order for interim or conservatory measures (either by the tribunal or an emergency arbitrator) will not constitute an arbitral award pursuant to the New York Convention, domestic procedural laws may (and often will) deny recognition at all.[656] It is therefore clearly desirable that the parties retain the right to apply to competent courts for intermediary relief, as their property, trade secrets or other rights may otherwise not be successfully protected.

In line with the suggestion made by the UNCITRAL model arbitration law[657], many domestic arbitration laws permit the parties to seek interim or conservatory relief through the courts of law.[658] However, considering that some national procedural rules do not provide the courts with explicit permission to that effect[659], the parties are well advised to clarify that any competent **domestic courts** should, notwithstanding the arbitration agreement, remain entitled to take preliminary measures. A judgment of a German Higher Regional Court illustrates the need for such a clarification: In the underlying case, the claimant (a German contractor for the engineering, construction and commissioning of a brewery in Algeria) had requested an interim injunction by a German court in order to prevent an allegedly unjustified drawing of a performance bond by the Algerian employer. Notwithstanding the explicit permission to issue interim orders pursuant to § 1033 of the German Code of Civil Procedure, the Higher Regional Court Nürnberg held that the choice of arbitration to be conducted in

367

---

thorough comparison of the arbitration institutions Simpson Thacher & Bartlett, *Comparison of International Arbitration Rules* (2nd edn Juris Publishing, USA 2002) 117.

[653] Germany: Art 1041 (1) German Code of Civil Procedure; Switzerland: Art 183 PILA.

[654] Art. 29 and Appendix V (Emergency Arbitrator Rules) ICC Arbitration Rules 2012. The rules on the emergency arbitrator will apply if the parties have not excluded them, Art. 29 (6) lit b ICC Arbitration Rules 2012.

[655] RA Schütze, *Schiedsgericht und Schiedsverfahren* (4th edn C.H. Beck, München 2007) para 253.

[656] P Hauser, "Eilrechtsschutz nach der neuen ICC-Schiedsordnung: Der "Emergency Arbitrator" [2013] RIW 364, 366. For further disadvantages compared to domestic court proceedings also J Grierson and A v Hooft, *Arbitrating under the 2012 ICC Rules* (Kluwer Law International, The Hague 2012) 63 f.

[657] See Art 17 UNCITRAL Model Law on International Commercial Arbitration 1985 with amendments as adopted in 2006.

[658] See for instance in Germany: § 1033 German Code of Civil Procedure; England: Art 44 Arbitration Act 1996; Switzerland: Art 183 PILA.

[659] With regard to remaining ambiguities in US Law JK Schäfer, "Ende eines Sonderweges: Gerichtlicher Eilrechtsschutz im Staat New York in internationalen Schiedsverfahren" [2006] SchiedsVZ 191 ff.

Switzerland expressed the parties' intention to exclude the jurisdiction of German courts in its entirety.[660]

368 These risks are non-existing if the parties agree (as it is suggested here) on the application of the **ICC Arbitration Rules**. Art 28 (2) of the ICC Arbitration Rules 2012 provides explicitly that the parties may apply to any competent judicial authority for interim or conservatory measures.[661] Accordingly, a choice of the ICC Rules without any further qualification will also incorporate Art 28 (2) into the arbitration clause. Against this background, the suggested subparagraph 2 is of a mere declaratory character and **strictly speaking not necessary**.

b) The alternative clause: Agreement on jurisdiction:

Subparagraph 1 and 2

369 § 14 (1) of the alternative clause contains an **agreement on jurisdiction** (respectively a "forum selection clause") providing for the exclusive jurisdiction of courts that remain to be selected by the seller. The seller can in particular either specify an individual court of first instance residing in a member state of the EU/EEA or choose the jurisdiction of the courts in one member state of the EU/EEA in general without further specifications.[662]

370 At least within the EU (and the EEA, with the exception of Liechtenstein), all domestic courts must accept an exclusive forum selection clause if only the requirements of Art 23 Brussels Regulation (or, as the case may be, the Lugano Convention) are fulfilled. Art 23 lit a of these instruments requires an agreement in writing, respectively the confirmation of an oral agreement in writing (or in a form which either accords with practices which the parties have established between themselves or are widely known and regularly observed usages of international trade that the parties are or ought to have been aware of). The **written-form requirement** is clearly fulfilled if the purchaser countersigns the main contract document and thereby declares his explicit acceptance of the International Sales Terms – a specific reference to the jurisdiction clause within the countersigned document (though suggested by the model form) is strictly speaking not necessary.[663]

Subparagraph 2

371 If the parties choose a venue outside the EU/EEA, the applicable national procedural laws of this jurisdiction will be decisive as to the scope, validity and effect of a forum selection clause. This also holds true with regard to the effect of an exclusive agreement on jurisdiction providing for a venue within the EU in Non-EU member states respectively with regard to an enforcement of a judgment rendered by a court within the EU outside the European Union as non-EU courts are not bound by the Brussels Regulation. If the seller nevertheless prefers litigation over arbitration

---

[660] OLG Nürnberg (27 Oct 2004) [2005] SchiedsVZ 51 f.

[661] Once the file has been transmitted to the arbitral tribunal, this right is subject to the existence of "appropriate circumstances". In any event, both application and any measures taken by a national court or other judicial authority must be notified to the ICC-Secretariat without delay.

[662] U Magnus in U Magnus and P Mankowski (eds), *Brussels I Regulation* (2nd edn Sellier, München 2011) Art 23 para 72.

[663] Briggs (n 623) para 7.4.

in this event, it is undoubtedly advisable to either opt for a **non-exclusive venue clause** or – as suggested by § 14 (2) – to provide for **an additional optional right** of the seller to bring an action before the courts located at the purchaser's place of business. Otherwise, the seller may end up in a situation where he can neither enforce a judgment rendered by the chosen court in his home jurisdiction abroad nor bring an action against the purchaser before a court in any other jurisdiction, as this court may deny its jurisdiction based on the exclusive forum selection clause.[664]

According to the author, an "unilateral jurisdiction agreement" is perfectly valid pursuant to the Brussels Regulation and should at least be respected by any court within the EU. That having said, however, the **French Cour de cassation** has recently taken the opposite view[665] by invalidating a corresponding agreement based on the assumption that an unilateral option should be considered as being contrary to the objectives of Art. 23 Brussels Regulation. Though this decision concerned a consumer contract, the reasoning of the court may also apply to B2B contracts.[666] Even though this judgment seems to be fundamentally flawed (all the more given that the Cour de cassation did not even deem it necessary to refer the matter to the European Court of Justice), the seller may also for this reason want to use the **suggested non-exclusive jurisdiction clause** instead. 371a

§ 14 (2) can and should also be deleted in its entirety once the **Hague Convention** of 30 June 2005[667] on Choice of Courts Agreements has come into force and both the state of jurisdiction and all potential enforcement states have acceded to this Convention. Otherwise the benefits of the Convention may be lost as the Convention only recognizes unfettered exclusive jurisdiction agreements.[668] 372

Subparagraph 3

Whether an exclusive forum selection clause also contains the parties' intention to derogate the jurisdiction of other courts even for **interim or conservatory measures** remains highly controversial.[669] Accordingly, the parties are for their mutual benefit well advised to explicitly keep that option open. 373

---

[664] See for such a case Schütze (n 617) para 184.
[665] Cour de Cassation (26 Sep 2012), Arrêt n° 983, File number 11–26.022; http://www.courdecassation.fr/jurisprudence_2/premiere_chambre_civile_568/983_26_24187.html.
[666] See R Fentiman,"Unilateral Jurisdiction Agreements in Europe" [2013] CLJ 24 ff. who provides an excellent critical review of this ill-judged decision.
[667] See n 624 above.
[668] See Art 3 lit a Hague Convention: For the purposes of this Convention a) 'exclusive choice of court agreement' means an agreement concluded by two or more parties that meets the requirements of paragraph c) and designates, for the purpose of deciding disputes which have arisen or may arise in connection with a particular legal relationship, the courts of one Contracting State or one or more specific courts of one Contracting State to the exclusion of the jurisdiction of **any other courts** [emphasis added].
[669] See, eg, BG (17 Sep 1999) BGE 125 III 451, 453: Exclusive forum selection clause ousts in principle (subject to certain exceptions) the jurisdiction of otherwise competent courts (pursuant to the Lugano Convention) also in relation to interim measures.

Appendix

I. The Sales Documentation Put Together

SALES CONTRACT

between

1. [...] (hereinafter "Seller")
2. [...] (hereinafter "Purchaser")

    Seller and Purchaser hereinafter also individually referred to as "Party" and collectively referred to as "Parties"

Seller agrees to deliver and Purchaser agrees to purchase the following contractual products including the scope of supply as further described in the enclosed Specifications pursuant to the terms and conditions below.

Contractual Products:	[...]
Contract Price:	EUR [...] plus VAT (if applicable). The Parties agree that the Purchaser is not entitled to pay the contract price in any other currency. Place of performance for the payment is the Seller's place of business.
Payment Terms:	Payment shall become due upon delivery of the Contractual Products in accordance with the Delivery Terms set forth below.
	Payment shall be effected via letter of credit against the following documents pursuant to § 2 (3) of the International Sales Terms:
	1. Commercial Invoice
	2. [...]
Delivery Terms:	[...] (INCOTERMS © 2010) subject to any amendments set forth in the International Sales Terms (see below).
Delivery Period:	[...]
Country of Use:	[...]
Terms & Conditions:	The attached International Sales Terms (including in particular the <u>arbitration agreement</u> stipulated in Art 14 of the International Sales Terms) [*alternatively: including the <u>forum selection clause</u> stipulated in Art 14 of the International Sales Terms*] shall apply to this sales transaction to the exclusion of any other terms and conditions.

_____   _____
Seller   Purchaser

_____   _____
Place, Date   Place, Date

Appendix

INTERNATIONAL SALES TERMS

§ 1 GENERAL PROVISIONS

(1) The following International Sales Terms shall apply to the supply of the contractual goods and related services (if any) by the Seller (hereinafter collectively referred to as the "Products") and shall together with the written Sales Contract signed by both parties and the agreed Technical Specifications of the Products (if any) collectively constitute the entire contract between the parties (hereinafter the "Contract). No other terms and conditions shall apply, including the terms contained in the Purchaser's general terms and conditions or referred to by the Purchaser, whether or not such terms conflict with or supplement these International Sales Terms and regardless of whether or not the Seller has explicitly objected to such terms.

(2) The International Sales Terms shall apply to the present Contract with the Purchaser. They shall by means of a framework agreement also apply to all future contracts concluded with the Purchaser, whose preponderant object is the supply of Products or related spare parts.

(3) The International Sales Terms shall not apply if the Products are intended for personal, family or household use by the Purchaser.

§ 2 TERMS OF PAYMENT

(1) The stipulated contract price is exclusive of value added tax. The Purchaser shall at Seller's request provide the Seller with the necessary documentation required by the competent tax authorities as evidence of an export tax exemption. The Purchaser shall reimburse the Seller for any value added taxes levied on the seller in the country of dispatch or the country of destination due to either the agreed terms of delivery, any failure to duly provide the requested documentation referred to above or any other circumstances attributable to the Purchaser. Any taxes, fees, duties and other charges which are levied on the Seller in connection with the performance of the Contract in the country of destination of the Products (if any) shall be solely borne by the Purchaser and the Purchaser agrees to pay or reimburse the Seller for any such taxes which the Seller is required to pay.

(2) If the Parties have not agreed on other terms of payments, all payments shall be made to the bank account notified by the Seller without any reservation or deduction. All bank charges and fees shall be borne by the Purchaser.

(3) If the Contract provides for payment by means of a letter of credit, the Purchaser shall within two (2) weeks after the conclusion of the Contract open an irrevocable and transferable letter of credit in accordance with and subject to the Uniform Customs and Practice for Documentary Credits published by the International Chamber of Commerce (UCP 600) in favor of the Seller in the amount of the Contract Price, confirmed by a first class European bank with a branch at Seller's place of business and available at sight payment against the presentation of the documents further described in the Contract. The letter of credit shall have an expiry date of at least four (4) months from the contractual delivery date respectively the end of the contractual delivery period. All bank charges and fees shall be at the Purchaser's expense.

(4) If the Seller does not receive payment from the Purchaser when such payment has become due, the Seller is entitled to charge interest at an annual rate of eight (8) percentage points above the rate for main refinancing operations of the European Central Bank (ECB) (http://www.ecb.int/home/html/index.en.html) as applicable throughout the period of delay. This provision shall apply mutatis mutandis if a letter of credit is not opened in time. Any further rights and remedies of the Seller provided by the Contract or under the applicable governing law shall remain unaffected.

(5) The Purchaser may only set off claims against the Seller in accordance with the governing law of the Contract that are owed in the same currency as the corresponding claim of the Seller arising out of the Contract and that are either undisputed between the Parties or have been finally adjudicated. The aforementioned rule shall apply mutatis mutandis to any right of retention of the Purchaser.

I. The Sales Documentation Put Together

§ 3 TERMS OF DELIVERY

(1) The Seller may withhold delivery until due payments have been made (or, as the case may be, a letter of credit has been opened) by the Purchaser in accordance with the Contract and all other obligations owed by the Purchaser under the Contract that are necessary for the performance of the delivery of the Products have been discharged.

(2) Partial deliveries of the Products shall be permitted throughout the delivery period.

(3) In case of a delay in delivery or any other performance owed by the Seller under the Contract, the Seller shall only be liable for damages if the delay was caused negligently or intentionally. Seller's liability for any damages shall in this case be limited to an amount of 0.5 % of the Contract Price for the Products (net) for each full week of delay up to a maximum amount of 5 % of the Contract Price (net) in the aggregate. Any claim for damages shall also be capped at this maximum amount if the Purchaser declares the avoidance of the Contract due to the delay. This limitation of liability shall not apply in any of the events stipulated in § 6 (5)[670] of the present International Sales Terms.

(4) The time of delivery agreed upon between the Parties shall not be of the essence. Accordingly and subject to any further prerequisites of the applicable governing law of this Contract, the Purchaser is only entitled to declare the Contract avoided by reason of any delay if the delay is attributable to the Seller, the Purchaser has threatened the Seller with avoidance in writing after the date of delivery and an additional period of time of reasonable length, at least however […] weeks, has not resulted in the delivery of the Products. § 10 (Force Majeure) shall remain unaffected.

(5) If delivery is delayed at the Purchaser's request or otherwise for reasons attributable to the Purchaser by more than fourteen (14) days after notice was given of the readiness for dispatch by the Seller, the Seller may charge the Purchaser liquidated storage costs for each commenced month thereafter amounting to 0.5 % of the Contract Price of the Products up to a maximum of 5 % of the Contract Price. The Seller remains entitled to claim further proven general damages in excess of the liquidated amount. Other rights and remedies provided by this Contract and/or applicable governing law, in particular the right to declare the Contract avoided, shall remain unaffected.

(6) Unless otherwise explicitly agreed in writing by the Seller, the Purchaser shall be solely responsible for the installation and erection of the Products.

[alternatively]

§ 3 TERMS OF DELIVERY

(1) The Seller may withhold delivery until due payments have been made by the Purchaser (or, as the case may be, a letter of credit has been opened) in accordance with the Contract and all other obligations owed by the Purchaser under the Contract that are necessary for the performance of delivery have been discharged.

(2) Partial deliveries of the Products shall be permitted throughout the delivery period.

(3) In case of a delay in delivery or any other performance owed under the Contract that was caused intentionally or negligently by the Seller, the Seller shall pay liquidated damages amounting to 0.5 % of the Contract Price for the Products (net) for each full week of delay up to an overall maximum of 5 % of the Contract Price (net) in the aggregate for any event of delay provided the Purchaser can prove that he has suffered any loss at all. The liquidated damages payable under this clause shall subject to § 3 (4) below constitute the sole and exclusive remedy of the Purchaser for delay. This limitation of liability shall not apply in any of the events stipulated in § 6 (5) of these International Sales Terms below.

(4) The time of delivery agreed upon between the Parties shall not be of the essence. Accordingly and subject to any further prerequisites of the applicable governing law of this Contract, the

---

[670] This reference must be replaced with a reference to § 6 (2) International Sales Terms if the second alternative of § 6 is used (see below).

Appendix

Purchaser is only entitled to declare the Contract avoided by reason of any delay if the delay is attributable to the Seller, the Purchaser has threatened the Seller with avoidance in writing after the date of delivery and an additional period of time of reasonable length, at least however [...] weeks, has not resulted in the delivery of the Products. In case of an avoidance of the contract pursuant to this § 3 (4), the Purchaser is entitled to claim further proven general damages in excess of the liquidated damages payable up to a maximum amount of 5 % of the Contract Price. For the avoidance of doubt, all damage claims (liquidated plus general damage claims) shall in the aggregate be capped at an amount of 10 % of the Contract Price. § 10 (Force Majeure) shall remain unaffected.

(5) If delivery is delayed at the Purchaser's request or otherwise for reasons attributable to the Purchaser by more than fourteen (14) days after notice was given of the readiness for dispatch by the Seller, the Seller may charge the Purchaser liquidated storage costs for each commenced month thereafter amounting to 0.5 % of the Contract Price of the respective Products up to a maximum of 5 % of the Contract Price. The Seller remains entitled to claim further proven general damages in excess of the liquidated amount. Other rights and remedies provided by this Contract and/or applicable governing law, in particular the right to declare the Contract avoided, shall remain unaffected.

(6) Unless otherwise explicitly agreed in writing by the Seller, the Purchaser shall be solely responsible for the installation and erection of the Products.

§ 4 TRANSFER OF TITLE

(1) Title to the Products shall not pass to the Purchaser until the Seller has unconditionally received the full amount of the contract price due under this Contract. The transfer of risk shall remain unaffected by this retention of title.

(2) Until title to the Products has passed to the Purchaser pursuant to the foregoing, the Purchaser shall insure the Products with a reputable insurance company for their full replacement value against all risks and shall keep the Products in good repair and condition. Until transfer of title, the Purchaser is not entitled to pledge, transfer ownership as security, lease or otherwise dispose of the Products without Seller's prior written approval. The Purchaser may however resell the Products in the ordinary course of business provided he receives payment from his customer or retains title so that the property is transferred to Purchaser's customer only after fulfillment of the customer's obligation to pay.

(3) If the relevant domestic property laws do not recognize a retention of title or provide for additional requirements such as but not limited to registration requirements etc., the Purchaser undertakes to support the Seller at Seller's request in order to either fulfill any of these requirements or to establish a comparable security interest for the Seller in relation to the Products. Costs reasonably incurred by the Seller in this regard shall be borne by the Purchaser.

§ 5 QUALITY DEFECTS AND DEFECTS OF TITLE

(1) In case the Products do not conform with the contractual obligations as to quantity, quality or description ("Quality Defects") or are not free from enforceable rights of third parties, including but not limited to enforceable rights based on intellectual property ("Defects of Title") already at the time of transfer of risk, the Purchaser shall have the remedies provided by the UN Convention on Contracts for the International Sales of Goods (CISG) subject to the following provisions. These remedies (as amended hereafter) shall constitute Purchaser's sole and exclusive remedies for any Quality Defect or Defect of Title. The Purchaser shall in particular not be entitled to rescind the contract based on any mistake as to the actual condition of the Products.

Quality Defects

(2) The Products shall only be deemed to be non-conforming if they do not comply already at the time of transfer of risk with the specifications laid down in this Contract, which shall conclusively describe the applicable conformity standard of the Products. In the absence of agreed specifications, the Products shall only be deemed defective if they are at the time of

transfer of risk not fit for the purpose for which products of the same description would ordinarily be used. The application of any further conformity standards implied by law or otherwise shall be explicitly excluded. The Seller shall in particular not be responsible for the fitness of the Products for any particular purpose or for compliance of the Products with any legal requirements existing outside of Seller's country of residence.

(3) Accordingly, the Seller shall not be responsible for any non-conformity arising after the transfer of risk such as but not limited to any defect due to faulty use, maintenance or modifications of the Products, use of unsuitable spare parts, defective installation or erection by the Purchaser or any third party not acting on behalf of the Seller, natural wear and tear or damage or any other external influences not attributable to the Seller.

(4) In case of delivery of non-conforming Products, the Seller shall at his option and subject to any further restrictions pursuant to the applicable governing law either repair any defect or replace any Products or any portion thereof that are non-conforming. The Seller shall be given adequate time and opportunity to remedy the defect. For this purpose, the Purchaser shall grant the Seller access to the Products. Additional costs incurred by the Seller due to the relocation of the Products to a place other than the original place of destination shall be borne by the Purchaser. A right of the Purchaser to claim delivery of substitute Products shall be explicitly excluded.

(5) The Purchaser shall have the right to a reduction of the contract price pursuant to the applicable governing law once either two attempts of the Seller to make good the defect have failed or the Seller has not undertaken such remedial measures within a reasonable time after receipt of a notice indicating a Quality Defect and lapse of an additional final respite set by the Purchaser. Subject to any further limitations set forth in § 6 below and by the applicable governing law, the same prerequisites shall apply for any claim for damages in lieu of performance. If the Quality Defect amounts to a fundamental breach of contract, the Purchaser is in this event alternatively entitled to declare the contract avoided subject to any further preconditions and restrictions set forth by the applicable governing law.

(6) Any and all remedies of the Purchaser for any Quality Defect are conditional upon prompt notice to be given by the Purchaser no later than seven (7) calendar days after the Purchaser has discovered or ought to have discovered the defect in accordance with his duty to examine the Products. The Purchaser shall examine the Products after handover within as short a period as is practicable in the circumstances whereas the period of time for the examination of the Products shall in any event not exceed a period of fourteen (14) days commencing upon handover of the Products. The Purchaser is not entitled to rely on any excuse for its failure to give the required notice. The Seller is not entitled to rely on this § 5 (6) if the lack of conformity relates to facts that he has or ought to have been aware of at the time of handover of the goods and which he did not disclose to the Purchaser.

Defects of Title

(7) The Products shall only have a deficiency in title if they are not free from enforceable rights of third parties that exist already at the time of transfer of risk. Third parties' enforceable rights founded on intellectual property shall only be deemed to constitute Defects of Title to the extent that a) the intellectual property right is registered in the country of use specified in the Contract and such right is based on the identical invention disclosed and claimed in a property right registered and made public in Seller's country of residence and b) the ordinary use of the Products as foreseen in the Contract by the Purchaser is thereby impeded.

(8) If the Purchaser will be refrained from the regular use of the Products due to industrial or intellectual property rights in the Products of any third party, Seller shall upon Purchaser's request subject to the conditions and limitations stated in § 5 (7) at Seller's discretion and cost either:

Appendix

(a) procure for the Purchaser the right to use the Product, or
(b) provide the Purchaser with a non-infringing replacement product or modify the Product so that it becomes non-infringing, provided that the replacement product/modified Product meets substantially the same functional specifications as the Product.
(c) refund the purchase price to the Purchaser upon return of the Products less a reasonable amount of depreciation for any period of use of the Products.

If Seller has not undertaken such remedial measures within a reasonable time after receipt of notice of default by the Purchaser, the Purchaser may subject to any preconditions under governing law declare the avoidance of the Contract and (subject to the limitations set forth in § 6 below) claim damages.

(9) The Seller shall only be liable for any Defect of Title if the Purchaser gives Seller prompt written notice pursuant to the applicable governing law, neither consents to any judgment or decree nor undertakes any other act in compromise of any claim without first obtaining Sellers' written consent. The Purchaser is not entitled to rely on any excuse for his failure to give the required notice. The Seller is not entitled to rely on a delayed notice of the Purchaser if he knew of the right or claim of the third party and the nature of it at the time of handover of the Products.

(10) The Purchaser loses the right to rely on a Quality Defect of the Products or on a Defect of Title if he does not give the Seller notice thereof at the latest within a period of one (1) year from the date of handover of the Products to the Purchaser, regardless of whether the defect has been or ought to have been detected by that time. This provision shall not apply if the defect relates to facts that the Seller has been or ought to have been aware of at the time of handover of the goods and which he did not disclose to the Purchaser.

§ 6 LIMITATION OF DAMAGE CLAIMS

(1) Without prejudice to further limitations set forth below in this § 6 or elsewhere, damage claims of the Purchaser shall in any event only exist in case of negligence or intentional misconduct attributable to the Seller.

(2) Without prejudice to § 3 (Delay in Delivery) but notwithstanding anything to the contrary elsewhere, the Seller shall in no event and irrespective of the legal basis (contract, tort, indemnity or any other area of law) be liable to the Purchaser for loss of profit or revenue, wasted overhead, loss of production, loss of use, loss of data, cost of capital, cost of substitute goods, property damage external to the Products and any damage, expenditure or loss arising from such damage, any incidental, indirect or consequential damage or any of the foregoing suffered by any third party.

(3) Without prejudice to any further limitation of liability stipulated in this § 6 or elsewhere, Seller's overall liability arising from or connected to this Contract shall irrespective of the legal basis (contract, tort, indemnity or any other area of law) in the aggregate be limited to the Contract Price.

(4) The limitation of liability stipulated in the preceding subparagraphs of this § 6 shall apply regardless of whether any such damage or loss has been directly caused by the Seller or any of his subcontractors, agents, advisors or employees acting on his behalf.

(5) The aforementioned limitations of liability shall not apply in the following events for whose occurrence the burden of proof shall rest with the Purchaser:
a) gross negligence or willful misconduct attributable to the Seller. They do however apply in case of gross negligence of any other party acting for the Seller, including without limitation Seller's subcontractors, agents, advisors and employees but excluding Seller's legal representatives and executive staff.
b) in case of bodily injury culpably caused by an act or omission attributable to the Seller or
c) insofar as mandatory law provides otherwise.

(6) All limitations of liability stipulated in this § 6 shall also apply for the benefit of the Seller's subcontractors, agents, advisors, directors and employees.
[alternatively]

§ 6 EXCLUSION OF DAMAGE CLAIMS

(1) Without prejudice to § 3 (Delay in Delivery) but notwithstanding anything to the contrary elsewhere, the Seller shall in no event and irrespective of the legal basis (contract, tort, indemnity or any other area of law) be liable to the Purchaser for any damages, losses or expenditures, caused by defective products or otherwise, arising from or related to this Contract. This exclusion of liability applies regardless of whether any such damages, losses or expenditures have been directly caused by the Seller or by any of his subcontractors, agents, advisors or employees acting on his behalf.

(2) § 6 (1) shall not apply in the following events for whose occurrence the burden of proof shall rest with the Purchaser:

a) gross negligence or willful misconduct attributable to the Seller. § 6 (1) does however apply in case of gross negligence of any other party acting on behalf of the Seller, including without limitation Seller's subcontractors, agents, advisors and employees but excluding Seller's legal representatives and executive staff.

b) in case of bodily injury culpably caused by an act or omission attributable to the Seller or

c) in so far as mandatory laws provide otherwise.

(3) § 6 (1) shall to the same extent apply for the benefit of the Seller's subcontractors, agents, advisors, directors and employees.

§ 7 LIMITATION OF ACTIONS

(1) It is expressly agreed that the Purchaser cannot bring an action based on a quality defect before the arbitral tribunal or any court of law nor plead the existence of any such defect as a defense against any action of the Seller based on the non-performance by the Purchaser after one (1) year from the handover of the Products to the Purchaser and regardless of whether the defect has been or ought to have been detected by that time.

(2) § 7 (1) shall also apply in relation to any claims of the Purchaser based on concurring claims under tort arising from defective Products.

(3) The statute of limitations of one year cannot be invoked by the Seller if it can be proven that he willfully deceived the Purchaser.

(4) Remedial measures of the Seller in case of any defect, including but not limited to either repair or replacement of the Products or any parts thereof shall not trigger the commencement of a new limitation period. Any such remedial measure by the Seller or any third party acting on his behalf shall not be deemed to constitute a tacit acknowledgement of debt or liability on the part of the Seller.

§ 8 EXPORT CONTROL REGULATIONS

(1) Delivery obligations of the Seller are subject to the condition that required export licenses are issued and that no other restrictions imposed by mandatory export control regulations of the European Union, the United States of America or any other relevant jurisdiction (regardless whether these restrictions were at the time of contract conclusion foreseeable or not) exist. In the event that the delivery of the Products is prevented by export control regulations or other legally mandated restrictions for more than three (3) months from the scheduled delivery date, both parties are entitled to declare the avoidance of the Contract.

(2) The Purchaser undertakes to comply with all export control regulations of the national export control authorities applicable to him, in particular the authorities in the European Union and in the United States of America. In particular, the Purchaser undertakes not to directly or indirectly export or re-export the Products to any country for which such export may be prohibited by the aforementioned regulations. Failure to comply strictly with all laws relating to

embargoes, sanctions, export and re-export applicable to the Purchaser shall entitle the Seller to declare the avoidance of the Contract.

§ 9 AVOIDANCE OF THE CONTRACT BY THE SELLER

Without prejudice to any such right or other remedies provided by the applicable governing law of this Contract, the Seller is entitled to declare the Contract avoided without any further preconditions if

a) the Purchaser fails to make payment of the Contract Price to the Seller under this Contract within thirty (30) days after it has become due and payable, or fails to open a letter of credit pursuant to the Contract within such period after the due date, or

b) the Purchaser fails to perform his contractual obligations whose performance is necessary for the delivery of the Products or to take delivery pursuant to the Contract within fourteen (14) days after request of the Seller in that regard, or

c) a material deterioration of the Purchaser's creditworthiness has occurred or insolvency proceedings relating to the assets of the Purchaser are applied for or commenced.

§ 10 CONFIDENTIALITY

(1) The Parties shall keep all know-how, data and any other information (collectively hereinafter "Information") received from the respective other Party under this Contract confidential with respect to any third parties and shall use the Information solely for the purpose of this Contract.

(2) The confidentiality obligation shall not apply to Information which

a) is in the public domain at the time of disclosure or later becomes part of the public domain without any breach of this confidentiality obligation,

b) was known to the receiving Party prior to disclosure by the disclosing Party,

c) is disclosed to the receiving Party by a third party without any breach of a confidentiality obligation towards the disclosing Party,

d) has been independently developed by the receiving Party.

The receiving Party bears the burden of proof that any one of the foregoing requirements for an exemption is fulfilled.

(3) The confidentiality obligations stipulated in this § 10 shall remain in force after the Parties have discharged their performance obligations. They shall also survive an avoidance of this Contract.

§ 11 FORCE MAJEURE

(1) Neither party shall be in breach of this Contract if and to the extent that the performance of the Contract is prevented or made excessively onerous by an Event of Force Majeure as defined below in § 11 (2). However, no ground for relief under this § 11 shall exist if the non-performing party could have reasonably expected both the impediment and its effects upon its ability to perform at the time of the conclusion of the Contract or reasonably avoided or overcome it or its effects.

(2) Any event that is beyond either party's reasonable control shall be deemed to constitute an "Event of Force Majeure" regardless of whether such event occurs before or after the conclusion of the Contract. An Event of Force Majeure shall include but shall not be limited to natural disasters or catastrophic events, nuclear accidents, fire, flood, typhoons or earthquakes, terrorism, acts or omissions by governmental authorities, allocations or restrictions upon the use of materials or manpower, war, riots, sabotage or revolutions, strikes or lockouts.

(3) If either Party claims that an Event of Force Majeure has occurred affecting its performance, it shall promptly notify the other Party. If the Event of Force Majeure continues for a period of ninety (90) calendar days or more upon notice, either Party may terminate the Contract in writing after to the lapse of that period.

(4) § 11 shall not prejudice any further exemption provisions provided either by these International Sales Terms or the applicable governing law.

§ 12 MISCELLANEOUS

(1) This Contract contains the entire understanding between the Parties and fully replaces any other agreements or understandings between the Parties on its subject matter entered into before the conclusion of this Contract. Accordingly, this § 12 (1) shall prevail over Arts 8 (3) and 11 CISG.

(2) No amendment to this Contract shall be valid unless made in writing. The same shall apply with regard to any amendment to this written form requirement. For the avoidance of doubt, the written form requirement shall be deemed complied with in any case of exchange of communications via E-mail or facsimile.

(3) Should any of the provisions of this Contract be or become invalid or otherwise unenforceable, this shall not affect the validity and enforceability of the remaining contractual provisions. The invalid or unenforceable provision will be automatically replaced by a valid and/or operative provision which most effectively serves the economic purpose and effect intended by the original provision.

(4) The Purchaser is not entitled to assign any rights or claims arising from or related to this Contract to any third party without the prior written consent of the Seller.

§ 13 GOVERNING LAW

(1) This Contract is governed by Swiss material law to the inclusion of the United Nations Convention on Contracts for the International Sale of Goods (CISG).

(2) The material laws of Switzerland shall also apply with regard to any non-contractual obligations arising from or related to this contract, in particular any concurring claims under tort. *This choice of law does however not extend to obligations arising out of an act of unfair competition, the restriction of competition or an infringement of intellectual property rights.*

§ 14 ARBITRATION

(1) All disputes arising from or related to the Contract, regardless of their legal basis (contract, tort or otherwise), shall be submitted to the International Court of Arbitration of the International Chamber of Commerce (ICC) and shall be finally settled under the ICC Arbitration Rules 2012 (hereinafter the "Rules") by one (1) arbitrator appointed in accordance with the Rules. The language to be used in the arbitration proceedings shall be English. The seat of arbitration shall be [...] Switzerland.

(2) The parties remain, however, entitled to apply to any competent judicial authority for interim or conservatory measures in accordance with the Rules.

[alternatively]

§ 14 EXCLUSIVE JURISDICTION

(1) Without prejudice to § 14 (2) and § 14 (3) below, the Parties agree to submit any dispute arising from or related to the Contract, regardless of its legal basis (contract, tort or otherwise) to the exclusive jurisdiction of the courts of [...].

(2) The Seller remains entitled to bring an action also at the principal place of business of the Purchaser.

(3) Both parties remain entitled to apply to any competent judicial authority for interim or conservatory measures.

[alternatively]

§ 14 NON-EXCLUSIVE JURISDICTION

The Parties agree to submit any dispute arising from or related to the Contract, regardless of its legal basis (contract, tort or otherwise) to the non-exclusive jurisdiction of the courts of [...].

II. The United Nations Convention on Contracts for the International Sale of Goods

[reproduced with permission of UNCITRAL]

The States Parties to this Convention,

Bearing in mind the broad objectives in the resolutions adopted by the sixth special session of the General Assembly of the United Nations on the establishment of a New International Economic Order, Considering that the development of international trade on the basis of equality and mutual benefit is an important element in promoting friendly relations among States,

Being of the opinion that the adoption of uniform rules which govern contracts for the international sale of goods and take into account the different social, economic and legal systems would contribute to the removal of legal barriers in international trade and promote the development of international trade,

Have agreed as follows:

Part I. Sphere of application and general provisions

CHAPTER 1. SPHERE OF APPLICATION

Article 1

(1) This Convention applies to contracts of sale of goods between parties whose places of business are in different States:
(a) when the States are Contracting States; or
(b) when the rules of private international law lead to the application of the law of a Contracting State.

(2) The fact that the parties have their places of business in different States is to be disregarded whenever this fact does not appear either from the contract or from any dealings between or from information disclosed by, the parties at any time before or at the conclusion of the contract.

(3) Neither the nationality of the parties nor the civil or commercial character of the parties or of the contract is to be taken into consideration in determining the application of this Convention.

Article 2

This Convention does not apply to sales:
(a) of goods bought for personal, family or household use, unless the seller, at any time before or at the conclusion of the contract, neither knew nor ought to have known that the goods were bought for any such use;
(b) by auction;
(c) on execution or otherwise by authority of law;
(d) of stocks, shares, investment securities, negotiable instruments or money;
(e) of ships, vessels, hovercraft or aircraft;
(f) of electricity.

Article 3

(1) Contracts for the supply of goods to be manufactured or produced are to be considered sales unless the party who orders the goods undertakes to supply a substantial part of the materials necessary for such manufacture or production.

(2) This Convention does not apply to contracts in which the preponderant part of the obligations of the party who furnishes the goods consists in the supply of labour or other services.

Article 4

This Convention governs only the formation of the contract of sale and the rights and obligations of the seller and the purchaser arising from such a contract. In particular, except as otherwise expressly provided in this Convention, it is not concerned with:
(a) the validity of the contract or of any of its provisions or of any usage;
(b) the effect which the contract may have on the property in the goods sold.

Article 5

This Convention does not apply to the liability of the seller for death or personal injury caused by the goods to any person.

Article 6

The parties may exclude the application of this Convention or, subject to article 12, derogate from or vary the effect of any of its provisions.

CHAPTER II. GENERAL PROVISIONS

Article 7

(1) In the interpretation of this Convention, regard is to be had to its international character and to the need to promote uniformity in its application and the observance of good faith in international trade.

(2) Questions concerning matters governed by this Convention which are not expressly settled in it are to be settled in conformity with the general principles on which it is based or, in the absence of such principles, in conformity with the law applicable by virtue of the rules of private international law.

Article 8

(1) For the purposes of this Convention statements made by and other conduct of a party are to be interpreted according to his intent where the other party knew or could not have been unaware what that intent was.

(2) If the preceding paragraph is not applicable, statements made by and other conduct of a party are to be interpreted according to the understanding that a reasonable person of the same kind as the other party would have had in the same circumstances.

(3) In determining the intent of a party or the understanding a reasonable person would have had, due consideration is to be given to all relevant circumstances of the case including the negotiations, any practices which the parties have established between themselves, usages and any subsequent conduct of the parties.

Article 9

(1) The parties are bound by any usage to which they have agreed and by any practices which they have established between themselves.

(2) The parties are considered, unless otherwise agreed, to have impliedly made applicable to their contract or its formation a usage of which the parties knew or ought to have known and which in international trade is widely known to, and regularly observed by, parties to contracts of the type involved in the particular trade concerned.

Article 10

For the purposes of this Convention:
(a) if a party has more than one place of business, the place of business is that which has the closest relationship to the contract and its performance, having regard to the circumstances known to or contemplated by the parties at any time before or at the conclusion of the contract;

(b) if a party does not have a place of business, reference is to be made to his habitual residence.

Article 11

A contract of sale need not be concluded in or evidenced by writing and is not subject to any other requirement as to form. It may be proved by any means, including witnesses.

Article 12

Any provision of article 11, article 29 or Part II of this Convention that allows a contract of sale or its modification or termination by agreement or any offer, acceptance or other indication of intention to be made in any form other than in writing does not apply where any party has his place of business in a Contracting State which has made a declaration under article 96 of this Convention. The parties may not derogate from or vary the effect of this article.

Article 13

For the purposes of this Convention 'writing' includes telegram and telex.

Part II. Formation of the contract

Article 14

(1) A proposal for concluding a contract addressed to one or more specific persons constitutes an offer if it is sufficiently definite and indicates the intention of the offeror to be bound in case of acceptance. A proposal is sufficiently definite if it indicates the goods and expressly or implicitly fixes or makes provision for determining the quantity and the price.

(2) A proposal other than one addressed to one or more specific persons is to be considered merely as an invitation to make offers, unless the contrary is clearly indicated by the person making the proposal.

Article 15

(1) An offer becomes effective when it reaches the offeree.

(2) An offer, even if it is irrevocable, may be withdrawn if the withdrawal reaches the offeree before or at the same time as the offer.

Article 16

(1) Until a contract is concluded an offer may be revoked if the revocation reaches the offeree before he has dispatched an acceptance.

(2) However, an offer cannot be revoked:
(a) if it indicates, whether by stating a fixed time for acceptance or otherwise, that it is irrevocable; or
(b) if it was reasonable for the offeree to rely on the offer as being irrevocable and the offeree has acted in reliance on the offer.

Article 17

An offer, even if it is irrevocable, is terminated when a rejection reaches the offeror.

Article 18

(1) A statement made by or other conduct of the offeree indicating assent to an offer is an acceptance. Silence or inactivity does not in itself amount to acceptance.

(2) An acceptance of an offer becomes effective at the moment the indication of assent reaches the offeror. An acceptance is not effective if the indication of assent does not reach the offeror within the time he has fixed or, if no time is fixed, within a reasonable time, due account being taken of the circumstances of the transaction, including the rapidity of the means of communication employed by the offeror. An oral offer must be accepted immediately unless the circumstances indicate otherwise.

II. The United Nations Convention on Contracts for the International Sale of Goods

(3) However, if, by virtue of the offer or as a result of practices which the parties have established between themselves or of usage, the offeree may indicate assent by performing an act, such as one relating to the dispatch of the goods or payment of the price, without notice to the offeror, the acceptance is effective at the moment the act is performed, provided that the act is performed within the period of time laid down in the preceding paragraph.

Article 19

(1) A reply to an offer which purports to be an acceptance but contains additions, limitations or other modifications is a rejection of the offer and constitutes a counteroffer.

(2) However, a reply to an offer which purports to be an acceptance but contains additional or different terms which do not materially alter the terms of the offer constitutes an acceptance, unless the offeror, without undue delay, objects orally to the discrepancy or dispatches a notice to that effect. If he does not so object, the terms of the contract are the terms of the offer with the modifications contained in the acceptance.

(3) Additional or different terms relating, among other things, to the price, payment, quality and quantity of the goods, place and time of delivery, extent of one party's liability to the other or the settlement of disputes are considered to alter the terms of the offer materially.

Article 20

(1) A period of time of acceptance fixed by the offeror in a telegram or a letter begins to run from the moment the telegram is handed in for dispatch or from the date shown on the letter or, if no such date is shown, from the date shown on the envelope. A period of time for acceptance fixed by the offeror by telephone, telex or other means of instantaneous communication, begins to run from the moment that the offer reaches the offeree.

(2) Official holidays or non-business days occurring during the period for acceptance are included in calculating the period. However, if a notice of acceptance cannot be delivered at the address of the offeror on the last day of the period because that day falls on an official holiday or a non-business day at the place of business of the offeror, the period is extended until the first business day which follows.

Article 21

(1) A late acceptance is nevertheless effective as an acceptance if without delay the offeror orally so informs the offeree or dispatches a notice to that effect.

(2) If a letter or other writing containing a late acceptance shows that it has been sent in such circumstances that if its transmission had been normal it would have reached the offeror in due time, the late acceptance is effective as an acceptance unless, without delay, the offeror orally informs the offeree that he considers his offer as having lapsed or dispatches a notice to that effect.

Article 22

An acceptance may be withdrawn if the withdrawal reaches the offeror before or at the same time as the acceptance would have become effective.

Article 23

A contract is concluded at the moment when an acceptance of an offer becomes effective in accordance with the provisions of this Convention.

Article 24

For the purposes of this Part of the Convention, an offer, declaration of acceptance or any other indication of intention 'reaches' the addressee when it is made orally to him or delivered by any other means to him personally, to his place of business or mailing address or, if he does not have a place of business or mailing address, to his habitual residence.

Part III. Sale of goods

CHAPTER I. GENERAL PROVISIONS

Article 25

A breach of contract committed by one of the parties is fundamental if it results in such detriment to the other party as substantially to deprive him of what he is entitled to expect under the contract, unless the party in breach did not foresee and a reasonable person of the same kind in the same circumstances would not have foreseen such a result.

Article 26

A declaration of avoidance of the contract is effective only if made by notice to the other party.

Article 27

Unless otherwise expressly provided in this Part of the Convention, if any notice, request or other communication is given or made by a party in accordance with this Part and by means appropriate in the circumstances, a delay or error in the transmission of the communication or its failure to arrive does not deprive that party of the right to rely on the communication.

Article 28

If, in accordance with the provisions of this Convention, one party is entitled to require performance of any obligation by the other party, a court is not bound to enter a judgement for specific performance unless the court would do so under its own law in respect of similar contracts of sale not governed by this Convention.

Article 29

(1) A contract may be modified or terminated by the mere agreement of the parties.

(2) A contract in writing which contains a provision requiring any modification or termination by agreement to be in writing may not be otherwise modified or terminated by agreement. However, a party may be precluded by his conduct from asserting such a provision to the extent that the other party has relied on that conduct.

CHAPTER II. OBLIGATIONS OF THE SELLER

Article 30

The seller must deliver the goods, hand over any documents relating to them and transfer the property in the goods, as required by the contract and this Convention.

Section I. Delivery of the goods and handing over of documents

Article 31

If the seller is not bound to deliver the goods at any other particular place, his obligation to deliver consists:
(a) if the contract of sale involves carriage of the goods–in handing the goods over to the first carrier for transmission to the purchaser;
(b) if, in cases not within the preceding subparagraph, the contract relates to specific goods, or unidentified goods to be drawn from a specific stock or to be manufactured or produced, and at the time of the conclusion of the contract the parties knew that the goods were at, or were to be manufactured or produced at, a particular place–in placing the goods at the purchaser's disposal at that place;
(c) in other cases–in placing the goods at the purchaser's disposal at the place where the seller had his place of business at the time of the conclusion of the contract.

Article 32

(1) If the seller, in accordance with the contract or this Convention, hands the goods over to a carrier and if the goods are not clearly identified to the contract by markings on the goods, by shipping documents or otherwise, the seller must give the purchaser notice of the consignment specifying the goods.

(2) If the seller is bound to arrange for carriage of the goods, he must make such contracts as are necessary for carriage to the place fixed by means of transportation appropriate in the circumstances and according to the usual terms for such transportation.

(3) If the seller is not bound to effect insurance in respect of the carriage of the goods, he must, at the purchaser's request, provide him with all available information necessary to enable him to effect such insurance.

Article 33

The seller must deliver the goods:
(a) if a date is fixed by or determinable from the contract, on that date;
(b) if a period of time is fixed by or determinable from the contract, at any time within that period unless circumstances indicate that the purchaser is to choose a date; or
(c) in any other case, within a reasonable time after the conclusion of the contract.

Article 34

If the seller is bound to hand over documents relating to the goods, he must hand them over at the time and place and in the form required by the contract. If the seller has handed over documents before that time, he may, up to that time, cure any lack of conformity in the documents, if the exercise of this right does not cause the purchaser unreasonable inconvenience or unreasonable expense. However, the purchaser retains any right to claim damages as provided for in this Convention.

Section II. Conformity of the goods and third party claims

Article 35

(1) The seller must deliver goods which are of the quantity, quality and description required by the contract and which are contained or packaged in the manner required by the contract.

(2) Except where the parties have agreed otherwise, the goods do not conform with the contract unless they:
(a) are fit for the purposes for which goods of the same description would ordinarily be used;
(b) are fit for any particular purpose expressly or impliedly made known to the seller at the time of the conclusion of the contract, except where the circumstances show that the purchaser did not rely, or that it was unreasonable for him to rely, on the seller's skill and judgement;
(c) possess the qualities of goods which the seller has held out to the purchaser as a sample or model;
(d) are contained or packaged in the manner usual for such goods or, where there is no such manner, in a manner adequate to preserve and protect the goods.

(3) The seller is not liable under subparagraphs (a) to (d) of the preceding paragraph for any lack of conformity of the goods if at the time of the conclusion of the contract the purchaser knew or could not have been unaware of such lack of conformity.

Article 36

(1) The seller is liable in accordance with the contract and this Convention for any lack of conformity which exists at the time when the risk passes to the purchaser, even though the lack of conformity becomes apparent only after that time.

(2) The seller is also liable for any lack of conformity which occurs after the time indicated in the preceding paragraph and which is due to a breach of any of his obligations, including a

breach of any guarantee that for a period of time the goods will remain fit for their ordinary purpose or for some particular purpose or will retain specified qualities or characteristics.

Article 37

If the seller has delivered goods before the date for delivery, he may, up to that date, deliver any missing part or make up any deficiency in the quantity of the goods delivered, or deliver goods in replacement of any non-conforming goods delivered or remedy any lack of conformity in the goods delivered, provide that the exercise of this right does not cause the purchaser unreasonable inconvenience or unreasonable expense. However, the purchaser retains any right to claim damages as provided for in this Convention.

Article 38

(1) The purchaser must examine the goods, or cause them to be examined, within as short a period as is practicable in the circumstances.

(2) If the contract involves carriage of the goods, examination may be deferred until after the goods have arrived at their destination.

(3) If the goods are redirected in transit or redispatched by the purchaser without a reasonable opportunity for examination by him and at the time of the conclusion of the contract the seller knew or ought to have known of the possibility of such redirection or redispatch, examination may be deferred until after the goods have arrived at the new destination.

Article 39

(1) The purchaser loses the right to rely on a lack of conformity of the goods if he does not give notice to the seller specifying the nature of the lack of conformity within a reasonable time after he has discovered it or ought to have discovered it.

(2) In any event, the purchaser loses the right to rely on a lack of conformity of the goods if he does not give the seller notice thereof at the latest within a period of two years from the date on which the goods were actually handed over to the purchaser, unless this time-limit is inconsistent with a contractual period of guarantee.

Article 40

The seller is not entitled to rely on the provisions of articles 38 and 39 if the lack of conformity relates to facts of which he knew or could not have been unaware and which he did not disclose to the purchaser.

Article 41

The seller must deliver goods which are free from any right or claim of a third party, unless the purchaser agreed to take the goods subject to that right or claim. However, if such right or claim is based on industrial property or other intellectual property, the seller's obligation is governed by article 42.

Article 42

(1) The seller must deliver goods which are free from any right or claim of a third party based on industrial property or other intellectual property, of which at the time of the conclusion of the contract the seller knew or could not have been unaware, provided that the right or claim is based on industrial property or other intellectual property:

(a) under the law of the State where the goods will be resold or otherwise used, if it was contemplated by the parties at the time of the conclusion of the contract that the goods would be resold or otherwise used in that State; or

(b) in any other case, under the law of the State where the purchaser has his place of business.

(2) The obligation of the seller under the preceding paragraph does not extend to cases where:

II. The United Nations Convention on Contracts for the International Sale of Goods

(a) at the time of the conclusion of the contract the purchaser knew or could not have been unaware of the right or claim; or

(b) the right or claim results from the seller's compliance with technical drawings, designs, formulae or other such specifications furnished by the purchaser.

Article 43

(1) The purchaser loses the right to rely on the provisions of article 41 or article 42 if he does not give notice to the seller specifying the nature of the right or claim of the third party within a reasonable time after he has become aware or ought to have become aware of the right or claim.

(2) The seller is not entitled to rely on the provisions of the preceding paragraph if he knew of the right or claim of the third party and the nature of it.

Article 44

Notwithstanding the provisions of paragraph (1) of article 39 and paragraph (1) of article 43, the purchaser may reduce the price in accordance with article 50 or claim damages, except for loss of profit, if he has a reasonable excuse for his failure to give the required notice.

Section III. Remedies for breach of contract by the seller

Article 45

(1) If the seller fails to perform any of his obligations under the contract or this Convention, the purchaser may:

(a) exercise the rights provided in articles 46 to 52;

(b) claim damages as provided in articles 74 to 77.

(2) The purchaser is not deprived of any right he may have to claim damages by exercising his right to other remedies.

(3) No period of grace may be granted to the seller by a court or arbitral tribunal when the purchaser resorts to a remedy for breach of contract.

Article 46

(1) The purchaser may require performance by the seller of his obligations unless the purchaser has resorted to a remedy which is inconsistent with this requirement.

(2) If the goods do not conform with the contract, the purchaser may require delivery of substitute goods only if the lack of conformity constitutes a fundamental breach of contract and a request for substitute goods is made either in conjunction with notice given under article 39 or within a reasonable time thereafter.

(3) If the goods do not conform with the contract, the purchaser may require the seller to remedy the lack of conformity by repair, unless this is unreasonable having regard to all the circumstances. A request for repair must be made either in conjunction with notice given under article 39 or within a reasonable time thereafter.

Article 47

(1) The purchaser may fix an additional period of time of reasonable length for performance by the seller of his obligations.

(2) Unless the purchaser has received notice from the seller that he will not perform within the period so fixed, the purchaser may not, during that period, resort to any remedy for breach of contract. However, the purchaser is not deprived thereby of any right he may have to claim damages for delay in performance.

Article 48

(1) Subject to article 49, the seller may, even after the date for delivery, remedy at his own expense any failure to perform his obligations, if he can do so without unreasonable delay and

without causing the purchaser unreasonable inconvenience or uncertainty of reimbursement by the seller of expenses advanced by the purchaser. However, the purchaser retains any right to claim damages as provided for in this Convention.

(2) If the seller requests the purchaser to make known whether he will accept performance and the purchaser does not comply with the request within a reasonable time, the seller may perform within the time indicated in his request. The purchaser may not, during that period of time, resort to any remedy which is inconsistent with performance by the seller.

(3) A notice by the seller that he will perform within a specified period of time is assumed to include a request, under the preceding paragraph, that the purchaser make known his decision.

(4) A request or notice by the seller under paragraph (2) or (3) of this article is not effective unless received by the purchaser.

Article 49

(1) The purchaser may declare the contract avoided:
(a) if the failure by the seller to perform any of his obligations under the contract or this Convention amounts to a fundamental breach of contract; or
(b) in case of non-delivery, if the seller does not deliver the goods within the additional period of time fixed by the purchaser in accordance with paragraph (1) of article 47 or declares that he will not deliver within the period so fixed.

(2) However, in cases where the seller has delivered the goods, the purchaser loses the right to declare the contract avoided unless he does so:
(a) in respect of late delivery, within a reasonable time after he has become aware that delivery has been made;
(b) in respect of any breach other than late delivery, within a reasonable time:
  (i) after he knew or ought to have known of the breach;
  (ii) after the expiration of any additional period of time fixed by the purchaser in accordance with paragraph (1) of article 47, or after the seller has declared that he will not perform his obligations within such an additional period; or
  (iii) after the expiration of any additional period of time indicated by the seller in accordance with paragraph (2) of article 48, or after the purchaser has declared that he will not accept performances.

Article 50

If the goods do not conform with the contract and whether or not the price has already been paid, the purchaser may reduce the price in the same proportion as the value that the goods actually delivered had at the time of the delivery bears to the value that conforming goods would have had at that time. However, if the seller remedies any failure to perform his obligations in accordance with article 37 or article 48 or if the purchaser refuses to accept performance by the seller in accordance with those articles, the purchaser may not reduce the price.

Article 51

(1) If the seller delivers only a part of the goods or if only a part of the goods delivered is in conformity with the contract, articles 46 to 50 apply in respect of the part which is missing or which does not conform.

(2) The purchaser may declare the contract avoided in its entirety only if the failure to make delivery completely or in conformity with the contract amounts to a fundamental breach of the contract.

Article 52

(1) If the seller delivers the goods before the date fixed, the purchaser may take delivery or refuse to take delivery.

(2) If the seller delivers a quantity of goods greater than that provided for in the contract, the purchaser may take delivery or refuse to take delivery of the excess quantity. If the purchaser takes delivery of all or part of the excess quantity, he must pay for it at the contract rate.

CHAPTER III. OBLIGATIONS OF THE PURCHASER

Article 53

The purchaser must pay the price for the goods and take delivery of them as required by the contract and this Convention.

Section I. Payment of the price

Article 54

The purchaser's obligation to pay the price includes taking such steps and complying with such formalities as may be required under the contract or any laws and regulations to enable payment to be made.

Article 55

Where a contract has been validly concluded but does not expressly or implicitly fix or make provision for determining the price, the parties are considered, in the absence of any indication to the contrary, to have impliedly made reference to the price generally charged at the time of the conclusion of the contract for such goods sold under comparable circumstances in the trade concerned.

Article 56

If the price is fixed according to the weight of the goods, in case of doubt it is to be determined by the net weight.

Article 57

(1) If the purchaser is not bound to pay the price at any other particular place, he must pay it to the seller:
(a) at the seller's place of business; or
(b) if the payment is to be made against the handing over of the goods or of documents, at the place where the handing over takes place.

(2) The seller must bear any increase in the expenses incidental to payment which is caused by a change in his place of business subsequent to the conclusion of the contract.

Article 58

(1) If the purchaser is not bound to pay the price at any other specific time, he must pay it when the seller places either the goods or documents controlling their disposition at the purchaser's disposal in accordance with the contract and this Convention. The seller may make such payment a condition for handing over the goods or documents.

(2) If the contract involves carriage of the goods, the seller may dispatch the goods on terms whereby the goods, or documents controlling their disposition, will not be handed over to the purchaser except against payment of the price.

(3) The purchaser is not bound to pay the price until he has had an opportunity to examine the goods, unless the procedures for delivery or payment agreed upon by the parties are inconsistent with his having such an opportunity.

Article 59

The purchaser must pay the price on the date fixed by or determinable from the contract and this Convention without the need for any request or compliance with any formality on the part of the seller.

Appendix

Section II. Taking delivery

Article 60

The purchaser's obligation to take delivery consists:
(a) in doing all the acts which could reasonably be expected of him in order to enable the seller to make delivery; and
(b) in taking over the goods.

Section III. Remedies for breach of contract by the purchaser

Article 61

(1) If the purchaser fails to perform any of his obligations under the contract or this Convention, the seller may:
(a) exercise the rights provided in articles 62 to 65;
(b) claim damages as provided in articles 74 to 77.

(2) The seller is not deprived of any right he may have to claim damages by exercising his right to ther remedies.

(3) No period of grace may be granted to the purchaser by a court or arbitral tribunal when the seller resorts to a remedy for breach of contract.

Article 62

The seller may require the purchaser to pay the price, take delivery or perform his other obligations, unless the seller has resorted to a remedy which is inconsistent with this requirement.

Article 63

(1) The seller may fix an additional period of time of reasonable length for performance by the purchaser of his obligations.

(2) Unless the seller has received notice from the purchaser that he will not perform within the period so fixed, the seller may not, during that period, resort to any remedy for breach of contract. However, the seller is not deprived thereby of any right he may have to claim damages for delay in performance.

Article 64

(1) The seller may declare the contract avoided:
(a) if the failure by the purchaser to perform any of his obligations under the contract or this Convention amounts to a fundamental breach of contract; or
(b) if the purchaser does not, within the additional period of time fixed by the seller in accordance with paragraph (1) of article 63, perform his obligation to pay the price or take delivery of the goods, or if he declares that he will not do so within the period so fixed;

(2) However, in cases where the purchaser has paid the price, the seller loses the right to declare the contract avoided unless he does so:
(a) in respect of late performance by the purchaser, before the seller has become aware that performance has been rendered; or
(b) in respect of any breach other than late performance by the purchaser, within a reasonable time:
   (i) after the seller knew or ought to have known of the breach; or
   (ii) after the expiration of any additional period of time fixed by the seller in accordance with paragraph (1) of article 63, or after the purchaser has declared that he will not perform his obligations within such an additional period.

Article 65

(1) If under the contract the purchaser is to specify the form, measurement or other features of the goods and he fails to make such specification either on the date agreed upon or within a reasonable time after receipt of a request from the seller, the seller may, without prejudice to any other rights he may have, make the specification himself in accordance with the requirements of the purchaser that may be known to him.

(2) If the seller makes the specification himself, he must inform the purchaser of the details thereof and must fix a reasonable time within which the purchaser may make a different specification. If, after receipt of such a communication, the purchaser fails to do so within the time so fixed, the specification made by the seller is binding.

CHAPTER IV. PASSING OF RISK

Article 66

Loss of or damage to the goods after the risk has passed to the purchaser does not discharge him from his obligation to pay the price, unless the loss or damage is due to an act or omission of the seller.

Article 67

(1) If the contract of sale involves carriage of the goods and the seller is not bound to hand them over at a particular place, the risk passes to the purchaser when the goods are handed over to the first carrier for transmission to the purchaser in accordance with the contract of sale. If the seller is bound to hand the goods over to a carrier at a particular place, the risk does not pass to the purchaser until the goods are handed over to the carrier at that place. The fact that the seller is authorized to retain documents controlling the disposition of the goods does not affect the passage of the risk.

(2) Nevertheless, the risk does not pass to the purchaser until the goods are clearly identified to the contract, whether by markings on the goods, by shipping documents, by notice given to the purchaser or otherwise.

Article 68

The risk in respect of goods sold in transit passes to the purchaser from the time of the conclusion of the contract. However, if the circumstances so indicate, the risk is assumed by the purchaser from the time the goods were handed over to the carrier who issued the documents embodying the contract of carriage. Nevertheless, if at the time of the conclusion of the contract of sale the seller knew or ought to have known that the goods had been lost or damaged and did not disclose this to the purchaser, the loss or damage is at the risk of the seller.

Article 69

(1) In cases not within articles 67 and 68, the risk passes to the purchaser when he takes over the goods or, if he does not do so in due time, from the time when the goods are placed at his disposal and he commits a breach of contract by failing to take delivery.

(2) However, if the purchaser is bound to take over the goods at a place other than a place of business of the seller, the risk passes when delivery is due and the purchaser is aware of the fact that the goods are placed at his disposal at that place.

(3) If the contract relates to goods not then identified, the goods are considered not to be placed at the disposal of the purchaser until they are clearly identified to the contract.

Article 70

If the seller has committed a fundamental breach of contract, articles 67, 68 and 69 do not impair the remedies available to the purchaser on account of the breach.

Appendix

CHAPTER V. PROVISIONS COMMON TO THE OBLIGATIONS OF THE SELLER AND OF THE PURCHASER

Section I. Anticipatory breach and instalment contracts

Article 71

(1) A party may suspend the performance of his obligations if, after the conclusion of the contract, it becomes apparent that the other party will not perform a substantial part of his obligations as a result of:
(a) a serious deficiency in his ability of perform or in his creditworthiness; or
(b) his conduct in preparing to perform or in performing the contract.

(2) If the seller has already dispatched the goods before the grounds described in the preceding paragraph become evident, he may prevent the handing over of the goods to the purchaser even though the purchaser holds a document which entitles him to obtain them. The present paragraph relates only to the rights in the goods as between the purchaser and the seller.

(3) A party suspending performance, whether before or after dispatch of the goods, must immediately give notice of the suspension to the other party and must continue with performance if the other party provides adequate assurance of his performance.

Article 72

(1) If prior to the date for performance of the contract it is clear that one of the parties will commit a fundamental breach of contract, the other party may declare the contract avoided.

(2) If time allows, the party intending to declare the contract avoided must give reasonable notice to the other party in order to permit him to provide adequate assurance of his performance.

(3) The requirements of the preceding paragraph do not apply if the other party has declared that he will not perform his obligations.

Article 73

(1) In the case of a contract for delivery of goods by instalments, if the failure of one party to perform any of his obligations in respect of any instalment constitutes a fundamental breach of contract with respect to that instalment, the other party may declare the contract avoided with respect to that instalment.

(2) If one party's failure to perform any of his obligations in respect of any instalment gives the other party good grounds to conclude that a fundamental breach of contract will occur with respect to future installments, he may declare the contract avoided for the future, provided that he does so within a reasonable time.

(3) A purchaser who declares the contract avoided in respect of any delivery may, at the same time, declare it avoided in respect of deliveries already made or of future deliveries if, by reason of their interdependence, those deliveries could not be used for the purpose contemplated by the parties at the time of the conclusion of the contract.

Section II. Damages

Article 74

Damages for breach of contract by one party consist of a sum equal to the loss, including loss of profit, suffered by the other party as a consequence of the breach. Such damages may not exceed the loss which the party in breach foresaw or ought to have foreseen at the time of the conclusion of the contract, in the light of the facts and matters of which he then knew or ought to have known, as a possible consequence of the breach of contract.

Article 75

If the contract is avoided and if, in a reasonable manner and within a reasonable time after avoidance, the purchaser has bought goods in replacement or the seller has resold the goods, the party claiming damages may recover the difference between the contract price and the price in the substitute transaction as well as any further damages recoverable under article 74.

Article 76

(1) If the contract is avoided and there is a current price for the goods, the party claiming damages may, if he has not made a purchase or resale under article 75, recover the difference between the price fixed by the contract and the current price at the time of avoidance as well as any further damages recoverable under article 74. If, however, the party claiming damages has avoided the contract after taking over the goods, the current price at the time of such taking over shall be applied instead of the current price at the time of avoidance.

(2) For the purposes of the preceding paragraph, the current price is the price prevailing at the place where delivery of the goods should have been made or, if there is no current price at that place, the price at such other place as serves as a reasonable substitute, making due allowance for differences in the cost of transporting the goods.

Article 77

A party who relies on a breach of contract must take such measures as are reasonable in the circumstances to mitigate the loss, including loss of profit, resulting from the breach. If he fails to take such measures, the party in breach may claim a reduction in the damages in the amount by which the loss should have been mitigated.

Section III. Interest

Article 78

If a party fails to pay the price or any other sum that is in arrears, the other party is entitled to interest on it, without prejudice to any claim for damages recoverable under article 74.

Section IV. Exemption

Article 79

(1) A party is not liable for a failure to perform any of his obligations if he proves that the failure was due to an impediment beyond his control and that he could not reasonably be expected to have taken the impediment into account at the time of the conclusion of the contract or to have avoided or overcome it or its consequences.

(2) If the party's failure is due to the failure by a third person whom he has engaged to perform the whole or a part of the contract, that party is exempt from liability only if:
(a) he is exempt under the preceding paragraph; and
(b) the person whom he has so engaged would be so exempt if the provisions of that paragraph were applied to him.

(3) The exemption provided by this article has effect for the period during which the impediment exists.

(4) The party who fails to perform must give notice to the other party of the impediment and its effect on his ability to perform. If the notice is not received by the other party within a reasonable time after the party who fails to perform knew or ought to have known of the impediment, he is liable for damages resulting from such nonreceipt.

(5) Nothing in this article prevents either party from exercising any right other than to claim damages under this Convention.

Appendix

Article 80

A party may not rely on a failure of the other party to perform, to the extent that such failure was caused by the first party's act or omission.

Section V. Effects of avoidance

Article 81

(1) Avoidance of the contract releases both parties from their obligations under it, subject to any damages which may be due. Avoidance does not affect any provision of the contract for the settlement of disputes or any other provision of the contract governing the rights and obligations of the parties consequent upon the avoidance of the contract.

(2) A party who has performed the contract either wholly or in part may claim restitution from the other party of whatever the first party has supplied or paid under the contract. If both parties are bound to make restitution, they must do so concurrently.

Article 82

(1) The purchaser loses the right to declare the contract avoided or to require the seller to deliver substitute goods if it is impossible for him to make restitution of the goods substantially in the condition in which he received them.

(2) The preceding paragraph does not apply:
(a) if the impossibility of making restitution of the goods or of making restitution of the goods substantially in the condition in which the purchaser received them is not due to his act or omission;
(b) the goods or part of the goods have perished or deteriorated as a result of the examination provided for in article 38; or
(c) if the goods or part of the goods have been sold in the normal course of business or have been consumed or transformed by the purchaser in the course of normal use before he discovered or ought to have discovered the lack of conformity.

Article 83

A purchaser who has lost the right to declare the contract avoided or to require the seller to deliver substitute goods in accordance with article 82 retains all other remedies under the contract and this Convention.

Article 84

(1) If the seller is bound to refund the price, he must also pay interest on it, from the date on which the price was paid.

(2) The purchaser must account to the seller for all benefits which he has derived from the goods or part of them:
(a) if he must make restitution of the goods or part of them; or
(b) if it is impossible for him to make restitution of all or part of the goods or to make restitution of all or part of the goods substantially in the condition in which he received them, but he has nevertheless declared the contract avoided or required the seller to deliver substitute goods.

Section VI. Preservation of the goods

Article 85

If the purchaser is in delay in taking delivery of the goods or, where payment of the price and delivery of the goods are to be made concurrently, if he fails to pay the price, and the seller is either in possession of the goods or otherwise able to control their disposition, the seller must take such steps as are reasonable in the circumstances to preserve them. He is entitled to retain them until he has been reimbursed his reasonable expenses by the purchaser.

Article 86

(1) If the purchaser has received the goods and intends to exercise any right under the contract or this Convention to reject them, he must take such steps to preserve them as are reasonable in the circumstances. He is entitled to retain them until he has been reimbursed his reasonable expenses by the seller.

(2) If goods dispatched to the purchaser have been placed at his disposal at their destination and he exercises the right to reject them, he must take possession of them on behalf of the seller, provided that this can be done without payment of the price and without unreasonable inconvenience or unreasonable expense. This provision does not apply if the seller or a person authorized to take charge of the goods on his behalf is present at the destination. If the purchaser takes possession of the goods under this paragraph, his rights and obligations are governed by the preceding paragraph.

Article 87

A party who is bound to take steps to preserve the goods may deposit them in a warehouse of a third person at the expense of the other party provided that the expense incurred is not unreasonable.

Article 88

(1) A party who is bound to preserve the goods in accordance with article 85 or 86 may sell them by any appropriate means if there has been an unreasonable delay by the other party in taking possession of the goods or in taking them back or in paying the price or the cost of preservation, provided that reasonable notice of the intention to sell has been given to the other party.

(2) If the goods are subject to rapid deterioration or their preservation would involve unreasonable expense, a party who is bound to preserve the goods in accordance with article 85 or 86 must take reasonable measures to sell them. To the extent possible he must give notice to the other party of his intention to sell.

(3) A party selling the goods has the right to retain out of the proceeds of sale an amount equal to the reasonable expenses of preserving the goods and of selling them. He must account to the other party for the balance.

Part IV. Final provisions

Article 89

The Secretary-General of the United Nations is hereby designated as the depositary for this Convention.

Article 90

This Convention does not prevail over any international agreement which has already been or may be entered into and which contains provisions concerning the matters governed by this Convention, provided that the parties have their places of business in States parties, to such agreement.

Article 91

(1) This Convention is open for signature at the concluding meeting of the United Nations Conference on Contracts for the International Sale of Goods and will remain open for signature by all States at the Headquarters of the United Nations, New York until 30 September 1981.

(2) This Convention is subject to ratification, acceptance or approval by the signatory States.

(3) This Convention is open for accession by all States which are not signatory States as from the date it is open for signature.

Appendix

(4) Instruments of ratification, acceptance, approval and accession are to be deposited with the Secretary-General of the United Nations.

Article 92

(1) A Contracting State may declare at the time of signature, ratification, acceptance, approval or accession that it will not be bound by Part II of this Convention or that it will not be bound by Part III of this Convention.

(2) A Contracting State which makes a declaration in accordance with the preceding paragraph in respect of Part II or Part III of this Convention is not to be considered a Contracting State within paragraph (1) of article 1 of this Convention in respect of matters governed by the Part to which the declaration applies.

Article 93

(1) If a Contracting State has two or more territorial units in which, according to its constitution, different systems of law are applicable in relation to the matters dealt with in this Convention, it may, at the time of signature, ratification, acceptance, approval or accession, declare that this Convention is to extend to all its territorial units or only to one or more of them, and may amend its declaration by submitting another declaration at any time.

(2) These declarations are to be notified to the depositary and are to state expressly the territorial units to which the Convention extends.

(3) If, by virtue of a declaration under this article, this Convention extends to one or more but not all of the territorial units of a Contracting State, and if the place of business of a party is located in that State, this place of business, for the purposes of this Convention, is considered not to be in a Contracting State, unless it is in a territorial unit to which the Convention extends.

(4) If a Contracting State makes no declaration under paragraph (1) of this article, the Convention is to extend to all territorial units of that State.

Article 94

(1) Two or more Contracting States which have the same or closely related legal rules on matters governed by this Convention may at any time declare that the Convention is not to apply to contracts of sale or to their formation where the parties have their places of business in those States. Such declarations may be made jointly or by reciprocal unilateral declarations.

(2) A Contracting State which has the same or closely related legal rules on matters governed by this Convention as one or more non-Contracting States may at any time declare that the Convention is not to apply to contracts of sale or to their formation where the parties have their places of business in those States.

(3) If a State which is the object of a declaration under the preceding paragraph subsequently becomes a Contracting State, the declaration made will, as from the date on which the Convention enters into force in respect of the new Contracting State, have the effect of a declaration made under paragraph (1),provided that the new Contracting State joins in such declaration or makes a reciprocal unilateral declaration.

Article 95

Any State may declare at the time of the deposit of its instrument of ratification, acceptance, approval or accession that it will not be bound by subparagraph (1) (b) of article 1 of this Convention.

Article 96

A Contracting State whose legislation requires contracts of sale to be concluded in or evidenced by writing may at any time make a declaration in accordance with article 12 that any provision of article 11, article 29, or Part II of this Convention, that allows a contract of sale or its modification or termination by agreement or any offer, acceptance, or other indication of intention to be made in any form other than in writing, does not apply where any party has his place of business in that State.

Article 97

(1) Declarations made under this Convention at the time of signature are subject to confirmation upon ratification, acceptance or approval.

(2) Declarations and confirmations of declarations are to be in writing and be formally notified to the depositary.

(3) A declaration takes effect simultaneously with the entry into force of this Convention in respect of the State concerned. However, a declaration of which the depositary receives formal notification after such entry into force takes effect on the first day of the month following the expiration of six months after the date of its receipt by the depositary. Reciprocal unilateral declarations under article 94 take effect on the first day of the month following the expiration of six months after the receipt of the latest declaration by the depositary.

(4) Any State which makes a declaration under this Convention may withdraw it at any time by a formal notification in writing addressed to the depositary. Such withdrawal is to take effect on the first day of the month following the expiration of six months after the date of the receipt of the notification by the depositary.

(5) A withdrawal of a declaration made under article 94 renders inoperative, as from the date on which the withdrawal takes effect, any reciprocal declaration made by another State under that article.

Article 98

No reservations are permitted except those expressly authorized in this Convention.

Article 99

(1) This Convention enters into force, subject to the provisions of paragraph (6) of this article, on the first day of the month following the expiration of twelve months after the date of deposit of the tenth instrument of ratification, acceptance, approval or accession, including an instrument which contains a declaration made under article 92.

(2) When a State ratifies, accepts, approves or accedes to this Convention after the deposit of the tenth instrument of ratification, acceptance, approval or accession, this Convention, with the exception of the Part excluded, enters into force in respect of that State, subject to the provisions of paragraph (6) of this article, on the first day of the month following the expiration of twelve months after the date of the deposit of its instrument of ratification, acceptance, approval or accession.

(3) A State which ratifies, accepts, approves or accedes to this Convention and is a party to either or both the Convention relating to a Uniform Law on the Formation of Contracts for the International Sale of Goods done at The Hague on 1 July 1964 (1964 Hague Formation Convention) and the Convention relating to a Uniform Law on the International Sale of Goods done at The Hague on 1 July 1964 (1964 Hague Sales Convention) shall at the same time denounce, as the case may be, either or both the 1964 Hague Sales Convention and the 1964 Hague Formation Convention by notifying the Government of the Netherlands to that effect.

(4) A State party to the 1964 Hague Sales Convention which ratifies, accepts, approves or accedes to the present Convention and declares or has declared under article 92 that it will not be bound by Part II of this Convention shall at the time of ratification, acceptance, approval or accession denounce the 1964 Hague Sales Convention by notifying the Government of the Netherlands to that effect.

(5) A State party to the 1964 Hague Formation Convention which ratifies, accepts, approves or accedes to the present Convention and declares or has declared under article 92 that it will not be bound by Part III of this Convention shall at the time of ratification, acceptance, approval or accession denounce the 1964 Hague Formation Convention by notifying the Government of the Netherlands to that effect.

Appendix

(6) For the purpose of this article, ratifications, acceptances, approvals and accessions in respect of this Convention by States parties to the 1964 Hague Formation Convention or to the 1964 Hague Sales Convention shall not be effective until such denunciations as may be required on the part of those States in respect of the latter two Conventions have themselves become effective. The depositary of this Convention shall consult with the Government of the Netherlands, as the depositary of the 1964 Conventions, so as to ensure necessary co-ordination in this respect.

Article 100

(1) This Convention applies to the formation of a contract only when the proposal for concluding the contract is made on or after the date when the Convention enters into force in respect of the Contracting States referred to in subparagraph (1) (a) or the Contracting State referred to in subparagraph (1) (b) of article 1.

(2) This Convention applies only to contracts concluded on or after the date when the Convention enters into force in respect of the Contracting States referred to in subparagraph (1)(a) or the Contracting State referred to in subparagraph (1)(b) of article 1.

Article 101

(1) A Contracting State may denounce this Convention, or Part II or Part III of the Convention, by a formal notification in writing addressed to the depositary.

(2) The denunciation takes effect on the first day of the month following the expiration of twelve months after the notification is received by the depositary. Where a longer period for the denunciation to take effect is specified in the notification, the denunciation takes effect upon the expiration of such longer period after the notification is received by the depositary.

DONE at Vienna, this day of eleventh day of April, one thousand nine hundred and eighty, in a single original, of which the Arabic, Chinese, English, French, Russian and Spanish texts are equally authentic.

IN WITNESS WHEREOF the undersigned plenipotentiaries, being duly authorized by their respective Governments, have signed this Convention.

III. Excerpts from the Swiss Code of Obligations (Obligationenrecht)[671] and other relevant Swiss statutes

[reproduced with permission of the Federal Chancellery of the Swiss Confederation]

Validity of the Contract

Art 19

(1) The terms of a contract may be freely determined within the limits of the law.

(2) However, where the defect pertains only to certain terms of a contract, those terms alone are void unless there is cause to assume that the contract would not have been concluded without them.

Art 20

(1) A contract is void if its terms are impossible, unlawful or immoral.

(2) However, where the defect pertains only to certain terms of a contract, those terms alone are void unless there is cause to assume that the contract would not have been concluded without them.

---

[671] Given that English is not an official language of the Swiss Confederation, the english translation of the Swiss Code of Obligations that is used in this book has no legal force. The translation has been provided by the Federal Chancellery of the Swiss Confederation and can also be downloaded under http://www.admin.ch/opc/en/classified-compilation/19110009/index.html.

III. Excerpts from the Swiss Code of Obligations

Art 24

(1) An error is fundamental in the following cases in particular:
1. […]
4. where the error relates to specific facts which the party acting in error considered in good faith to be a necessary basis for the contract.

Limitation of Liability

Art 100

(1) Any agreement purporting to exclude liability for unlawful intent or gross negligence in advance is void.

(2) At the discretion of the court, an advance exclusion of liability for minor negligence may be deeemd void provided the party excluding liability was in the other party's service at the time the waiver was made or the liability arises in connection with commercial activities conducted under official licence.

(3) The specific provisions governing insurance policies are unaffected.

Art 101

(1) A person who delegates the performance of an obligation or the exercise of a right arising from a contractual obligation to an associate, such as a member of his household or an employee is liable to the other party for any loss or damage the associate causes in carrying out such tasks, even if their delegation was entirely authorised.

(2) This liability may be limited or excluded by prior agreement.

(3) If the obligee is in the obligor's service or if the liability arises in connection with commercial activities conducted under official licence, any exclusion of liability by agreement may apply at most to minor negligence.

Interest Rate in case of default on payment

Art 104

(1) A debtor in default on payment of a pecuniary debt must pay default interest of 5 % per annum even where a lower rate of interest was stipulated by contract.

(2) Where the contract envisages a rate of interest higher than 5 %, whether directly or by agreement of a periodic bank commission, such higher rate of interest may also be applied while the debtor remains in default.

(3) In business dealings, where the normal bank discount rate at the place of payment is higher than 5 %, default interest may be calculated at the higher rate.

Set- Off

Art 124

(1) A set-off takes place only if the debtor notifies the creditor of his intention to exercise his right of set-off.

(2) Once this has occurred, to the extent that they cancel each other out, the claim and countervailing claim are deemed to have been satisfied as of the time they first became susceptible to set-off.

(3) The special customs relating to commercial current accounts are unaffected

Art 126

The debtor may waive his right of set-off in advance.

Appendix

Statute of Limitations

Art 127

All claims become time-barred after ten years unless otherwise provided by federal civil law.

Art 129

The limitation periods laid down under this Title may not be altered by contract.

Art 134

(1) The limitation period does not commence and, if it has begun, is suspended:
1. [...]
6. for as long as the claim cannot be brought before a Swiss court.

(2) The limitation period begins or resumes at the end of the day on which the cause of prevention or suspension ceases to obtain.

(3) The specific provisions of debt collection and bankruptcy are unaffected.

Art 135

The limitation period is interrupted:
1. if the debtor acknowledges the claim and in particular if he makes interest payments or part payments, gives an item in pledge or provides surety;
2. by debt enforcement proceedings, an application for conciliation, submission of a statement of claim or defence to a court or arbitral tribunal, or a petition for bankruptcy.

Art 210

(1) An action for breach of warranty of quality and fitness becomes time-barred two years after delivery of the object to the buyer, even if he does not discover the defects until later, unless the seller has assumed liability under warranty for a longer period.

(2) The period amounts to five years where defects in an object that has been incorporated in an immovable work in a manner consistent with its nature and purpose have caused the work to be defective.

(3) In the case of cultural property within the meaning of Article 2 paragraph 1 of the Cultural Property Transfer Act of 20 June 2003, actions for breach of warranty of quality and fitness become time-barred one year after the buyer discovered the defect but in any event 30 years after the contract was concluded.

(4) An agreement to reduce the limitation period is null and void if:
 a. the limitation period is reduced to less than two years, or less than one year in the case of second-hand goods;
 b. the object is intended to be used by the buyer or his or her family; and
 c. the seller is acting in the course of his or her professional or commercial activities.

(5) The defence of defective goods remains available to the buyer provided he has notified the seller within the limitation period.

(6) The seller may not invoke the limitation period if it is proved that he wilfully misled the buyer. The foregoing does not apply to the 30-year period under paragraph 3.

Contractual Penalties

Art 160

(1) Where a penalty is promised for non-performance or defective performance of a contract, unless otherwise agreed, the creditor may only compel performance or claim the penalty.

(2) Where the penalty is promised for failure to comply with the stipulated time or place of performance, the creditor may claim the penalty in addition to performance provided he has not expressly waived such right or accepted performance without reservation.

(3) The foregoing does not apply if the debtor can prove that he has the right to withdraw from the contract by paying the penalty.

Art 161

(1) The penalty is payable even if the creditor has not suffered any loss or damage.

(2) Where the loss or damage suffered exceeds the penalty amount, the creditor may claim further compensation only if he can prove that the debtor was at fault.

Art 163

(1) The parties are free to determine the amount of the contractual penalty.

(2) The penalty may not be claimed where its purpose is to reinforce an unlawful or immoral undertaking or, unless otherwise agreed, where performance has been prevented by circumstances beyond the debtor's control.

(3) At its discretion, the court may reduce penalties that it considers excessive.

Assignment of Rights and Claims

Art 164

(1) A creditor may assign a claim to which he is entitled to a third party without the debtor's consent unless the assignment is forbidden by law or contract or prevented by the nature of the legal relationship.

(2) The debtor may not object to the assignment on the grounds that it was excluded by agreement against any third party who acquires the claim in reliance on a written acknowledgement of debt in which there is no mention of any prohibition of assignment.

Art 165

(1) An assignment is valid only if done in writing.

(2) No particular form is required for an undertaking to enter into an assignment agreement.

Tort Liability and Statute of Limitations applying for claims under tort

Art 41

(1) Any person who unlawfully causes loss or damage to another, whether wilfully or negligently, is obliged to provide compensation.

(2) A person who wilfully causes loss or damage to another in an immoral manner is likewise obliged to provide compensation.

Art 60

(1) A claim for damages or satisfaction becomes time-barred one year from the date on which the injured party became aware of the loss or damage and of the identity of the person liable for it but in any event ten years after the date on which the loss or damage was caused.

(2) However, if the action for damages is derived from an offence for which criminal law envisages a longer limitation period, that longer period also applies to the civil law claim.

(3) Where the tort has given rise to a claim against the injured party, he may refuse to satisfy the claim even if his own claim in tort is time-barred.

Appendix

Article 8 of the Swiss Federal Act Against Unfair Competition

Art 8 Use of abusive terms and conditions[672]

The use of general terms and conditions, which provide, in a manner that is contrary to the principles of good faith, for a significant and unjustified imbalance between the contractual rights and the contractual duties to the detriment of consumers, does in particular amount to an abusive trade practice.

---

[672] Translation by the author.

Index

agreement on jurisdiction 351, 353, 369–373
- ~ and provisional measures 373
  see also Brussels Regulation
  see also Hague Convention on Choice of Court Agreements

alternative dispute resolution 354–356
- adjudication 356
- multistep dispute resolution 354

antitrust law
  see competition and antitrust laws

arbitration 13, 126–128, 338–340, 342, 345–368
- ad-hoc ~ 347, 348, 359
- ~ agreement 128, 342, 346, 348, 349, 357–365
- ~ and choice of law
  see governing law, choice of
- ~ and provisional measures 366–368
- institutional ~ 347, 348, 357, 366
- ~ laws 342, 348, 349, 362, 364, 367
- mandatory laws and ~ *see there*
- New York Convention *see there*
- seat of ~ 349

assignment
- anti- ~ clause 102, 322, 334–336
- ~ pursuant to Swiss law 12, 76, 101, 102

avoidance of the contract
- applicable limitation periods 90, 94
- ~ by the purchaser 26, 52, 68, 69, 90, 195, 221, 226, 245, 246, 266, 281, 303
- ~ by the seller 26, 71, 72, 227, 303, 305–308
- legal consequences of an ~ 70
  see also fundamental breach
- ~ pursuant to the CISG 26, 27, 52, 54, 59–61, 68–70

battle of forms 155, 156, 163–169, 205
- knock out rule 164, 167, 168
- last shot rule 164–166, 168
- rejection clause 164, 205

bill of lading 172, 175, 176, 183, 195

blue pencil test 261

bodily injury 58, 74, 76, 83, 110, 112, 114, 153, 154, 220, 265, 267, 278, 342, 353

Brussels Regulation (44/2001/EC) 351, 370, 371

CESL 114a-114c

choice of court agreement
  see agreement on jurisdiction

choice of law
  see governing law, choice of

CISG
- advantages of the ~ 7–12
- introduction into the ~ 14–73
  see avoidance of the contract
  see conformity of the goods
  see consumer contracts
  see damages
  see delay

  see delivery of substitute goods
  see fundamental breach
  see liability
  see price reduction
  see repair
  see restitution
  see retention right
  see specific performance
  see transfer of risk
  see validity of the contract

Code of Obligations (Obligationenrecht)
  see assignment
  see damages
  see formation of contract
  see indemnity
  see liability
  see limitation of liability
  see limitation periods
  see liquidated damages
  see penalties
  see private international law
  see public policy
  see set-off
  see tort
  see validity of the contract

competition and antitrust laws 115, 129, 132–139, 312
- EU competition laws 132–134, 136–139, 312
  - Regulation (330/2010/EU), 134, 136, 138, 139, 312
- non-compete obligation 138
- resale price maintenance 136
- territorial and customer sales restrictions 137
- tying 139
- US antitrust laws 132, 134, 136–139
  - Sherman Act 134

confidentiality
- breach of ~ 310
- confidentiality clause 309–312
- unfair competition laws and protection of confidentiality *see there*

conflict of laws
  see private international laws

conformity of the goods
- ~ pursuant to the CISG 32, 36, 39–43, 55, 57, 236–239, 247, 283, 286, 291, 292
  see also defects

consumer contracts
- choice of court in ~ 351
- choice of law in ~ 337
- implied quality standards in ~ 237
- relationship of ~ with the CISG 207
- unfair terms in ~ 86, 207, 239, 267

contemplation rule 64, 66, 252

contra proferentem doctrine 87, 260, 278, 328

179

contract price 21, 22, 34, 59, 60, 69–71, 94, 131, 151, 156, 165, 170–172, 174, 179, 195, 209, 225, 228, 229, 232, 254, 259, 266, 281, 343, 344
– ~ and contract formation 21, 22, 165
– applicable limitation period for payment of ~ 94
– determination of ~ 170, 171
– maturity of ~ 71, 172
– reduction of ~ *see there*
– refund of ~ 254, 266, 281
– security of ~ 228, 229, 232
see also payment terms
contractual penalties
see penalties
cut-off period 12, 92, 256, 285, 286, 291, 292, 296
damages
– claim for ~ 133, 151, 185, 263
  – applicable limitation periods 90
  – in lieu of performance 58, 60, 71, 151, 244–246
  – pursuant to Swiss law 85, 90, 102, 106, 113, 114
  – pursuant to the CISG 51, 52, 54, 57–67, 70–72, 185, 214, 223, 225, 246, 258, 263, 302
– consequential ~ 3, 264, 272–281
– foreseeability of ~ 57, 64–67, 220, 258
  see also contemplation rule
– general ~ 103, 106, 114, 220, 221, 223, 225, 226, 266, 274
– incidental ~ 264, 274
– indirect ~ 264, 272–275, 277–279
– liquidated ~ *see there*
see also liability
see also limitation of liability
DCFR 58, 339
default
see delay
defect 3, 5, 11, 26, 32, 36, 41, 43–47, 49–51, 55, 57, 58, 60, 65, 67, 68, 75, 85, 90–94, 110–114, 116, 153, 234, 235, 241–243, 246, 249–256
– defects of title 36, 44–47, 50, 57, 94, 250–254, 256
– hidden ~ 49, 50, 235, 255
– liability for ~
  see liability
– quality defects 26, 36, 41–43, 47, 48, 50, 53, 55, 57, 58, 60, 65, 67, 68, 75, 85, 90–93, 110–114, 116, 153, 241–243, 246, 247, 249, 253–255
– uncurable ~ 32
see also conformity of the goods
defects notification period 5, 283
see also cut-off period
see also limitation period
see also warranty period
delay
– ~ as a fundamental breach under the CISG 31, 34, 72
– ~ in delivery 4, 31, 53, 103, 106, 181, 185, 195, 219–222, 224–226, 257, 263, 302
– ~ in payment 34, 72, 73, 76
see also interest
delivery
– delay in delivery *see there*
– delivery date 31, 37, 181, 189, 191, 195, 213, 218, 219
see also delay in delivery

– delivery obligations 185, 188–190, 195–203, 303, 304
– delivery of substitute goods
  – applicable limitation period 90
  – contractual exclusion of ~ 244
  – pursuant to the CISG 26, 32, 52, 53, 55, 243
– delivery terms 156, 212, 219–226
  – INCOTERMS *see there*
  – partial delivery 219
Draft Common Frameof Reference
see DCFR
Dual Use Regulation (428/2009/EC)
See export control laws
duties and taxes 200, 202, 209–212
– INCOTERMS 202, 212, 2000 200
– VAT *see there*
enforcement
see recognition and enforcement
entire agreement clause
see merger clause
Euro crisis 171a
examination of the goods
see notification of defects
exchange control regulations 150–152
– IMF-Treaty 150–152
– mandatory laws *see there*
exclusive jurisdiction
see agreement on jurisdiction
exemption clause
see limitation of liability clause
export control regulations 115, 129, 140, 142–149, 185, 186, 191–195, 302–304, 340
– European export control laws 142–145, 303
  – Dual Use Regulation (428/2009/EC) 142–145
– export authorizations
  see export licenses
– export licenses 142–144, 147, 185, 186, 191–195, 301, 303
– mandatory laws *see there*
– US export control laws 146–149, 303
  – Commerce Control List (CCL) 147
  – Export Administration Regulations (EAR) 146–148
  – Office of Foreign Trade Control (OFAC) 148
  – Specially Designated Nationals and Blocked Persons Lists 148
FIDIC
– FIDIC conditions 2, 5, 220, 283, 354
force majeure
– ~ clause 314–321
– delineation of ~ from hardship 315
– ~ event 63, 314, 318
– ICC ~ clause 318
formation of the contract
– ~ under Swiss law 77
– ~ under the CISG 16, 20–24, 45, 74, 157, 164, 168
frustration of the contract 314
fundamental breach
– by the purchaser 33–35, 72, 305, 306
– by the seller 29–32, 55, 68, 222, 243, 266, 302
– pursuant to the CISG 10, 26–35, 55, 68, 69, 72, 222, 243, 266, 302

Index

governing law
- choice of the ~ 338, 340
  - and arbitration 338–340, 345
- ~ clause 18, 337–342
- impact of ~ 1–13, 73, 76, 167, 282, 283, 287, 298, 314, 321, 323, 335
- limitations of ~ 115–154
  see also mandatory laws
- supplementary ~ 7, 12, 13, 73, 75, 76, 103, 214, 216, 287
gross negligence
  see negligence
guarantee of durability 43, 241, 286–291, 299
Hague Convention on Choice of Courts Agreements 353, 372
hardship
- ~ clause 315
- relationship of ~ with force majeure clause 315
- UPICC *see there*
ICC
- ~ arbitration rules 13, 127, 338, 347, 357, 358, 360, 361, 368
- ~ court 357, 360, 361
- force majeure clause *see there*
- INCOTERMS *see there*
- ~ model international sale contract 2, 4, 220, 317
impossibility
- ~ of performance 30, 76, 105, 314
- ~ to make restitution 70
INCOTERMS 31, 38, 185–204, 212, 222, 301
- ~ 2010 185–203, 212, 301
indemnity
- ~ as part of claim for damages 58
- ~ clause 153, 252, 265
- pursuant to Swiss law 265
insolvency
- ~ laws 227, 228
- ~ of the purchaser 35, 227
intellectual property rights 44–46, 250–254, 309
  see also defects in title
intentional misconduct 4, 220, 267, 316
interest
- determination of ~ rate 73, 76, 209, 214, 215
- in case of default with payment 73, 214
International Chamber of Commerce
  see ICC
Late Payment Directive (2011/35/EU) 215, 228
letter of credit 173–184, 209, 213, 218, 228, 306
- back to back ~ 182
- bill of lading *see there*
- confirmed ~ 180, 181, 213
- documents 183
- principle of autonomy 176
- principle of strict compliance 176
- silent confirmation of ~ 180
- UCP 176, 177, 179–183
lex contractus
  see governing law
lex mercatoria 339

liability 3–5, 10, 11, 41–47, 62–64, 66–67, 74, 76, 77, 81, 83–85, 110–114, 116, 154, 195, 220, 224, 234, 257–259, 262–267, 269–271, 278, 280, 282, 288, 299, 300, 303, 314, 316, 319
- fault ~ 11, 62, 111, 270, 271, 314, 316
- in case of bodily injury
  see bodily injury
- limitation of ~ *see there*
- product liability *see there*
- pursuant to Swiss law 110–114, 267
- strict ~10, 11, 44, 62, 112, 114, 269–271, 314, 316
- time limitations on ~
  see limitation periods
- ~ towards third parties 116
  see also limitation of liability
limitation of actions
  see limitation periods
limitation of liability
- ~ clause 4, 83–85, 167, 220, 224–226, 245, 257, 259, 263–268, 273–279, 281
- ~ and third parties 265
- exclusion of liability 245, 263–265
- ~ in case of bodily injury 83, 267
- ~ in case of delay in delivery 220, 224–226
- ~ pursuant to Swiss law 83–85, 220, 266–268
- warranty disclaimer as hidden ~ 239
  see also damages
  see also liability
limitation periods
- clause on ~ 291–300
- delineation from cut-off periods 5, 256, 285
- delineation from guarantees of durability 43, 287–290
- governing law of ~ 282
- ~ pursuant to Swiss law 12, 77, 90–95, 256, 292–297
  - discontinuation of ~ 96, 299
  - suspension of ~ 96, 97
liquidated damages
- ~ clause 76, 103, 107, 220, 221, 223, 225, 310
- delineation of ~ from penalties 104
- ~ pursuant to Anglo-American law 6, 105, 108, 109
- ~ pursuant to Swiss law 108, 109
litigation 340, 345, 346, 350–356, 371
- agreement on jurisdiction *see there*
- Hague Convention on Choice of Court Agreements *see there*
Lugano Convention 351, 370, 373
lump sum payment clause 107–109, 310
mandatory laws
- ~ and arbitration 126–128, 340, 349, 362
- general impact of ~ 1, 115–117
- overriding mandatory ~ 117, 119–129, 207, 340
  - competition and antitrust laws 132
  - exchange control regulations 150
  - export control regulations 140
- simple/domestic ~ 117–121, 207, 337
  see also public policy

181

Index

merger clauses 239, 322–329
   see also parol evidence rule
negligence
 - delineation of ~ from strict liability 62
 - gross ~ 4, 84, 85, 220
New York Convention 127, 346, 348, 353, 361, 363, 364
non-assignment clause
   see assignment
non-compete obligations
   see competition and antitrust laws
non-disclosure agreement
   see confidentiality clause
no-oral modification clause
   see written form requirement
notification of defects
 - contractual clause on ~ 247–249
 - notification periods 5, 47–51, 92, 247, 248
 - pursuant to the CISG 47–51, 254–256, 292
ordre public
   see public policy
Orgalime
 - ~ S 2012 2, 3, 224, 265, 317
parol evidence rule
 - pursuant to the CISG 326
 - pursuant to US law 325
payment
 - currency of ~ 171
 - ~ of duties and taxes
   see duties and taxes
 - ~ of transport 189, 194
 - ~ terms 156, 172–183
   see also contract price
   see also letter of credit
 - clause on ~ terms 209–215
PECL 325, 339
penalties
 - delineation of ~ from liquidated damages 104
 - ~ pursuant to Anglo-American law 105
 - ~ pursuant to Swiss law 76, 104–107
price reduction
 - applicable limitation period 90
 - contract clause on ~ 245, 246, 266
 - ~ remedy under the CISG 51–54, 57
Principles of European Contract Law
   see PECL
private international laws
 - Rome I Regulation see there
 - Rome II Regulation see there
 - Swiss private international law
   see also governing law
   - ~ and arbitration 133, 338, 342, 362, 366, 367
   - characteristic contractual obligation 18
   - in general 79
   - internal situation 118, 337
   - law governing assignment 335
   - law governing limitation periods 282
   - mandatory laws see there
   - property laws 130
Product Liability Act 112, 113
public policy
 - ~ as restriction for exemption clauses 267

 - barrier for recognition and enforcement 346
 - competition law 133
 - transnational ~ 126, 340
 - ~ under Swiss law 80, 83, 88, 133, 267
recognition and enforcement
 - ~ of arbitral awards 127, 346
 - ~ of judgments of courts of law 346, 351–353
   see also Brussels Regulation
   see also Hague Convention on Choice of Court Agreements
   see also New York Convention
reduction
   see price reduction
reformation clause
   see severability clause
repair
 - ~ as remedy under the CISG 32, 52, 53, 55, 58, 243
 - impact of ~ on limitation periods 290, 298, 299
 - relationship with limitation of liability 266, 281
resale price maintenance
   see competition and antitrust laws
reservation of title
   see retention of title
restitution
 - limitation periods in relation to ~ 94
 - restitution claim 68, 70, 152, 227, 228, 266, 281
 - scope of restitution under CISG 58, 68, 70
retention of title
 - ~ clause 131, 227–233
 - current account ~ clause 229
 - prolonged ~ clause 229
retention right
 - ~ of the purchaser 172
 - ~ of the seller 218
 - ~ pursuant to the CISG 75, 218
Rome I Regulation (593/2008/EC)
 - ~ and arbitration 338
   see also governing law, choice of
 - characteristic contractual obligation 18
 - consumer contracts 207
 - internal situation 118–120, 337
 - law governing assignment 335
 - law governing formation of contract 20, 168
 - law governing limitation periods 282
 - mandatory laws see there
 - relationship with international conventions 20
Rome II Regulation (864/2007/EC)
 - ~ and arbitration 338
 - ~ and choice of law 342
 - pre-contractual liability 1
 - product liability 154, 342
Sales of Goods Act
 - retention of title 131
 - specific performance
   see ~ pursuant to Anglo American law
 - transfer of risk 231
 - warranties 40, 42, 237, 251
set-off
 - no ~ clause 216, 217
 - ~ rights 12, 209, 216
 - ~ under Swiss law 76, 98–100, 216

severability clause 322, 332, 333
- preservative part of ~ 332
- reformation clause 333

specific performance
- ~ as a remedy under the CISG 52, 54–56, 245, 254, 314
- damages in lieu of ~ *see there*
- limitation period in relation to ~ 94
- ~ pursuant to Anglo-American law 56

taxes
see duties and taxes

termination of the contract
see avoidance

tort
- applicable law 116, 153, 154
- concurring claims under tort pursuant to Swiss law 75–77, 83, 85, 93, 110–113
  - limitation periods 93
  - Product Liability Act *see there*

trade terms
see INCOTERMS

transfer of property
- applicable law 129–131
- ~ as primary obligation of the seller 36, 185
  see also retention of title
- duties of purchaser before ~ in case of retention of title 232

transfer of risk
- ~ pursuant to INCOTERMS *see there*
- ~ pursuant to the CISG 38
- relationship with transfer of property 231
- relevance for determination of defects 42, 235, 241, 289

transfer of title
see transfer of property

UCC
- anticipatory repudiation 69
- battle of forms 167
- choice of law 118, 337
- cumulative remedies 54
- formation of the contract 24
- frustration of the contract *see there*
- limitation of liability 267, 274
- limitation periods 283, 290, 299
- notification of defects 47
- parol evidence rule *see there*
- penalty clauses
  see penalties
- retention of title 131
- rights of third parties 58, 153
- specific performance *see there*
- warranties 40, 237, 239, 251

UCP
see letter of credit

UN Convention on Contracts for the International Sale of Goods
see CISG

uncertainty rule 87, 261

UNCITRAL 15, 17, 346, 347, 367
- ~ arbitration rules 347
- ~ model law on arbitration 346, 367

unfair competition laws
- protection of confidentiality 309
- unfair contract terms 82

unfair contract terms
see validity of the contract

UNIDROIT Principles of International Commercial Contracts 2010
see UPICC

Uniform Commercial Code
see UCC

Uniform Customs and Practice for Documentary Credits
see UCP

United Nations Commission on International Trade Law
see UNCITRAL

United Nations Convention on the Recognition and Enforcement of Foreign Arbitral Awards
see New York Convention

unusual terms rule 87

UPICC
- as governing law 339
- battle of forms 167
- contemplation rule 64
- contra proferentem rule 260
- contractual penalties 105
- determination of interest rate 73, 214
- effect of anti-assignment clause 102
- hardship 314
- merger clause 325

validity of the contract 4, 12, 74, 76, 80–89, 129, 133, 157, 168, 207, 332
- ~ and the CISG 74
- ~ under Swiss law 80–89

value added tax
see VAT

VAT
- VAT Directive (2006/112/EC) 210–212
  see also taxes and duties

warranties
- ~ claims 90–92, 94, 256, 282, 293, 334, 343
- disclaimer of ~ 234, 239
- evergreen ~ 298
- express warranties 40, 237, 288, 399
- ~ extending to future performance
  see guarantee of durability
- implied warranties 40, 237, 239, 399
- ~ periods 283, 288, 290, 291, 299
- third party ~ 58
- use in international commercial contracts 6

warranty of durability
see guarantee of durability

willful misconduct
see intentional misconduct

written form requirement
- contractual ~ 322–324, 329–331
- ~ for choice of court agreements 370